The *NEW* RULES of
ATTACHMENT

The *NEW* RULES of
ATTACHMENT

How to Heal Your Relationships, Reparent Your Inner Child, and Secure Your Life Vision

Dr. Judy Ho, PhD, ABPP, ABPdN

balance

New York   Boston

Copyright © 2024 by Judy Ho

Jacket design by Jim Datz

Jacket copyright © 2024 by Hachette Book Group, Inc.

Balance
Hachette Book Group
1290 Avenue of the Americas
New York, NY 10104
GCP-Balance.com
twitter.com/GCPBalance
instagram.com/GCPBalance

First Edition: March 2024

Balance is an imprint of Grand Central Publishing. The Balance name and logo are registered trademarks of Hachette Book Group, Inc.

The publisher is not responsible for websites (or their content) that are not owned by the publisher.

Balance books may be purchased in bulk for business, educational, or promotional use. For information, please contact your local bookseller or the Hachette Book Group Special Markets Department at special .markets@hbgusa.com.

Library of Congress Control Number: 2023948879

ISBNs: 9781538741429 (hardcover), 9781538741443 (ebook)

Printed in the United States of America

LSC-C

Printing 1, 2024

This book is dedicated to Luca, who reminds me
every day of the beauty of life and wonders of the world.
You have taught me so much about myself and
given me the greatest gift of all.

CONTENTS

Introduction: The Big Deal with Attachment ix

ATTACHMENT
Chapter 1: Attachment Theory 3
Quiz: What's My Attachment Style? 13
Chapter 2: Attachment Style and Your Self-Concept 31
Chapter 3: The Influence of Attachment on Your Life Vision 45

THE SECURE ATTACHMENT STYLE
Chapter 4: Secure Attachment: The Connected Explorer 69

THE AVOIDANT ATTACHMENT STYLE
Chapter 5: Avoidant Attachment: Fiercely Independent 105
Chapter 6: Healing the Avoidant Attachment Style 123

THE ANXIOUS ATTACHMENT STYLE
Chapter 7: Anxious Attachment: The Worried Warrior 171
Chapter 8: Healing the Anxious Attachment Style 185

THE DISORGANIZED ATTACHMENT STYLE
Chapter 9: Disorganized Attachment: Surveillance Specialists 233
Chapter 10: Healing the Disorganized Attachment Style 259

CONTENTS

Conclusion: Your Resilient Self **311**

Appendix A: Style Triggers and Timely Tips **315**
Appendix B: Self-Compassion Strategies **325**
Appendix C: Self-Concept Boosters **329**

Acknowledgments **337**

Notes **339**

The Big Deal with Attachment

Most people come to see me because they are struggling, and they are looking for ways to turn their lives around. You may find that some of their concerns are familiar: Susan can't seem to achieve the goals she sets for herself and has often self-sabotaged her good efforts along the way. Stuart is unsatisfied with his relationships and has trouble connecting meaningfully with others. Anne is plagued by negative self-talk that makes her feel unworthy of better outcomes, and she is suspicious of those who show genuine concern for her. Conner's struggles with depression and shame lead him to isolate himself from friends and family and to stop pursuing his dreams. Bart's insecurities about his worth drive his anxiety symptoms and a shaky self-esteem, which lead to clinging behavior in relationships.

By the time my patients get to me, they've usually been through a few cycles of making progress and then slipping back into their old struggles. Some of my patients tell me they feel hopeless and doubt that anything can really help them get back on track. They've thrown in the metaphorical towel and have accepted the "raw deal" they've been handed in life. Their thinking gets stuck in: I'll *never* have a good relationship, I'll *never* have a job I love, I'll *never* reach my goals or any of my dreams.

In these moments of deep pain, frustration, and anguish, many of my patients search for the bigger answers. They want to know why they find themselves in similar situations over and over again—and repeat patterns that don't serve their lives but they can't seem to shake. And their big existential questions deserve big answers.

As a clinical and forensic neuropsychologist, one of my primary specialties is helping people gain insight into the roots of their mental health and life struggles. I go beyond identifying the problems they're currently experiencing to discover why these problems are happening in the first place. Without understanding the origins of these difficulties, it can be challenging to develop a long-term strategy to manage the difficult thoughts, troubling emotions, and challenging situations that every person faces throughout their life.

More often than not, discovering those origins requires diving deep—all the way back to when we were children. So many of the challenges and struggles we continue to experience as adults have their roots in the patterns we learned in early childhood. And when I say early, I mean as far back as the first few months to years of life, when we form ideas about ourselves and the world around us. These early learning experiences continued to impact how my clients currently tried to create physical and psychological safety for themselves, their beliefs about how people were likely to respond to them, and how they approached relationships, their careers, and the goals they set for themselves in different areas of life. It created a default for how they interacted with the world, and even when these ideas were unproductive, unhelpful, and caused stress and discontent, they couldn't break free from those beliefs. The perspective they developed about themselves and the world that underlay their nagging negative self-talk, recurring emotional struggles, and unhelpful behavior patterns was due to *attachment*.

You may have heard of attachment by talking with your friends, seen a self-quiz on social media, read articles online, or discovered this concept at your therapist's office. From my side of the couch, attachment is a fundamental aspect of human development that has a huge impact on our overall well-being throughout our lives. At its most basic level, attachment refers to the first emotional bond that forms between you and your primary caregiver(s). This first crucial bond, designed to keep you alive and thriving during a time when you can't possibly care for yourself, sets the stage for the development of who you are, what you believe (particularly about yourself), and how you will interact with others.

We come into the world as blank slates, ready to learn everything we can from our social world, so experiences and the lessons learned that occur during childhood tend to stick with us into adulthood. Because these situations and interactions with our primary caregivers occur at a time when we are learning how the world works as well as who we are and our role in what happens, we come to believe how we responded to a situation then is a rule that should be applied to all other similar situations in the future. Even as we grow older, come into our own, and gain control over our environment, our inner child's memories and experiences continue to impact us—sometimes in unhelpful ways. Your inner child is a metaphorical "little you," the part of your psyche that is still childlike, innocent, and full of wonder. It is also the part of you that might harbor some unhealed wounds. Your inner child likely has needs that were not met, and you learned how to deal with that the best you could—but from a child's perspective and abilities. That's why it is common, as adults, when we are scared, confused, and longing for unconditional support, to feel the way we did when we were children and we did not get what we needed from our caregivers.

Because we form our attachments as a result of the connection we have with our caregivers—in many ways, the people who modeled what it is like to experience love, support, and be in a relationship—attachment theory is referenced most often regarding romantic relationships. As the thinking goes: The way you learned to love is the way you will love, and receive love from, others. But as it turns out, our attachment style has an even further reaching (and commonly overlooked!) impact on our lives. Your attachment style doesn't just determine what you expect in relationships; it becomes the foundation of your self-concept—the way you think about yourself and what makes up who you are: your thoughts, feelings, behaviors, attitudes, likes and dislikes, as well as what you value. Attachment experiences create templates for how you experience and interpret your social world and, by extension, how you take care of your needs and help you to predict how others are likely to respond to you. Secure attachment relationships typically result in more positive and balanced internal working models, meaning that you're more likely to hold yourself in high esteem, have satisfactory and lasting relationships, and believe that you deserve good things in life. Insecure attachment generally leads to lower self-esteem, a shaky sense of identity, and doubts about self-worth and whether good things should happen to you—including loving and symbiotic relationships with others.

Because the influences of insecure attachment can be so far-reaching, sometimes people ask me if it is too late for them to heal their childhood wounds and traumas, fearing that the answer might be yes. But each time, I answer them with a resounding and confident "No, it's never too late to heal your attachment." It doesn't matter how old you are or where you are in life, whether you're partnered or single, working or retired, estranged from your family, or feel burned from craving real connection but not getting it. The truth is, you only need one person with whom you can form a secure attachment in order to see your transformation to a secure attachment style. And it all starts with a secure attachment to yourself.

Developing secure attachment won't transform you into someone with a million best friends, instantly establish deep intimacy with your romantic partner, or allow you to land your dream job tomorrow, but it will help you begin to consistently believe in yourself and promote a healthy and stable self-concept that will pave the way toward confidently approaching all areas of your life with a deep sense of belonging and resilience.

You'll have a much better toolkit in your arsenal to cope with stressful situations and to adjust to transitions throughout your life, such as moving to a new place, becoming a parent, taking on bigger responsibilities at work, planning for retirement, or becoming the caregiver for your aging parents. Being securely attached gives you the confidence to face whatever challenges come your way, to believe that good things are possible for you, and to know that you have a hand in creating these positive outcomes for yourself.

The tools in this book are those I have developed and refined through years of work with my clients to resolve their attachment issues, and I know that they can help you to build the stable and healthy attachment bond you deserve with *yourself*, the one person who has been with you from the very beginning and will be with you throughout your life. There is a version of you who has experienced all the good and bad you have encountered, the quiet observer who has seen everything that has happened, taken all the valuable lessons from each situation, and is now the wiser and more empowered part of you who can guide your inner child to self-development, deeper insight, and ultimate healing. This will be the foundation from which you can redefine who you are and what is possible for you. The life you desire is truly within your reach, and you can transform how you feel about yourself and how you interact with the world.

HOW TO USE THIS BOOK

The goal of this book is to help you break free from the negative cycles of insecure attachment and develop your ability to be securely attached. No matter what happened in your past, you can work from where you are today—seeking change.

In the first chapters, you'll become familiar with the core concepts of attachment theory, its impact on self-concept, and how both inform your life vision. To make sure you have an idea of where you're headed on this healing journey, in chapter 4, I will explain the characteristics of secure attachment and how these Connected Explorers meet challenges in different areas of their lives.

The quiz on page 13 will reveal your attachment style, and you can jump straight to the chapters that will address your avoidant, anxious, or disorganized style. There, you'll find insights into how your attachment developed and how it has impacted you throughout your development from childhood to now. You'll learn the most common traits of your style and how those characteristics manifest and play out in your life—in self-concept, in relationships, with family and friends, at work, and in goal pursuits. In the chapters focused on healing your style, you'll take a deep dive into a range of activities specifically designed to help you change the internal working models that keep you stuck and move you closer to achieving a secure attachment style. Every activity is supported by scientific research to help you counter the imbalance in your attachment style with practical tips that you can implement immediately in your daily life to, in effect, reprogram yourself toward a more secure way of interacting with others.

Before we jump in, I have a few important tips on how you can get the most out of this book. First, I highly recommend keeping a journal as you work through the exercises in this book. The physical act of writing can keep your mind engaged and bring a sense of calm, focus, and mindfulness to the task, but just as important, your journal will also give you a record of your thoughts and feelings, which you can review later to note your progress. A journal doesn't have to be a bound book—it can be whatever works best for you. Write in pen, marker, or pencil in a spiral notebook, on blank pages, or lined pages. You can even write on loose sheets of paper if you prefer, but if you do so I recommend collecting them in a folder, so they are gathered in one place for easy review. You can also use your journal for another purpose—it is possible that when you are first learning about attachment struggles and the consequences they have had on your life, you might experience grief, anger, or sadness for the things that have happened in the past; feel free to write about the thoughts and feelings that come up for you. All these emotional responses are completely normal and part of processing these deeper issues that have affected you. Through identifying and processing these feelings, you can continue to move forward to learn solutions and coping techniques to overcome such challenging internal reactions by doing the exercises in the book.

I'm a solution-oriented person, so I understand that you may feel the urge to rush through the material as quickly as possible. But keep in mind that the issues that have developed in your life did not arise overnight, so it will take some time and patience to work through what you are learning. Developing a solid foundation is important so that you can experience long-term benefits and resolve the recurrent problems in your life once and for all. So, please, take the time to fully absorb the information and discover how it applies to your life. I encourage you to take on all the exercises—even if you think they may not apply to you. Give them your best shot and work them all the way through. If something doesn't feel helpful and doesn't become a useful tool for you, that's okay. The only way you'll know is if you give it a try. This approach also ensures that whatever ends up in your toolbox after you have tried all the exercises will be the most effective and personalized strategies for you.

In the same vein, consistent practice will solidify your understanding and help you retrain your mind to let go of old patterns and adopt new ones. Revisit chapters when you need to, make time to regularly review exercises that have been particularly helpful for you, and keep working at it, especially when you find the influences of your old attachment style slipping back into your life.

Finally, if there is someone in your life who is embarking on a similar self-development journey, consider talking with them about what you're learning, and encourage each other to use your newfound skills to manage life's problems big and small. Self-development, when done right, isn't always going to feel comfortable; lift each other up when needed and lean on this connection, which will help you to persevere when the going gets tough.

It is my greatest hope that the information and exercises in this book will guide you on your healing journey and that your new secure attachment style will allow you to find success in all areas of your life. No matter what you've been through, I know you can take charge of your life today and learn the tools to live a more empowered, satisfying, and joyful life.

Let's dive in.

ATTACHMENT

CHAPTER 1

Attachment Theory

Human beings crave connection. It is fundamental to who we are as a species and a necessary ingredient to thriving in this world. We all need to feel the support of community, enjoy time with our friends and loved ones, contribute positively at work with our colleagues, reach our desired goals, and form satisfying romantic relationships. All these meaningful human connections and experiences are influenced by the interactions and support we had with our parents or caregivers when we were young. In fact, some of the most important factors that contribute to your ability to form meaningful, satisfying relationships with people throughout your life, your skills in regulating emotions, and your path to self-development and growth are present beginning when you are an infant.

Psychiatrist John Bowlby, who developed attachment theory, believed that our early experiences with parents, caregivers, and other important adults have a profound impact on our social, emotional, and cognitive development. Dr. Bowlby's theory of attachment suggests that human beings are born biologically preprogrammed to form attachment, or as he described it, a "lasting psychological connectedness,"[1] because this helps us survive. He was highly influenced by a 1937 study by Nobel laureate

Konrad Lorenz, which showed attachment was innate in goslings who were typically hatched away from their biological mothers.[2] Immediately after the goslings hatched, Lorenz was the first biological being they encountered, and the baby geese began following Lorenz around, the result of a process called "imprinting." They recognized Lorenz as their "mother" and formed a strong bond with him. They came to lean on Lorenz for survival and protection.

Through his own observations, Dr. Bowlby came to believe that young humans require an affectional bond (much like the imprinting of Lorenz's geese) with at least one primary caregiver for positive social and emotional development. This attachment bond, a deep and emotional connection that develops between an infant and their primary caregiver(s), is based on the child's biological need for survival and their psychological need for security. After all, human infants quite literally cannot live without their parents, unlike the newborns of some other species.

As soon as they are born, infants cry to attract the attention of caregivers. As they grow older, they begin to smile, babble, and interact in meaningful ways with the adults around them, especially their primary caregiver. This is often the mother but can equally be the father, grandparent, or any caregiver who provides the majority of the child's care and responds most often to their needs. By the end of the first year, babies can display a wide range of behaviors designed to maintain closeness with caring adults. This includes following and clinging to the caregiver (especially when frightened or in a new situation), becoming upset at the caregiver's departure, greeting the caregiver when they return, and exploring and learning about their environment in a relaxed way when the caregiver is present and available. By their second year of life, babies begin to take notice of others' goals and feelings in addition to their own and can change their behaviors to increase the chances of reaching their own goals.

Essentially, the baby and their caregivers are engaged in a dance: How does the parent respond to their child's needs? What behaviors are rewarded, and which are punished? Does the baby feel soothed and comforted, safe, and attended to when they cry? These repeated interactions teach the child whether their caregivers are consistent, whether they can be counted on for help, and how best to get their needs met.

The quality of that dance determines what Dr. Bowlby called the attachment bond: our first template of how we relate to others. Having secure attachment bonds enables a child to feel protected and able to explore their environment, interact with familiar as well as new people, and learn important skills while knowing that they have a safe haven to return to when they feel scared or threatened. In the long run, secure attachment is the foundation that lets you engage with the world, knowing that you have a safe place to come back to; learn to organize your feelings, thoughts, and actions; and understand where and how to seek care and comfort. However, many people suffer attachment wounds during these crucial developmental stages. These attachment issues occur at a time in a child's life when they have very little control over their circumstances, and they require the adults around them to help them feel safe and to meet their basic needs. It is understandable, then, that most people who have experienced attachment wounds early in life perceive a loss of control and subsequently develop rigid and inflexible rules for how they should think, feel, and behave, all aimed at shielding them from further hurt, pain, and disappointment.

To understand the influences of attachment bonds and what happens when they go awry, Dr. Bowlby's collaborator, Dr. Mary Ainsworth, devised a study that classified the four attachment styles we know today: secure, avoidant, anxious, and disorganized.

THE STRANGE SITUATION

The Strange Situation Procedure is a standardized procedure devised by Dr. Ainsworth in the 1970s to observe attachment security in children within the context of caregiver relationships. Dr. Ainsworth was a developmental psychologist who worked with Dr. Bowlby and was strongly influenced by his ideas about attachment. As suggested by its name, the Strange Situation was designed to present children with an unfamiliar but not overwhelmingly frightening experience. The study was conducted with infants between the ages of nine and eighteen months and took place in an unfamiliar environment that was likely to heighten the child's need for their parent. The procedure involved a series of eight episodes lasting approximately three minutes each, in which a mother, child, and stranger were introduced, separated, and reunited. Based on the infant's reactions to these different situations, the infants were classified into four different attachment styles.[3]

During the procedure, the parent and the infant are first left alone while the infant explores the room full of toys. Then an adult stranger enters the room and talks for a minute to the parent, after which the parent leaves the room. The stranger stays with the infant for a few minutes, and then the parent returns and the stranger leaves. During the session, a video camera records the child's behaviors, which are later coded and analyzed.

Dr. Ainsworth knew from her research that a child's attachment is largely influenced by their primary caregiver's sensitivity to their needs for safety and security, so she was specifically interested in observing:

1. The amount of exploration that the child engages in (such as playing with new toys).
2. The child's reactions to their caregiver's departure each time.
3. The child's reunion behaviors with the caregiver.
4. The child's reactions to the stranger when they are alone without the caregiver.

Based on the patterns of behavior she observed, she categorized the children in the study into four attachment styles:

Secure: These infants explored freely while their caregiver was present; engaged somewhat comfortably with the stranger, especially if their caregiver encouraged such interactions; were noticeably upset when the caregiver left; and were generally happy and welcoming of the caregiver's return.

Avoidant: These infants either avoided or ignored the caregiver and did not explore much regardless of who was present. They showed little emotion when the caregiver left or during their reunion. This apathy is a cover for their internal distress, which was shown in an early study that measured the heart rate of these infants.[4]

Anxious: These infants explored relatively little even when the caregiver was present. They were more wary of the stranger than other infants in the study, and when their caregiver departed, they were highly distressed and some screamed or cried inconsolably. When the caregiver returned, there was some ambivalence on the part of the child. They may have appeared to be angry or continued to cry.

Disorganized: Infants with disorganized attachment showed pronounced displays of fear, contradictory behaviors (such as following and clinging to the caregiver quickly followed by anger toward the caregiver), as well as freezing behaviors or dissociation (seemingly disconnecting from the world around them and being minimally responsive to environmental stimulation). This attachment style can be somewhat unpredictable and is not easily categorized because the infants showed contradictory patterns of behavior, clinging to their caregiver one minute and becoming angry or aggressive with them in the next.

Even as we grow and become less dependent on our caregivers, the influence of early attachment stays with us, because of the ideas we've developed about ourselves, other people, and the world around us based on our early attachment relationships. Over time, these beliefs are further molded by our perceptions and experiences, influence our behaviors, and are held in our memories. Psychologists call this system of thoughts, memories, beliefs, feelings, and actions about yourself and others the *internal working models*, essentially your inner guidance system. Your internal working models serve as templates for how you interact with the world and create expectations about what will happen when you do. While they continue to change and develop over time, a child's baseline inner working models are usually well established by the time they are just a few years old.

It may seem strange to imagine that something you have no control over in your infancy can impact you for years after, but that's exactly what happens: Unless you work to heal your style, the beliefs you internalized as a child can persist and influence you throughout your life. This occurs because our brains tend to favor information that confirms our mental models. It's challenging to accept new information that requires us to reevaluate and potentially change our existing belief systems. Holding on to our long-standing, deeply held mental models is less cognitively demanding, time-consuming, and emotionally uncomfortable than challenging preestablished ideas that have been with us since we were learning about how the world works. By default, our brains will stay with these established ideas unless we do something to actively shake them up.

THE IMPACT OF ATTACHMENT IN ADULTHOOD

None of these attachment styles—secure, avoidant, anxious, or disorganized—make you inherently good or bad. That said, your early attachment bonds have a strong influence over whether you *believe* you are fundamentally good or bad (and therefore whether you deserve good things in life or not) and whether you feel loved and cared for. Your early attachment style shapes your self-concept—a constellation of beliefs you hold about yourself—which tells you how to navigate your life and how to achieve the outcomes you want. It forms the basis for how you handle different situations as you grow older, from forging new relationships and working with others, to setting and attaining your goals, and preparing you to face new, challenging situations. In short, attachment influences everything you do because it tells you who you think you are.

The unhealed attachment wounds in all the insecure attachment styles (avoidant, anxious, disorganized) can lead to codependency in relationships and intergenerational transmission of problematic attachment. At its most extreme, insecure attachment can make it challenging to navigate even simple day-to-day tasks like deciding what to eat or whether or not to exercise. Those with attachment wounds may question themselves and experience significant self-doubt. They may distance themselves from people and make excuses for their absence, occupying themselves with endless projects and distractions. A person with insecure attachment may create negative self-fulfilling prophecies; for example, believing that no one cares about them, they withdraw from others and preclude those people from the chance to show that they care. People with insecure attachment are also likely to engage in self-defeating interactions, for example, being highly suspicious and paranoid of their partner without cause until they finally push that person away. These behaviors of the insecurely attached can occur without much conscious thought and yet have real-world negative consequences.

These behaviors lead to developing few positive, healing bonds with others, and they interfere with reaching coveted goals in life. Without secure social bonds, people are likely to develop physical ailments and chronic illnesses, suffer from depression or anxiety, and struggle with substance abuse. They can also experience existential crises and feel they lack motivation and purpose. In fact, many common concerns I hear in my practice—from relationship issues to challenges in the workplace—stem from problems in the attachment bond.

The realization of just how instrumental your caregivers were in determining your attachment style can make this work challenging for a lot of people. If your childhood was stressful or traumatic, it's especially easy to get caught in a cycle of blame and anger with your caregivers for your current struggles, or struggle with shame if you perceive your emotional vulnerability and need for connection as weaknesses. It's important to remember that all children will do whatever they can to seek approval, care, safety, protection, and belonging. This survival instinct is natural and necessary. As a young child, you were simply trying to adapt the best you could to your situation, to ensure your survival in that moment. You were also trying to minimize potential threats in the future by internalizing some of these life lessons and banking your coping style for later challenges and interactions.

Regardless of your parents' own imperfections and missteps, the work ahead is about you wanting to change the ways you behave and the beliefs you hold about yourself today. You don't need to merely fantasize about what your life could have been if your childhood was better. Your life is your own, and healing is possible for you no matter what style you developed in childhood. This can also be an opportunity to practice understanding and compassion for your parents: Their own struggles—financial, physical, emotional, relational—and unhealed attachments all played into their parenting style. More often than not, they did the very best they could for you.

꒰

Although many people identify most with one primary attachment style, it is worthwhile to note that some find they have one predominant attachment style followed by a secondary attachment style. Sometimes, people can develop more than one attachment style in response to relating to different caregivers. One caregiver may have been flexible and generally present, while another primary caregiver was unpredictable and not consistently emotionally available. As a result, you may have developed both a secure attachment style as well as an anxious attachment style, and which style expresses itself depends on the situation or the person.

While some readers may find that one attachment style pervades all the major domains of life, others may find that they switch among different styles in different contexts. For example, someone who is secure in relationships may find themselves anxious at work, or someone who is secure in their friendships and goal attainment might find that they are avoidant with their family. If this is you, review the chapters that apply to both of your attachment styles and work through all the exercises that are contained within them.

Some problematic attachment scripts may be more detrimental than others and take a person further from healing and personal growth. As you work through the rest of the book, you may choose to focus on the attachment style that you feel is most negatively impacting you, and then turn to the work related to your secondary attachment style once you've made some progress in healing the attachment style that is most challenging.

There are people who believe that once your attachment style has formed, it remains that way for the long haul. Certainly, there have been psychologists in the past who subscribe to the idea that there is a "sensitive period" during which people form their attachment bonds, and once that sensitive period has passed, you're stuck with what you're given. I don't believe that's true, and I've seen people of all ages break free of their insecure attachments that were formed in childhood.

If you walk away with only one lesson from this chapter (and this book), let it be this: Secure attachment and all its benefits are achievable at *any* age and stage of your life. You don't have to wait for other people or circumstances to heal your past wounds and create better outcomes—you simply need to commit to the process, learn to trust that you are capable of positive change, and watch your life transform for the better. But first, you'll need to determine your attachment style.

Quiz: What's My Attachment Style?

You may already have a suspicion about your attachment style from reading the descriptions in chapter 1, but this quiz will help you to gain insight into which style most closely aligns with your behavior and beliefs about yourself, and to see if there are any areas of your life where you exhibit different types of attachment. For each of the questions, circle the option that you feel describes you best. If more than one seems to describe you, choose which one describes you more of the time. If you are unsure of how to answer, think about how this question may apply to you when you are in a new, stressful, or unfamiliar environment. The shadow of your insecure attachment style will likely emerge in challenging situations.

CHILDHOOD

Would you describe yourself as a curious and exploratory child?

   A. Yes, and especially if my primary caregiver was around.
   B. Yes, and I explored rather well whether my primary caregiver was around or not.
   C. I explored more with my primary caregiver present than if they were not there, but was still very cautious and a bit nervous.
   D. No, I was very scared to explore, and a lot of things felt frightening or foreign to me.

How do you think your primary caregiver felt about you?

A. I consistently felt valued and loved by them.

B. My primary caregiver seemed to care a lot about other things—they seemed busy and often distracted, so I relied more on myself.

C. It was hard to know how they felt about me; sometimes they were very doting and other times they were distant.

D. My primary caregiver was unpredictable, neglectful, and/or abusive. I had a confusing relationship with them.

What usually happened when your primary caregiver left you alone with others to look after you or play with you?

A. I missed their presence but then gradually warmed up to others who were around.

B. I found ways to make myself feel better without asking others for help.

C. I was very sad and scared without them and had a hard time doing things until they returned.

D. I was extremely upset and even inconsolable for long periods of time when they left. When they returned, I was still mad at them for leaving and would express my upset to them.

How did you respond to new people you were introduced to if your primary caregiver(s) was/were also around?

A. If my caregiver seemed to support it, I was pretty comfortable being social with new people.

B. I didn't necessarily care that much about interacting with them—I could play on my own and entertain myself.

C. Even with my caregiver there, I had difficulty warming up to new people and felt nervous around them.

D. I was often more interested in doing things with these new people than my own caregiver(s).

How did your caregiver react when you expressed negative emotions?

A. They allowed me to express my feelings and comforted me.

B. My caregiver didn't like it when I expressed negative emvotions. They told me to stop being upset or to stop being sensitive.

C. They appeared to be very anxious or stressed when I was upset. Sometimes they were so upset themselves that they were not available to really support me.

D. My caregiver often reacted in a way that made me feel unsafe. I was afraid to set them off or lose their support.

Did you feel you could count on your caregiver(s) to support you?

A. For the most part, I felt that they would support me no matter what.

B. My caregiver(s) seemed to care for me more when I was achieving things or doing things for them. Sometimes they gave me responsibilities I wasn't equipped to handle as a child, so it felt like I was supporting them.

C. Sometimes they were supportive but almost overly so, in an intrusive or overprotective way. They seemed anxious about potential bad outcomes or consequences.

D. My caregiver disappointed me a lot, and over time I just learned to not expect much or any support from them at all.

RELATIONSHIPS—FAMILY

What is your relationship like with your family now?

A. Every family has its difficulties, but we generally get along well.

B. I'm pretty independent and don't feel particularly close to my family. Their opinion matters less to me than the opinions of non-familial people or my own opinions.

C. I find myself constantly seeking their validation and approval for things I do, or feeling like I don't know where I stand with them.

D. I have a lot of anger and resentment toward some members of my family, but I also want them to care about me and love me. It's very stressful every time I have to interact with them.

What do you remember about your parents' relationship growing up?

A. They generally seemed connected to each other in a positive way (and if they were not a couple, they seemed to co-parent effectively).

B. They seemed generally disconnected from each other, whether they were together as a couple or not.

C. I witnessed a number of arguments between them. One of them seemed more invested in the relationship than the other person and sometimes one or both of them would act more insecure about the relationship.

D. I witnessed or learned about severe arguments and even abuse. Sometimes I was the subject of their arguments or fights. They made me feel like it was my fault they didn't get along.

What are some of your most vivid memories with family members?

A. I remember a lot of the good times—happy memories of fun activities, trips we took as a family.

B. I remember my family congregating around my activities, particularly my achievements—and I remember being tasked with a lot of responsibilities starting at a young age.

C. I remember feeling left out a lot or not quite knowing where I belonged within the family. Sometimes I felt like I had to vie for family members' attention.

D. Many of my memories of my family are negative, and sometimes, I even feel like huge sections of my memories from childhood are missing or blurred.

What is your relationship like with siblings, if you have any (and/or other close familial peers, such as cousins with whom you spent a lot of time/grew up together)?

A. We generally get along, even if I do have some that I am closer to than others.

B. I am generally the favored one and I like it that way. If I am being honest, I sometimes feel competitive with my siblings.

C. I find myself feeling like my sibling or cousin is favored over me and wanting to prove myself to gain more positive attention.

D. I have a lot of confusing feelings about my siblings and/or cousins. Sometimes I love them and other times I want nothing to do with them.

RELATIONSHIPS—FRIENDSHIPS

How are you at making new friends and interacting with strangers?

A. I generally have very little problems making new friends or striking up conversations with new people.

B. I am generally independent and don't need a lot of friends to have a good time. But I have a fair number of acquaintances and new friends in my life most of the time, depending on what my interests are or who I am working with.

C. I really want to make friends but am often worried about whether people really like me. Sometimes I won't initiate a friendship unless I'm pretty sure they're going to reciprocate. I'm unlikely to start a conversation first with a stranger.

D. I want connection with others, but it has been hard to keep long-term friendships. I'm often hot and cold with them, and there isn't a lot of stability in my friendships.

How are you at opening up to others?

A. I can get to know a new person pretty easily and don't have much of a problem trusting people who seem trustworthy.

B. It takes me a long time to open up to people, but I don't mind learning about them first and can be a good listener.

C. I sometimes tell them a bit too much about myself too early, and I spend a lot of time making sure they like me. I tend to become very friendly and personal with people with whom I have professional relationships.

D. I really want to be close to people but find it very difficult to trust them. Sometimes I find myself testing them to make sure they aren't going to do something terrible to me, and I tend to get suspicious about what people's true intentions are.

What do you believe about friends?

A. Good ones may be hard to find, but I have some that I can trust through thick and thin, and they are almost like extended family members to me.

B. You don't really need many friends—and I don't really particularly depend on friends to do what I need to do on a daily basis.

C. You have to keep them interested and engaged or else they might forget about you, or make other friends that they find more important than you.

D. They are likely to disappoint you—so it's best to keep your guard up so that you aren't caught in a vulnerable spot when they do something to upset you.

How are you with long-term friendships?

A. I have a few close, long-term friends whom I cherish.

B. I tend to value my independence rather than deep emotional ties with people.

C. When I haven't spoken to them in a while, I wonder if they're upset with me. I sometimes wonder if I stop doing things for others whether they'll still care about me.

D. I tend to write people off quickly if they've made a mistake, so I don't tend to have long-term friendships.

RELATIONSHIPS—ROMANTIC

How do you usually feel and behave in romantic relationships?

A. I feel comfortable depending on my partner for emotional support. I can also depend on others for that support if my partner isn't available.

B. I'm not too attached to my romantic partners and tend to always have a life of my own. I don't tend to ask them for help when I'm going through something difficult.

C. Sometimes people describe me as clingy or too invested in my partners. When they're upset, I take on all their burdens and feel just as devastated as they do. And sometimes I act a bit jealous or possessive, and even suspect they are cheating on me for no reason.

D. Sometimes I act out in my relationships to test how much my partner loves me. Then I feel guilty and try to do things to make up for my actions.

What do you believe about your romantic life?

A. I'm confident there are and/or have been people who really care about and love me.

B. I think others care for and love me, but I don't invest too deeply in people or relationships—I also feel fine on my own.

C. I fall in love quickly and deeply but frequently wonder if people will love me back the same way.

D. I can't depend on others to meet my needs, so I keep them at arm's length. That way I'm not surprised when they leave me or do something to disappoint me.

How are you with breakups?
A. After a period of mourning, I can generally move on.
B. I seem to walk away pretty easily after a breakup, generally unscathed. And I'm not necessarily in a rush to get into another serious relationship after a breakup.
C. I have a difficult time recovering after a breakup. I feel pretty devastated without them and sometimes fear I'll end up alone.
D. I usually go through a period of acting out or somewhat impulsive behaviors. Sometimes I get on a string of rebound relationships or I do something self-destructive like drink too much or engage in severe emotional eating.

How do you approach closeness and emotional intimacy in romantic relationships?
A. I'm comfortable with closeness and intimacy with the right people.
B. I generally don't like to be too close with others, to rely on them too much, or to have them know too much about my inner thoughts. I tend to be more comfortable with physical, rather than emotional, intimacy.
C. I want desperately to be close to others, but find that I'm always the one who seeks that more than the people I'm in a relationship with.
D. I go back and forth between wanting closeness and being angry and pushing people away.

Which of these patterns best describes you in romantic relationships?
A. I'm excited about romantic relationships, enjoy dating, and

like being in meaningful relationships, but also fare okay or even well when I am single.

B. I like being in relationships to an extent, but I tend to prioritize other things in life over my romantic life.

C. I would describe myself as a serial monogamist—I don't generally like to be single.

D. I have a hard time being without my partner, but when they return, I feel suffocated and want to escape. Sometimes I'm angry or resentful toward my partner without a specific reason.

SELF-CONCEPT

How do you feel about yourself generally?

A. There's room for improvement, but I generally feel okay or good about myself.

B. I feel great about myself particularly when I am achieving my goals and making headway on accomplishments—especially if I am doing this better than other people.

C. I don't feel good about myself unless other people tell me I'm okay or reassure me in some way. I worry that others are more successful, attractive, or competent than me.

D. I sometimes despise or hate myself, and I don't know how to change that. I also frequently have feelings of emptiness and don't know why that happens.

What is your self-esteem dependent upon?

A. My self-esteem tends to depend on my own beliefs, thoughts, and feelings. I can feel okay or good about myself even if I have a challenging day.

B. My self-esteem is very dependent on what I do for a living, whether I am achieving my goals or feel I am accomplishing something important.

C. My self-esteem varies greatly depending on what is happening that day, how people treat me or respond to me.

D. My self-esteem is pretty erratic—I can't seem to figure out why some days I feel good and other days I feel terrible about myself.

How do you deal with negative thoughts?

A. I have good and bad days but can generally recover decently from negative thinking.

B. When I have negative thoughts, I try to avoid thinking about them or push them away.

C. I have a lot of self-deprecating thoughts, and sometimes it's hard to think positively.

D. My negative thoughts feel unmanageable at times. I sometimes or often believe I am deeply flawed and broken and that no one and nothing can fix me.

How are you at managing your physical and mental health?

A. I know it's important, so I try to develop good habits for my body and mind.

B. I pride myself on focusing on my own well-being. Sometimes important people in my life tell me that I focus more on my own well-being than on their needs.

C. I fall short of the goals I set for myself and feel that others have it better than me.

D. I find myself wondering if I really deserve to have good things happen to me, so sometimes I neglect or self-sabotage my physical and mental health.

How are you with being alone and on your own?

A. I enjoy being on my own, but also enjoy being with people I care about.

B. I highly value my independence and often prefer to do things on my own. It gives me a sense of accomplishment when I do something on my own that others do in groups.

C. I feel lost and anxious when I'm alone for too long. I try to avoid this by keeping myself busy with others—sometimes even doing activities I'm not that into just so I don't have to be alone.

D. I'm afraid of some of my own thoughts when I'm alone, so I often distract from these thoughts by doing things that help me escape my reality, like emotional eating, binge-watching TV, and even addictive behaviors like using alcohol and drugs too much.

Which of the below best describes your worldview?

A. There are plenty of people who are trustworthy, and a small handful who aren't.

B. It's better to invest in things rather than people, because people disappoint you. That's why I value independence more than deep emotional ties with people.

C. Most people don't tell you what they are really thinking, so you have to be proactive and try to find out the truth for yourself and make sure they don't mislead you.

D. Most people can't be trusted, and they'll hurt or even abuse you if they have the chance.

SCHOOL/WORK

What best describes your experience as a student (in childhood and adulthood if applicable)?

- A. I was generally confident and did fine in school with teachers and peers.
- B. I enjoyed excelling in school and relished doing better than other people.
- C. I was worried that I would say the wrong thing in class and sound stupid or that other students wouldn't like me, so I was somewhat timid and didn't initiate as much as I would like socially and/or academically.
- D. I had significant difficulty making friends or making consistent headway in my academics.

How did you interact with teachers when you were in school?

- A. I enjoyed positive attention from my teachers but was okay if I wasn't their favorite student.
- B. I strived to be the best and greatly enjoyed being rewarded with positive attention from teachers, especially if it was clear that I was one of their favorite students.
- C. I worked very hard to make sure my teachers liked me and sometimes or often worried that I didn't measure up to other students.
- D. I had a hard time bonding with teachers consistently. I acted out in class, sometimes for attention, and became angry or frustrated with many of my teachers.

How are you at work?

- A. I can focus on the tasks I'm assigned and do a pretty good job.
- B. I love focusing in on work, so much so that I sometimes neglect the social interactions in my workplace.
- C. I end up trying to make my supervisors and co-workers like me more than focusing on the tasks I'm assigned.

    D. I have difficulty holding on to jobs and can get into some pretty big conflicts with supervisors and co-workers.

How are you at getting along with colleagues?

    A. I can generally work well with most people.

    B. I tend to take the lead in almost all teamwork, and can be somewhat critical of others' approaches if I don't agree with them.

    C. I worry about whether my colleagues like and respect me, but sometimes have trouble speaking up in group settings.

    D. I have difficulty trusting others in groups and can get derailed from the purpose of the task or project due to interpersonal arguments or frustrations.

How are your relationships with supervisors and bosses?

    A. I can generally get along with them if I figure out their work style and what they expect from me.

    B. I generally get along well with supervisors because I work very hard to make sure I go above and beyond expectations, even if it is at the expense of my personal and social life.

    C. I am often nervous about whether I am meeting expectations and need reassurance from them to make sure I'm meeting goals.

    D. I have a lot of negative feelings with people in authority positions and will sometimes challenge them, so it can be hard to get along harmoniously with a supervisor or boss.

When you start a new job or get a promotion, what are you usually like?

    A. I feel good about my accomplishment and work to be effective at my job.

    B. I love the challenge of a new position and throw myself into becoming the best, sometimes at all costs.

    C. I constantly feel worried that I don't deserve my position and that someone might discover that I can't do my job as well as they thought.

    D. I have difficulty with new jobs and can feel a bit confused about what to aim for and where to go next in my career.

ATTAINING WANTS, GOALS, AND NEEDS

How are you at communicating your wants, needs, and opinions?

    A. I can assertively communicate my wants, needs, and opinions.

    B. I can sometimes be a bit forceful in asserting my wants and needs and, if I feel stifled, I get frustrated and upset.

    C. I tend to avoid talking about my own wants, needs, and opinions and try to take care of the needs of those around me.

    D. I often don't know what I want or need—my ideas can change often and somewhat randomly.

Do you feel comfortable asking for help when needed?

    A. I'm comfortable asking for help from people I love and trust.

    B. I don't like asking others for help and prefer to rely on myself.

    C. I'm uncomfortable with asking for help because I don't want to seem too needy or dependent.

    D. I don't bother asking people for help because they won't really want to help me anyway. But it makes me sad thinking about the fact that I have such little support.

How do you feel about communicating with important people in your life?

    A. I find it relatively easy to be emotionally open with people close to me. I feel comfortable expressing my opinion, even if it means disagreeing with someone I care about.

B. I don't generally like to talk too much about my deepest thoughts or feelings. I like to keep some things to myself.

C. I often worry that people in my life will stop loving me or that they might leave me. I have difficulty speaking assertively about my opinions, especially if it means disagreeing with someone I care about.

D. I go back and forth between wanting to tell people my inner-most thoughts and pushing them away.

How are you with dealing with people's feelings?

A. I am open to hearing others' feelings and feel comfortable taking care of them when they are upset, but if it becomes too taxing for me, I know to take a break or ask others to also help support the person I care about.

B. I am uncomfortable around people who seem highly emotional, and generally dislike conversations about emotions.

C. I become very mission driven to try to solve other people's emotional problems, even if it means that I suffer or have to give up some of the things I need or want to do that day.

D. I often think other people's negative emotions are about me, and may end up being confrontational with them when they're feeling upset.

How do you manage conflict with important people in your life?

A. I don't love conflict but can manage it.

B. I am pretty good with compartmentalizing conflicts, and can focus on something else until I have time to resolve the conflict.

C. If conflicts aren't resolved immediately, I get very anxious and scared about the state of that relationship.

D. When a conflict happens, it's easier to end the relationship than to try to work it out.

How are you at striving for and reaching goals?

A. I can reach most of my goals if I put in my best effort.

B. I'm really good at reaching goals, and when I'm upset about something that happened with other people, I tend to focus even harder on goals and achievements to make me feel better.

C. I try really hard to reach my goals but seem to always come up short. I question my own abilities and skills more often than others.

D. It really depends—sometimes I feel like I can reach my goals, but often right before I make headway I sabotage my own efforts and then beat myself up about it.

SCORING YOUR QUIZ

To find your primary attachment style, tally up the overall number of A, B, C, and D items you circled. The letter that you have circled the most is your dominant attachment style—this is the one that has the most universal influence on your beliefs about yourself and your interactions with others.

Because some people exhibit a different style depending on the situation or who you're with, I also recommend that you review your responses by section to see if your style is consistent. You may find that in certain domains of life, you display a more secure attachment style, while in others, you display a form of insecure attachment (or perhaps, two different forms of insecure attachment depending on domain of life).

	A's	B's	C's	D's
CHILDHOOD				
RELATIONSHIPS—FAMILY				
RELATIONSHIPS—FRIENDSHIPS				

RELATIONSHIPS—ROMANTIC				
SELF-CONCEPT				
SCHOOL/WORK				
ATTAINING WANTS, GOALS, AND NEEDS				
TOTAL OF ALL CATEGORIES				

Mostly A's: Secure—Connected Explorer

You have a generally positive view of self and others; your sense of self is not overly dependent on what others think of you, what happens on a given day, or your accomplishments in life. You're comfortable with emotional intimacy and can usually form healthy, stable relationships. You generally stay connected to people who matter to you while pursuing your individual goals.

Mostly B's: Avoidant—Fiercely Independent

Self-sufficiency and self-reliance are the watchwords of the Fiercely Independent. In fact, if this is your style, you probably feel more comfortable chasing achievements and praise than pursuing intimacy and relationships. You're very goal oriented, and it's likely hard for you to depend on others. Your parents may have set high expectations for you to take care of yourself even as a child, and now you generally fly solo and don't often ask for help even when you need it.

Mostly C's: Anxious—Worried Warrior

You tend to have high anxiety about your relationships and worry about being abandoned or rejected by others. You get a self-esteem boost when people are positive about you, and your self-esteem can get rocked if you don't get good feedback—even if it's about something minor. It can be tough for you to reach goals or even have the confidence that you can get what you want, and unless someone is fully cheering you on, you may give up on yourself. Your parents may have made you feel insecure about their love and care for you, so you've become overly concerned with earning others' approval through people-pleasing behaviors because this ensures their support and reduces your anxiety.

Mostly D's: Disorganized—Surveillance Specialist

You may see danger lurking around every corner and tend to be on high alert even when you don't necessarily need to be. This is because your parents may have been unpredictable or even abusive. As a result, it may be challenging for you to form stable relationships and manage conflicts in a consistent way. You may exhibit push-pull (or approach-avoid) dynamics in both relationships and goal pursuits. Your self-concept may vary more often than the other attachment styles.

〜

No matter what your current attachment style is, I want you to know that secure attachment and its benefits are within your reach. Attachment isn't a one-and-done: In adulthood, it's up to us how we want to strengthen, change, or maintain our attachment style. So, how do you obtain secure attachment and keep it, especially if you weren't given the opportunity to form positive attachment bonds earlier in life? Becoming securely attached starts with affirming yourself and developing a healthy self-concept that will pave the way to confidently approaching all the areas of your life with a deep sense of belonging and resilience. In fact, the key to healing attachment issues is working on self-concept, so let's take a look at what self-concept is and how it is related to attachment bonds.

CHAPTER 2

Attachment Style and Your Self-Concept

When I ask you who you are, what do you imagine? Do you see yourself as attractive, intelligent, funny? Pride yourself on being a self-taught artist? Perhaps you value adventure, integrity, or community? Do you think you're a compassionate and caring person who is a good friend and supportive family member? Maybe you're convinced you're not a morning person. All of these are examples of the many aspects that make up a person's self-concept—a collection of perceptions, thoughts, beliefs, feelings, and attitudes that one holds about oneself.

Self-concept is formed through a combination of experiences, social interactions, and cultural influences, from family background, peer groups, education and work experiences, and exposure to media messages. Having a healthy, stable, and resilient self-concept is crucial to experiencing success and fulfillment in all the domains of your life—and a healthy attachment bond is where it all begins. Self-concept may seem self-explanatory, but it's actually a nuanced, multifaceted idea with big implications for our mental health. When psychologists talk about self-concept, what we're really talking about are its three components: self-image, self-worth, and ideal self.[1]

Self-image is how you perceive yourself right now, in this moment. It does not necessarily reflect reality, and it can be altered by your thoughts, how you are feeling on a given day, and what you think about your behaviors and actions or what they signify to you. For example, on days you volunteer for a charity you might think of yourself as a generous person, while having an argument with a loved one over something trivial might lead you to view yourself as impatient. Your self-image can consist of social roles, personality traits, physical attributes, or abstract concepts of being. It's also possible to have a more lasting, generalized negative self-image such as believing you are unlovable or incompetent.

Self-worth is how much value you place on yourself and how much you like, respect, and accept yourself. Although self-esteem and self-worth are often used interchangeably, self-worth is thought to be more stable and enduring, whereas self-esteem can be more variable and situational. Self-esteem often comes from how others react to you, how you compare yourself to others (and whether you believe you measure up), how you identify yourself, and what roles you hold most dear in life. For example, the prestige or stigma related to particular roles in life may change, boost, or hurt your self-esteem depending on how much you believe those roles define a central part of you. In general, people with higher self-esteem tend to also have a stronger sense of self-worth because they have more positive and accepting views of themselves. On the other hand, people with lower self-esteem might also struggle with feelings of inadequacy, which can erode their sense of self-worth over time.

Ideal self is who you'd like to be. When your ideal self and your self-image are similar, with alignment in the thoughts, feelings, beliefs, and actions of both selves, you feel safe and stable as you go through life. If, however, your ideal self and your self-image have very little in common, that discrepancy can cause intense emotional discomfort.[2,3]

The intersection between how you feel about yourself in the moment, how much you like and respect yourself, and how closely your sense of self in the present aligns with who you aspire to be all factor into that bigger picture we call "self-concept."

Before we dive in to further understand the connection between self-concept and attachment, take a look at this quick self-concept snapshot. Your score will serve as a baseline to track any changes in self-concept as you begin to heal your attachment style. Remember, two major goals of healing your attachment wounds are to improve your self-concept and to meet the needs of your inner child. Once you have completed the exercises that help you to heal insecure attachment, you'll take this self-concept assessment again to notice the progress you're making.

SELF-CONCEPT SNAPSHOT

Read the statements below and choose the option that best describes you.

1 = not true, **2** = sometimes or partially true, **3** = mostly or definitely true

- If I had the opportunity, I wouldn't change many things about myself.
- I have confidence in my decision-making.
- I don't worry excessively about what others think of me.
- I like myself even when I am in conflict with someone else.
- I value myself even when I make mistakes.
- I believe my efforts contribute to my success.
- I have control over my reactions to difficult situations.
- I like myself.
- I can start and finish projects without others' help and approval.
- I have a clear sense of who I am.
- I have positive and admirable traits.
- I can overcome challenges when I try hard.

Add up your total score, which will range between 12 and 36. The higher your score, the stronger your self-concept.

SELF-CONCEPT AND ATTACHMENT

Almost every patient who comes to me in my private practice is struggling with some type of negative self-belief. They struggle with poor self-image and low self-worth, and think that their ideal self is likely to go unrealized in their lifetime. These deep-seated, strongly held negative beliefs can usually be traced back to their early childhood experiences and represent their greatest fears about how others might see them. What's even more challenging is that these negative self-beliefs act as self-fulfilling prophecies: We're convinced that we see ourselves accurately, and the rigidity of those self-perceptions gets in the way of healthy relationships, satisfying connections, and successful goal pursuits.

Our minds are naturally inclined to use simplified strategies to conserve mental energy and reduce cognitive load. In many ways this is adaptive and necessary (for example, when we have to make decisions without time to analyze the nitty-gritty), but this cognitive miserliness can lead to biases and errors in our thoughts and actions. This is why our attachment experiences have such a profound impact on us as we grow: The stories we learned from our caregivers become the simplified strategies we use to see the world and ourselves. They become shortcuts to our self-concept that are hard to shake for two reasons. The first is because they're so readily accessible. We are likely to quickly classify ourselves as being less capable, less worthy, or less lovable than others just because these thoughts have been with us and percolating for some time.

The second reason has to do with the brain's self-confirmation bias. Going back to that cognitive miserliness, our brains prefer confirming an existing belief—even when it's negative!—to creating a new one, so we are less likely to entertain a new idea or a new action that will change how we think about ourselves. We may even unconsciously seek evidence to further cement these existing unproductive beliefs. The influence of our self-concept goes beyond how we think about ourselves and impacts how we relate to others.

People with insecure attachment styles and, relatedly, negative self-concepts develop problematic *attachment scripts*, which are rigid, inflexible rules about how they should respond to different situations and people in their lives. When these scripts are followed, they create the disappointing results they've come to expect.

For example, if your self-beliefs tell you that you are unlovable, unworthy, and incapable, you may believe that no one can take care of your needs or that you don't deserve good things in life. You may say, "I'm terrible at relationships, so why bother?" and subconsciously activate a *script of detachment* where you immerse yourself in solitude, work, or other ways of achieving a self-fulfilling prophecy. You may go from job to job unable to find a stable working environment or develop connections with co-workers. Although you may feel lonely, you might vehemently deny the need for relationships because you are so busy with work or other solo activities. Because you feel unwelcome or that you don't fit in with the group, you may avoid family or other social gatherings.

Or you may have a gnawing, persistent worry that your loved ones don't care about you. You may have subconsciously activated a *script of dependency* where you may indiscriminately cling to any relationships, come on too strong, or ask for repeated reassurances that exhaust the people in your life with your emotional neediness. You may be on high alert to signs that others are displeased or detaching from you and engage in extreme people-pleasing behaviors to gain acceptance. This creates a vicious cycle where your self-esteem is attached to how others respond to you. Your self-perception can turn on a dime and cause you to feel a lack of control. You may have difficulty making decisions without input from other people and feel stressed or scared when you're alone for too long. You can find yourself obsessing over ways to avoid being hurt or rejected and running hot and cold with loved ones, and these erratic behaviors can provoke the very reactions from others that you most fear. It's a classic cycle of self-sabotage that strengthens your negative self-beliefs and makes it even more challenging for you to heal your attachment wounds.

WHAT MAKES UP YOUR SELF-CONCEPT?

Despite self-concept playing such an integral role in our daily lives, most of us are unfamiliar with the idea and the enormous impact it has on our behavior and who we are. So, let's pause and do an exercise that will help you to get to know yourself and take the time to think about who you are, what you think, and what you value.

EXERCISE: HOW I SEE MYSELF

Draw a circle on a piece of paper or in your journal, write your name in the middle, and then draw several spokes that radiate out from the circle (it will look a little like a sun).

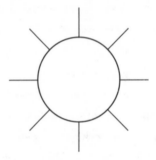

Now think about the characteristics, behaviors, and accomplishments that represent who you are. How do you see yourself? How would you introduce yourself to a stranger? What are the most important things to know about you, past, present, and future? At the ends of the spokes, write down what comes to mind, and feel free to add more lines if needed. Don't overthink this; simply write down what comes up without judging the result.

When you're done, look at your drawing and ask yourself the following questions:

- How many of the items are personality traits or characteristics that are internal aspects of yourself (*patient, adventurous, caring, hardworking, humorous*)?
- How many are physical descriptions (*the color of your hair, eyes, or your body type*)?
- How many are social roles (*mother, son, friend, teacher*)?
- How many are achievements (*college graduate, financially independent*)?
- How many are activities you engage in (*running, cooking, blogging*)?
- Did you list your job, where you live, what inspires you, or aspirations (traits you hope to embody or goals you wish to achieve)?
- What about more abstract, existential ideas about the self (such as *"I'm a human being"* or *"I'm a spiritual being"*)?

꙳

When my client Emily created her self-concept drawing, it took her quite a while to think about what to write. She paused often, wrote, and rewrote, and frankly, looked a bit perplexed by it. All in all, it took her about fifteen minutes to complete this exercise—a long time, especially because she was supposed to write down whatever first came to mind.

When I asked her why this exercise was difficult for her, she told me that it had been a long time since she had thought about who *she* was, what she wanted, and who she is at her core. Emily's experiences point to an anxious attachment that developed early in life in response to parents who, despite their best efforts, were not consistently available to Emily emotionally or physically. Emily's parents divorced when she was very little. In fact, she doesn't remember them being together as a couple. Her father had an untreated anxiety disorder and sometimes seemed a bit disengaged when Emily was around as he was often lost in his own thoughts. Her mother remarried when Emily was seven years old, and while her stepfather was a nice man, she never felt close to him. Sometimes Emily felt her mother was more interested in her new husband than in her, and it caused Emily to experience jealousy and feeling left out. Over time, Emily became a people pleaser and was constantly going out of her way to do things for others. She relied on other people's reactions to her to decide whether she felt good about herself.

Worried Warriors like Emily, who are anxiously attached, often put their focus outward, and by making sure others' needs are met, they neglect themselves and their own self-development. When we looked at what Emily wrote, it became clear that Emily focused on others at the expense of herself:

- Social roles in life: Most of her descriptors concerned her relationship to another person (*daughter, mother, girlfriend*)
- Characteristics and traits: Many of the characteristics she listed were negative (*procrastinator, irritable*)
- Physical attributes: The two she listed were neutral in tone (*green eyes, straight hair*)
- She did not list any achievements or goals
- She did not list any activities or her job
- She listed three aspirational qualities that she wanted to embody more of but didn't feel she was quite there yet (*insightful, compassionate, and motivated*, which in my opinion were already part of who she was, but she disagreed)

As we looked through her responses together, it was clear that Emily defined herself almost exclusively in relation to other people—no wonder her self-concept could change drastically from day to day! If she had a nice conversation with her mother, she was a "good" daughter. If she argued with her best friend, then she wasn't the "caring" person she aspired to be.

Depending on the specific interactions she had with the people whom she deemed important in her life, she could be left feeling any number of ways about herself.

Of course, humans are social beings, and a part of your self-concept is going to be derived from information you obtain from the outside world. For example, you know you have a great sense of humor because people laugh at your jokes, and they tell you they think you're funny. At some point, this belief sticks, and if you have a stable, resilient self-concept you don't necessarily need external feedback to confirm it. Just because your cousin doesn't laugh at one of your jokes today doesn't change your self-belief that you have a great sense of humor. You feel confident that you're a funny person based on your cumulative past experiences—it has become a constant belief you have about yourself that doesn't require confirmation from the outside world. If, however, your self-concept is insecure, you may end up as the class clown, constantly trying to confirm and prove that you're funny by performing for others and seeking their approval.

Connected Explorers, or those who are securely attached, tend to maintain balance in the various components that make up self-concept. Their self-descriptors include a range of categories and aren't too heavily focused on one at the expense of another. Their self-concept also strikes a balance between beliefs and ideas that are rooted within themselves and those concepts and ideas that rely on information from the outside world.

That balance is what gives secure attachment its power. We can't always predict how others might react, what mood they're in, or how much they want to engage with us on a given day. During these moments, having aspects of self, rooted within us, that are stable, consistent, and relatively impervious to change is important for us to feel good about ourselves and to carry out the things we have to do on a daily basis with efficiency and ease.

The world and the people around us change from moment to moment, as do our relationships with them. So, if your self-concept relies on one aspect of your life over another (such as an overidentification with a romantic relationship or a job), when that area isn't going well, it is easy to feel like, somehow, your whole self isn't worthwhile or lovable. These self-beliefs can then impact your functioning in other important areas of life.

However, if your self-concept is diversified, when you have an argument with your romantic partner or your boss offers you negative feedback, the other aspects of your self-concept can buffer you against negative self-beliefs. For example, if you're beating yourself up for being unproductive at work, you can go home, focus on being a parent, and feel good about honoring your top values of family and community.

BONUS EXERCISE: DIVERSIFYING YOUR SELF-CONCEPT

Look back at your self-concept drawing and make a conscious effort to add different categories related to how you see yourself. Add physical characteristics or personality traits if they were missing from your original exercise. Consider adding more abstract definitions of yourself (e.g., I'm a spiritual being) or different roles that are important to you (like being a sister, a volunteer, or a mentor). If you didn't list goals or accomplishments, this is a good opportunity to add a couple. If you feel that your original exercise showed an overdependence on certain people or relationships, expand your self-concept to include roles with other important people in your life. Fill in as many additional spokes as you'd like; the more multifaceted, the better!

Now, think about how you might nourish and strengthen one "spoke" of your self-concept. You are looking for ways to make this aspect of your self-concept take root within yourself so that it will be a solid part of who you are and not as dependent on the day-to-day influences of others.

When you have selected one "spoke" of your self-concept that you'd like to nourish, think of one way you could invest in, and strengthen, this aspect of yourself. How can you increase a skill, improve your mood, or make yourself feel like you are aligning more closely with this aspect of who you are? It would be helpful to think of something you can do right now, even if it's a small activity that takes only a few minutes, as well as think of something that you can do over a longer period of time (for instance, over the next week or month) that will continue to build upon your skill or investment in this area of yourself.

For example, if you wrote "knowledgeable," you could spend some time delving into a new topic of interest or reading a chapter in a book on your bookshelf that you've been meaning to get to. Over the next week, you might decide to finish the book or think about a way to expand your knowledge on a topic of interest by doing something to build your knowledge over time (like enrolling in an online course on graphic design). You could choose to invest time in one of your favorite activities (like working on a jigsaw puzzle) or revisit a past hobby (like buying some knitting supplies today and then over the course of the next month knitting a hat for your baby nephew) to affirm that you are a multifaceted person, and all aspects of yourself are worth cultivating and honoring.

Again, the purpose of diversifying your self-concept is so that you aren't overly reliant on any one aspect of it to fulfill your self-esteem needs. Take the time to invest in *all* the spokes in your wheel, but don't feel you need to nurture them all at once.

⤳

After Emily completed this exercise, she realized that she had stopped running, a hobby she used to enjoy and that represented an essential aspect of who she is, but that she had let fall to the wayside. She set an important goal for herself: to train for a marathon, which she had wanted to do for many years, but there was always something that got in the way. She began running three times a week, which improved her self-confidence. Additionally, she bonded with several co-workers over running, and they began a running group on Saturdays, which gave her a new circle of people for social support.

Emily told me that once she got back to herself and invested in these other areas of her self-concept, she began to feel her self-esteem increase every day. She became more confident in what she had to offer in a romantic relationship, and because she had other important and meaningful pursuits, she began to obsess less about how her romantic relationships were going.

Of course, old habits die hard, and she found herself feeling insecure from time to time. But she can now redirect herself by turning to something else that made her feel good about herself, and pretty soon, those negative thoughts and feelings lessened in intensity, and she didn't feel like she had to act on them as she had before (like calling the person she was dating several times if she hadn't heard from them in a day or two).

Although Emily's anxious attachment style was leading her to behave in ways that were counterproductive for her, by digging into her self-concept and taking the time to evaluate how she perceived who she is, she was able to refocus her attention on who she wants to be. Her efforts, in effect, can override the anxious attachment behaviors and beliefs that she developed as an infant. Now, as an adult, she can make positive changes to her self-concept and begin to pave the way for a self-concept that isn't as outwardly directed, but rather, feels more stable and resilient in the face of what she is doing and who she is with.

When we think about what it means to live well, to have a life that makes us happy, excited, and fulfilled, often what we're reaching for are aspects of our self-concept. As you've seen, the way you think about and feel toward yourself has a major impact on how you move through the world. A strong self-concept isn't about looking at things through rose-colored glasses or artificially building yourself up while struggling with imposter syndrome on the inside. Instead, a strong self-concept is rooted in self-acceptance. It's about embracing yourself just as you are, an imperfect human (like all humans) who, despite best intentions, might make mistakes, commit errors of judgment, or do things you regret. None of us gets it right all the time, and it would be impossible to live up to those types of expectations, but a healthy self-concept is one that takes a balanced and realistic view. You must be able to accept yourself, warts and all, before you can turn to other people or things in life to fulfill yourself. Without self-acceptance, you'll constantly be looking for the next thing to knock you down or for someone to disappoint you, and that negative expectation often results in self-fulfilling prophecies.

Now that we have a good sense of how your attachment style and self-concept relate to each other, it's time to talk about the third component of our trifecta. Both your attachment style and your self-concept tie into your life vision—the big picture of what you want your day-to-day life to look like. Your life vision is what we will explore in the next chapter.

CHAPTER 3

The Influence of Attachment on Your Life Vision

We all want to feel like we can thrive in our lives. We want to believe that we can accomplish all the things that we set our eyes and hearts on. But we will only get as far in life as we believe we are capable of going. And insecure attachment and a negative or shaky self-concept put limits on our dreams.

As you have seen, early attachment experiences can significantly impact your self-concept. And, throughout your life, the interplay of your attachment style and your self-concept continues to influence how you view yourself and what you expect in your interactions with others. But your attachment and self-concept together also impact what you believe is possible.

Your life vision is the ultimate picture of your hopes and desires and provides the rationale for your actions and decisions. It's the big picture of who you want to be, what you want to be known for, and what you want your life to look like, both on a day-to-day basis and on a bigger scale. A strong life vision helps you clarify what you want out of life, is rooted in your most cherished values, and helps determine how you go about your day-to-day activities in pursuit of this grand vision. It is a road map that turns your dreams into reality and drives you to live life to the fullest—on your own terms.

In tandem with your attachment style, your self-concept drives how you envision that your life will unfold. Secure attachment leads to a strong, generally positive self-concept that propels you to dream big and believe that you can achieve what you put your mind to. Your self-concept influences whether you think you should reach for the stars or settle, contributes to your beliefs about what you deserve out of life, and whether your life is likely to improve if you put in your full effort at creating positive change.

If you have insecure attachment, it's as if there is a program installed in you that is running interference whenever you try to establish relationships, both romantic and platonic; find success at work; and reach the goals you'd like to achieve. By first looking at the influence your attachment has had on your life, you can identify the areas where this interference has been the most powerful. When you know where you have been, you can then have a better chance at determining what you need to move forward toward the life vision you desire.

The series of exercises in this chapter will help you to develop snapshots of your past, present, and future, which will allow you to examine the influence that attachment has had on developing and maintaining your self-concept, how you function in the major domains of life, the goals you've set for yourself, and your ideas about how (and how likely) you are to achieve these objectives.

EXERCISE: YOUR LIFE-AT-A-GLANCE TIMELINE

It's rarely obvious to us how our past experiences are affecting the story of our life that we've come to know. To help you begin to see how your style has contributed to your recollection of important life events and how you tend to view yourself and how you view others, you're going to build a Life-at-a-Glance Timeline. By looking at the common themes among your memories and life events, you'll be able to see how your attachment style has influenced your life, as well as how you remember it.

To begin, open your journal to two blank side-by-side pages or use a blank eight-and-a-half-by-eleven-inch sheet of paper turned horizontally. With a vertical line marking the end of the line on the left, and a vertical line marking the end of the line on the right, draw a horizontal line across the page. Write your birthdate and year on the left, and the current date and year on the right.

Birth Date   **Today's Date**

Using hash marks along the line, start by filling in memorable dates and events as they come to mind, as well as your age at the time of the event. A simple way to do this is to give the hashmark a letter and then create a key to the event you are including on the timeline (see below for an example). However, feel free to get creative and use markers, colored pencils, stickers, or cut and paste photos or other memorabilia next to certain events—you can even break out a big piece of poster board if you want more room to work. However you style them, the points on your timeline should represent anything that is of importance to you; they can include events or experiences that evoke positive, negative, neutral, or mixed emotions.

Everyone's timeline will look different. A milestone that has importance for you may not be something of value to your partner or friend, and vice versa. If you're having trouble coming up with occasions to complete your timeline, these examples might spark ideas for you:

- Your earliest memory
- Significant moves/relocations
- Your first important friendship
- Your first romantic relationship
- When you first encountered your most memorable teachers, coaches, or other important adults
- Separation or divorce of your parents
- Graduation from high school, college, and/or graduate school
- The birth or death of a family member or important friend
- Job changes, promotions, and/or career shifts
- An award or achievement
- Any personal losses
- The end of an important romantic relationship
- Moving in with a partner
- Engagement and/or marriage
- Some of your most cherished memories
- Some of your most devastating memories
- Something you are proud of
- Something you regret
- An illness, injury, or surgery
- One of your happiest childhood moments
- A situation that helped you to grow personally

Once you have recorded your most important memories, review each of them in chronological order. Some questions you can ask yourself as you review your timeline:

- What feelings and thoughts arise as you read through your personal timeline?
- What themes stand out to you?
- Are there any discernible patterns for when some of your best and worst memories occurred?

- Are there any specific people in your life who are connected to your major timeline events?
- Are most of your timeline events a certain type (e.g., achievements, relationships)? Is anything glaringly missing?
- Where is the timeline most crowded, and where are events more scattered? Are there any large blanks?
- What was a particularly difficult period in your life?
- Were there periods that were relatively problem free?
- What painful memories are you still carrying with you today?

When one of my clients, Jonah, did this exercise, he noted the following milestones and accomplishments.

Jonah's Milestones:

A. Student body president (age 12)
B. Drum major of marching band (age 15)
C. Made it onto the high school varsity basketball team (age 16)
D. Valedictorian of high school (age 18)
E. Graduated from college with a double major in business and economics (age 22)
F. First marathon completed (age 23)
G. Second through fifth marathons completed (ages 24–26)
H. First major job promotion from analyst to associate (age 27)
I. Married Melanie (age 30)
J. Second job promotion from associate to vice president (age 32)
K. Birth of son (age 33)
L. Third job promotion to senior vice president (age 36)
M. Tenth marathon (age 36)

Jonah's timeline was almost entirely filled with his impressive achievements. There were comparably few relationship milestones, and there was no acknowledgment of negative or stressful events on his timeline.

Some of Jonah's non-recognition of his relationships and his ultra-focus on work came directly from his childhood experiences. Jonah's parents divorced when Jonah was seven years old, and although he wasn't surprised, he was very disappointed. The one thing that always brought his parents together, even after their divorce, was Jonah's achievements. His parents attended every marching band performance and most of his basketball games, and made it a point to celebrate big achievements, from his graduations to his promotions. These were some of the rare times they presented a united front. His father, jaded from his own relationships, told Jonah not to marry and "put his stock in himself." Jonah's mother had several serious relationships after she divorced Jonah's father, but each eventually fizzled out. Although Jonah is very close with his mother, he noticed that she was less attentive and available to him when she was in a relationship.

The events Jonah chose had their roots in the avoidant attachment style and coping behaviors he developed when he was a child. His parents were not always emotionally available, but their regard for and interest in him seemed based on his achievements, so he derived a lot of his self-esteem from his success in these events and activities. Jonah admitted that it was hard for him to invest in others, because he believes he is more likely to be disappointed by the actions of another person.

I challenged Jonah to review his timeline and insert important activities that were based on relationships, or those that represented loss. It was hard for him to put negative or challenging events and situations in his life on the timeline. He didn't want to have to come face-to-face with disappointment and loss, and it was hard for him to process his feelings regarding such events. He recognized relationship events, like his engagement to his wife, were significant and deserved to be included, although they didn't feel like "achievement" to him. Ultimately, he added the following:

- Parents' divorce (age 7)
- Moving away from home to attend college (age 18)
- Being turned down for first choice internship (age 21)
- Loss of grandfather (age 29)
- Engaged to Melanie (age 29)
- ACL surgery (with a slow recovery) (age 31)

When Jonah had finished, his timeline felt like a more genuine representation of his life's ups *and* downs rather than simply a résumé of achievements.

↶

What about you? Is your timeline balanced, or is it a bit skewed toward particular types of situations or events? Is there anything you can add to balance it out so that your timeline is representative of the full scope of the positives and negatives of your life?

Your attachment style has a lot to do with the balance of your timeline and the types of events you choose to include in this exercise. As you saw with Jonah's timeline, the Fiercely Independent tend to ascribe more meaning to events that highlight personal accomplishments, and they may exclude negative events from their timeline because they don't want to come face-to-face with the experiences that might have triggered their avoidant attachment in the first place. The Fiercely Independent often experience discomfort toward deeper probing of feelings and therefore tend to exclude events that involved heightened negative emotionality. They may also minimize their relationships with other people.

Worried Warriors tend to have more events on their timelines that relate to their relationships with others, or they include important events in the lives of their loved ones. They may also be slightly skewed toward events that relate to times when their anxious attachment style was triggered, for example, when they were excluded from a social group, or when they had to perform at work and felt they came up short and didn't meet expectations (whether that's objectively true or not).

Those with disorganized attachment tend to have more difficulty outlining their lives in a sequential way. Surveillance Specialists may find it challenging to organize the important events of their lives. They can't easily identify how they feel, especially when they are under significant stress. They are also likely to highlight events where feelings of abandonment, rejection, and confusion were triggered, and find it difficult to see themselves in a consistently positive light (therefore under-emphasizing events that highlight their accomplishments). They may be unable to fully recall certain memories and experience strong physiological reactions that resemble fight-or-flight responses when they reflect on these events.

EXERCISE: WHEEL OF LIFE

Now that you've explored your most prominent memories to date, let's take a look at your life in the present. This exercise gives you a bird's-eye view of how satisfied you are across various domains of your life. It pinpoints areas of strength, helps to identify areas that need attention, and provides the motivation for you to make changes to create a more fulfilling and meaningful life now.

The Wheel of Life concept is attributed to Paul J. Meyer, who founded the Success Motivation Institute in 1960. Over the years, many versions of this tool have emerged and are regularly used in therapy, business organizations, and motivational seminars. This is my version of the wheel, which I have shared with my clients. Many enjoy this exercise because it provides them with a great deal of insight into themselves and their lives and paves the way to make practical changes.[1]

Open your journal and draw a circle. Divide the circle into eight equal parts and label each of the sections of the pie with the following categories:

1. Family of origin relationships
2. Current family relationships
3. Physical health
4. Mental health
5. Work and career
6. Romantic relationships
7. Friendships
8. Self-image and self-esteem

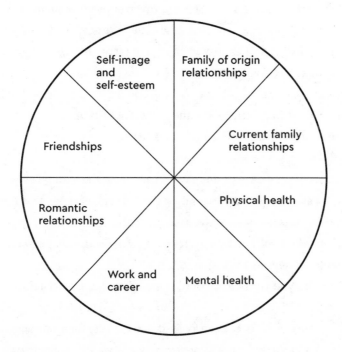

Now, by coloring in each piece of the pie, rank your current level of satisfaction, based on a scale of 0 to 10, where the outer boundary of the circle represents 10 and the middle point of the circle where all lines intersect represents a 0. Try to use the entire spectrum of number ratings.

A 10 rating does not mean that area of life is perfect or that there is no room for improvement; it simply means that you feel great about how that area of your life is going, it lights you up and nourishes you, and you don't have a desire to change anything right now.

Similarly, a rating of 0 doesn't mean that this area of your life is a catastrophe; rather, it means that you don't feel content in this area. Perhaps you have a strong motivation to change something in this aspect of your life to make it more meaningful or fulfilling for you.

A 5 rating might mean that you feel some satisfaction, but it is easy to see where there is room for improvement—perhaps you even have an idea of exactly how you might make this a 7 or 8, but you haven't had the time or energy to put a plan into action yet.

As you look at your Wheel of Life, how do you generally feel about what you see there? Ask yourself some questions to home in on your ratings in specific areas and make a note of your answers in your journal. Here are some to get you started:

- Which of these areas of life would you most like to improve?
- How are you currently spending time in each of these areas?
- Which area do you feel the best about?
- How might you emulate what's going well in one area to foster improvement in another area?
- Why do you think a particular area was low in satisfaction for you?
- Has one specific area been lower in satisfaction for a long time?
- If an area that has been consistently low was transformed to a 10, what would your daily life look like?
- What do you need from others in order to improve this specific area?

Let's look at an example. My client Annie's wheel looked like this:

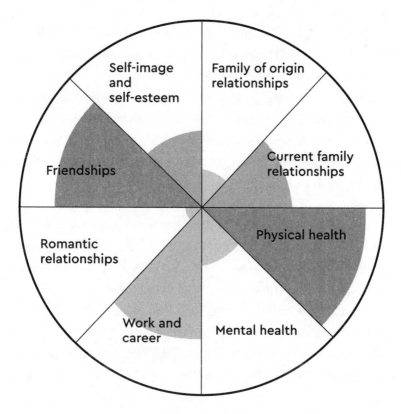

She felt good about her friendships, physical health, and career but realized that her family of origin, mental health, and especially her romantic relationships, which scored only a 1, needed improvement. As she reflected on her answers using the questions on page 54, she realized that she never felt truly comfortable or at ease in her romantic relationships. No matter how long she was dating the person, she often experienced a sense of precariousness, like something bad was about to happen. She had negative beliefs about her romantic partners and often thought, "They're not going to be around for long," or "Once they get to know the real me, they might decide they don't love me after all." These beliefs caused her to feel like she couldn't be herself in her relationships, let her hair down, and allow the chips to fall where they may. She felt that she had to continually earn the other person's affection and was sensitive to any cues that they might be losing interest, sometimes misinterpreting mundane actions as an indicator pointing toward the worst outcomes.

Understandably, she felt dissatisfied in her romantic relationships because she constantly felt as if she was second-guessing whether her partner cared about her or not. She often felt jealous, which led to conflict with her partners. In fact, she sometimes accused them of being unfaithful when they had done nothing, but she couldn't help herself. Now, after being in a relationship with Eric for a year, she still had many insecurities and sometimes felt like she didn't measure up to him. When she was especially stressed, she would become clingy and needy, because under duress it was hard for her to be alone with her thoughts. Her constant need for reassurance was sometimes overwhelming and uncomfortable for Eric, which caused him to pull away and reinforced Annie's worst fears.

The goal of your Wheel of Life is not to achieve a 10 in all areas. In fact, that is likely impossible! There are only so many hours in the day, and our energy is not infinite. Prioritizing one area typically means that you have to make sacrifices in another. The point of this activity is to give you a good understanding of the strengths in your life right now (and areas you can look to when you're going through challenging times, areas that will help you to be resilient and weather the storm). It also helps to identify what areas might need to be prioritized a bit more so that you can feel better about your quality of life and how you are spending each day.

As you review your Wheel of Life, you may notice that some of the patterns that emerge are a result of your earlier attachment experiences. Pay close attention to areas of dissatisfaction, which are likely to signal an earlier need that wasn't consistently met (for example, feelings of not being loved, because your parents didn't show unconditional caring toward you as a child) or suggest specific areas of low self-esteem (for example, challenges in taking charge of your own health when early experiences made you feel out of control with your own well-being).

Below is a brief overview of how attachment can impact each of these areas denoted on your wheel. The specific details about how your attachment style influences these domains—and what you can do to make changes—will be fully explained in subsequent chapters.

The Impact of Insecure Attachment

Knowing how your early belief systems influence what you've come to believe about how the world works and where you fit into it at your current juncture in life can offer important clues as to why you:

- **Struggle with intimacy as an adult**—An anxiously attached person may feel insecure in relationships, an avoidantly attached person may invest very little in intimate relationships, and an individual with disorganized attachment might oscillate between extreme trust and feeling disillusioned in their romantic relationships.
- **Have trouble connecting with others**—An anxiously attached person may feel that they are always setting aside their needs to cater to others; an avoidantly attached person might have many acquaintances but very few, if any, close confidants; and an individual with disorganized attachment might have an internal sense of emptiness even when they are around loved ones.
- **Stumble into the same patterns in your friendships and collegial relationships**—An anxiously attached person might find themselves second-guessing whether people truly like them, an avoidantly attached person might be accused of being overly focused on their own wishes at the expense of others, and an individual

with disorganized attachment might find that their friendships and collegial relationships are chaotic and drama-filled.

- **Have trouble setting and achieving goals**—An anxiously attached person may have trouble initiating new projects or making decisions without reassurance from others, an avoidantly attached person might overemphasize the importance of work goals and bucket list–type items over other goals that might balance their life, and an individual with disorganized attachment might find that they often sabotage their own efforts right before they're about to make a major breakthrough.
- **Can't seem to resolve the differences you have with certain family members**—An anxiously attached person might find themselves still seeking approval from their parents as an adult, an avoidantly attached person might choose to spend their spare time with others outside the family or by themselves, and an individual with disorganized attachment might find themselves under significant stress or even re-traumatized when they come into contact with their family of origin.
- **Behave in contradictory or self-sabotaging ways in close relationships**—An anxiously attached person might oscillate between being jealous and ingratiating, an avoidantly attached person might be very attentive in the early phases of dating but experience ambivalence as the relationship becomes more serious, and an individual with disorganized attachment might switch between idealizing their partner to being suspicious of them and setting up "tests" for them to prove their love.

Now that you've had the opportunity to pinpoint milestones in your past and how they have impacted you, as well as having clarified strengths and challenges in your present, you are prepared to move forward to gain a better understanding of how attachment also impacts your vision for your future. As you strengthen your life vision, this next visualization exercise asks you to turn your attention toward the future and focus on what you want out of life as you envision the days and years ahead.

EXERCISE: DISCOVERING YOUR LIFE VISION

Get into a comfortable position in your chair, or you can lie down if you wish. Gently close your eyes and take a few slow, deep breaths, breathing in through your nose and out through your mouth. Turn your attention to your current thoughts and start to observe them, as if they were clouds floating by in the sky. Imagine each thought is imprinted on a cloud that starts in the left peripheral part of your mind's eye. Each thought cloud then floats slowly across the sky toward the right peripheral part of your mind's eye, until each thought cloud disappears out of your visual field. If you find your attention drifting, try not to judge yourself, and gently guide your attention back to observing your thoughts.

Now imagine yourself slowly drifting to sleep. Your sleep is peaceful and refreshing. When you wake up, you discover that a miracle has occurred. Everything you ever wanted has materialized overnight, and you now have the life that you have always desired. It's not perfect, because there is no such thing, but you have a life that offers incredible meaning and rich experiences. You have no fear of failure nor any regrets, and people respect and cherish you and rarely disappoint you. If you put your mind toward a goal, you can achieve it with time and effort. The wounds of the past have healed, which allows you to move forward in love and confidence. You are honoring your most important values and making signif-icant strides toward self-actualization. You have achieved your ideal self, so that your self-image and your ideal self are completely aligned with each other.

Allow your mind to wander, taking in how you might feel if all of this has happened. Pay attention to the thoughts that you have in response to this vision. Think about what actions you might take first upon discovering these changes. What are some differences you might notice in the key areas of your life (family of origin relationships, current family relationships, physical health, mental health, work and career, romantic relationships, friendships, and self-image and self-esteem)? What is your job, and what does your day-to-day look like at work? Who are the most important people in your life—are they people from your family of origin, a romantic partner, or a couple of best friends? How do you feel about your physical and mental health? What are some ideas you have about your abilities to overcome challenges? What is your romantic partnership like if you have one? What is your relationship like with your child or children? What are some of the feelings you have as you consider who you are and how you feel about yourself?

Return your attention to your breathing and take a few more deep breaths in and out. Gently open your eyes and bring your awareness back to the room. Take time to record some of the thoughts and observations you had of your life vision. Perhaps note how this vision made you feel and think, and the actions you might take if this really was your new life. How might things be different with family, relationships, and so on?

Next, read through your journal entry and pay attention to how you feel. Now ask yourself these two questions—and be honest.

- Do you believe that your life vision fully captures your potential, or did you limit your own wishes and dreams in any way?
- Do you believe that your life vision is achievable with time

and effort, or do you think it's just a pipe dream that will never come to pass?

Your answers to these two questions—whether you believe your life vision captures your full potential, and whether you believe it is achievable—are extremely revealing. How you respond is directly linked to the attachment style you developed early in childhood.

THE CONNECTION BETWEEN LIFE VISION AND ATTACHMENT

For the securely attached, the Connected Explorers, their sense of self is stable, generally positive, and linked to the belief that they deserve and can attain positive outcomes through their individual efforts. During this life vision exercise, they generally aren't afraid to dream big and to imagine themselves operating at their full potential. They may approach this exercise with an inquisitive attitude and a positive mindset, excited to envision the potential for what's to come in their lives.

However, any of the insecure styles—avoidant, anxious, or disorganized— may struggle with attaining goals and achieving what they want in their lives, which is common because we tend to maintain our self-concept once it is established. They may hold themselves back from dreaming about what's possible because they're afraid to be disappointed, or they believe, either consciously or unconsciously, that they don't deserve good things.

Let's take a look at how this exercise worked for my client Jessica. When I asked her to do this life vision activity, she struggled because it was difficult for her to imagine a life in which her dreams come true. As she put it, "That just doesn't happen to me." Her disorganized attachment style was limiting her own ideas about what was achievable and the impact that her own desires and actions can have in her life. Once Jessica started to see how her past was informing her present (in her Wheel of Life exercise, where she noticed a lot of dissatisfaction over major areas) and even her thoughts about the future, she was stunned. She couldn't believe that, after all this time, her childhood was still in the driver's seat of her life—limiting her dreams, relationships, and her feelings about herself.

Jessica grew up in a chaotic and often neglectful home. Her father left her mother shortly after Jessica was born and was an inconsistent presence in her life. Sometimes he would show up and shower her with presents; other times he canceled plans with little notice, and weeks or months could go by without any contact. Between the ages of two and twelve, Jessica's mom had a succession of partners, and Jessica often witnessed their verbal arguments. Jessica tried to escape the chaos by going to her room and turning on music. One partner hit Jessica in front of her mother because Jessica refused to eat her dinner, and her mother defended his actions, doing nothing to protect Jessica. Thankfully, he wasn't around for long. Jessica's mother remarried when Jessica was twelve, and her stepfather was someone who never talked about his emotions and largely ignored Jessica. While there were fewer arguments in the house, there was also little interaction, and Jessica felt as if she was alone for a lot of her teen years.

These experiences showed Jessica that the adults in her life did not provide safety and stability. Now as an adult herself, Jessica was always on edge, anticipating something bad happening to her and, particularly in new or unfamiliar situations, was on high alert for potential danger.

She had little trust in others and watched for ways friends and colleagues as well as her family might seek to undermine or hurt her. She sought to distance herself from her family but often got pulled back in by some family drama—usually a separation between her mother and stepfather—which happened often. Each parent would reach out to Jessica for emotional support and to bad-mouth the other, which Jessica hated. At the same time, she was happy to have their attention, even if it arose from such negative circumstances.

Despite having a strong circle of female friends, Jessica often felt alone even when she was with people. With romantic partners, she struggled if the relationship was calm and stable because it felt unfamiliar. She grew up in chaos, and found comfort in the familiar, even if it wasn't healthy. As she said, "When there isn't chaos, I cause chaos…I guess it's all I know." The chaos she initiated would frustrate her partners, and the relationships would end, which confirmed Jessica's preexisting ideas about herself that she was somehow unlovable once people got to know the real her.

Her current partner, Scott, appeared to have an avoidant attachment style, which has worsened Jessica's insecurities about the relationship and led her to try to get Scott to "prove" that he cares about her. She openly flirted with other people in front of him, just to see if he would intervene. Scott found her behavior upsetting, didn't behave as Jessica hoped, and the situation always devolved into conflict.

Jessica's self-concept vacillated widely from day to day and sometimes from hour to hour. Her sense of self was often predicated on what was happening that day in her life or in the lives of those she was close to. There was very little stability in her life—and her self-image—as a result. Her boundaries in relationships were often very diffused, so that when she became excited about a new friend, she would take on all her friend's hobbies and their likes and dislikes. Sometimes she found herself overinvolved in her partner's life, trying to solve problems for them without being asked to do so. When Scott was having a bad day, Jessica had a bad day. If Scott felt angry, Jessica felt angry. If Scott was elated, so was Jessica.

In some ways, it makes sense that Jessica would struggle to imagine a full life vision. Experience had taught her inner child that she had to fend for herself because people in her life were unpredictable and could not be trusted to take care of her needs. Jessica had a difficult time believing that someone would love her consistently, wouldn't abruptly change their mind one day and out of the blue leave her. Her childhood was so erratic and seemingly without predictability that she thought all of her life, and particularly her close relationships, would be much the same.

Now that you have a bird's-eye view of your past, an assessment of your current situation, and a vision for your future, how do you feel? It's okay if seeing how attachment has shaped who you are to this point in life makes you feel a little sad, down, angry, or confused. That's all expected as you start making these connections.

The good news is that the attachment style that you developed during your early years does *not* have to determine your life going forward. No matter what your experiences were, you can reparent yourself—in essence, heal your own emotional wounds and unmet needs from your formative years. You can achieve secure attachment at any age and stage. Just by reading this book, you are already moving in a different direction—*you* are in control of how you manage your experiences going forward.

In the following chapters, we will explore how each attachment style manifests, and you'll gain the perspective, tools, and strategies you need to begin making positive changes in your life. You'll learn that the working models you absorbed as a child can be changed so that you can live a more fulfilling, satisfying, and meaningful life—and encourage bigger dreams while knowing that they are possible to achieve—rooted in a newfound secure attachment with yourself.

Before we launch into the work of your specific attachment style, I think it's important to take a moment to highlight that while you are doing some of this work, you may find yourself feeling all kinds of emotions. Some might be quite difficult, and you may even notice that your negative self-talk picks up as you reflect on some of the difficult moments of your life. Healing the patterns that you've been living out is hard work, and it takes time and gentleness. If, at any point, you find that you're feeling overwhelmed or struggling, I encourage you to use the self-compassion strategies I've included in Appendix B (page 325).

Self-compassion will help you to reduce self-criticism and enhance your motivation for personal growth, affirming that you are worthy of positive outcomes while you do the hard work to adopt different coping mechanisms and self-beliefs. With time and practice, you will be able to exercise self-compassion more regularly in your life and reap its benefits.

WHAT'S NEXT?

No matter your life vision, achieving it starts with building a new secure attachment. Safety, confidence, balance, and a stable sense of self—the building blocks of your best possible future—all start there. To better understand what you'd ultimately like to achieve in your life, the next chapter will clarify the gifts of secure attachment and show you what you can aspire to as you make changes in your attachment style.

THE SECURE
ATTACHMENT STYLE

CHAPTER 4

Secure Attachment:
The Connected Explorer

I have great news for you. People who believe they can change their attachment styles often do.[1] While you can't change the past and how your insecure attachment style (avoidant, anxious, disorganized) developed in the first place, you can work to connect with your inner child and build a new, secure attachment—this time, with your adult self.

Understanding the origins and characteristics at the core of your attachment style is essential to your healing, but before we get to the specifics, I want you to have a sense of what it is that you're striving toward. To that end, we're going to start by looking specifically at the behaviors and beliefs that accompany secure attachment. Knowing how secure attachment originates may also give you a jump start on incorporating some of these behaviors into your parenting or other interpersonal interactions, regardless of where you are on your attachment healing journey.

I also want you to know right up front that just because a person has a secure attachment style, it doesn't mean that everything in their life comes up roses or that somehow their childhood experiences were anywhere near perfection. Secure attachment isn't a guarantee that one's life will be smooth sailing. It simply means that the internal scripts they've developed about who they are, how people respond to them, and how the world works tend to be more balanced and realistic and favor effective problem-solving and coping under stressful situations.

That's why I like to call people with secure attachment "Connected Explorers." They generally stay connected to the people and values that are important to them while pursuing their goals. They comfortably navigate new terrain knowing that the secure base their caregivers provided (and that they now provide themselves through a strong self-concept) allows them to face life's varied situations and challenges from a firm grounding.

In many ways, you can think of their secure attachment style as a set of helpful tools for life that they were gifted by their caregivers and other positive early childhood experiences. That doesn't mean you can't have these tools, too—you might just have to work a bit harder or more intentionally to acquire them, which is why you're reading this book!

Individuals who are securely attached are generally capable of having strong, mutually fulfilling interpersonal relationships with people in all areas of their life. Their relationships tend to be healthy and balanced. They are perceived as valuable group members who don't stress too much about possible failure or rejection. They tend to exhibit high satisfaction with their jobs and work environments and their co-workers and have confidence in their ability to contribute. They also tend to report higher well-being and fewer symptoms of physical and mental stress compared to insecurely attached individuals (avoidant, anxious, disorganized).

For example, my client Tom started seeing me when, at thirty-two years old, he got laid off from his dream job as a software developer. It was a disappointing blow and represented a hard knock to his confidence. He is married with two children and was feeling discouraged because he hadn't been able to find a new job even after looking for several months. He was becoming concerned about being able to provide for his family and felt pressured to get a new job quickly. Additionally, Tom's brother is struggling with alcohol abuse and is currently in a residential treatment center. Tom's family expects him to be the primary person to intervene with his brother and take on being his support in recovery. Tom is happy to help his brother in any way he can; however, with the responsibility of his brother's welfare falling on his shoulders at a moment when he was worried about his job prospects, financial stability, and ability to care for his wife and kids in the way that he would like to, Tom was feeling overwhelmed.

What's notable about Tom's example is that he stayed connected and true to who he was and didn't shy away from accessing those other parts of himself that were also meaningful and valuable to him. While he was facing some objectively challenging circumstances, he was consistently able to reach out for support from friends and family. The job loss hit his self-esteem a bit hard, but because his self-esteem is not predominantly rooted in his achievements or his career, Tom is able to maintain his sense of self. He knows he is a loving husband, a caring father, and a supportive brother—and he values those qualities. During the past several months while he has been out of work, Tom has cherished the additional time he's been able to spend with his two young children, getting to walk them to school each morning, attend their after-school soccer practices, research community activities that the entire family can take part in, and even take time to do some work on their home. He also took up cooking and Roller-blading. He calls his brother every day to check in on how he's doing, and he visited him at the treatment center on several weekends.

Does he still feel overwhelmed and at times downright dejected by the lack of job prospects? Yes. Does he worry constantly about his brother? Yes. Does the concern about being able to pay their mortgage keep him up at night? Absolutely! But Tom is able to lean into other spheres of his identity. He understands that he is still a person of value and worth and thinks about how to engage in meaningful activities and contribute in the ways that he can, spending more time living out those aspects of who he is. The challenges he was facing did not derail him or impede his life vision.

He still believed he would be capable of getting his dream career back on track, and in the meantime, he capitalized on his other skills and nurtured his interests and relationships outside of work.

This equanimity, community, and unshakable sense of self is possible for you, too. So, let's look closer at what it means to be a Connected Explorer, from how secure attachment develops to the characteristics that guide the Connected Explorer's interactions with the world.

ORIGINS OF SECURE ATTACHMENT

Like all attachment styles, secure attachment develops in early childhood in response to experiences with caregivers. The parents of children who are securely attached are usually emotionally and physically present and available to the child when they are needed. They are protective but not overly so and give the child latitude to explore and learn about their environment. These parents are easy to spot on the playground. The parents of my son's friend Jackson are especially great at this. They let Jackson roam and play freely on his own while keeping an eye on him from a moderate distance. They keep an eye out for any real trouble he may encounter and step in if, for example, Jackson tries to climb a piece of equipment that is too big for him, but they will not yell at Jackson for doing so, just offer a simple redirection or give him help to climb. If Jackson falls and gets hurt, his parents will take care of him but aren't excessively anxious or concerned, and they communicate to Jackson that everything will be okay. Because they are close by and ready to give assistance, he views the parents as a stable source of support and care. You will often see securely attached children return to their parents periodically as they explore to get a quick hug, or they will give a little wave from a distance. Seconds later, they're back at play, exploring once more and feeling safe to do so, because they know their parent is nearby and available to help if needed.

In addition to providing physical safety for their kids, parents of securely attached children are attuned to the child's emotional needs.

When the child's behavior elicits a consistent, nurturing response from the parent, the child gains a sense of control over resolving issues. In a sense they learn to think, "When I do something or act in a certain way, I will get a certain response that helps me feel safe and solve the problem." Reaching out to others and getting help gives the child a path toward a healthy self-concept and strong self-esteem because they come to know that someone cares for them, that they deserve attention, and they are valued. This plants the seed for them to believe that their actions (and they as an individual) make a difference in the world.

By having a physical and emotional connection with their child, parents can help the child learn how to self-regulate—to effectively understand and manage their own thoughts and feelings to reach goals and solve problems. By being responsive to, and interacting with, their child, the parent is doing what is known as co-regulation—an interactive and two-way process between the parent and child that gradually results in a decrease in overall emotional distress and contributes to the emotional stability of both people.[2] The parent contributes to co-regulation by offering responsiveness and sensitivity and models self-regulation while providing care, affection, and support to their child, especially in times of stress. Effective co-regulation promotes self-sufficiency and allows children to feel safe to explore unfamiliar environments, learn new skills, and learn from their mistakes.[3]

Hugs, Hormones, and Happiness

Research has shown that parental affection in childhood is linked to health and happiness as the child grows, and leads as well to life-long positive outcomes, including higher self-esteem, improved academic performance, better parent-child communication, higher empathy and moral development, increased happiness, and fewer psychological and behavior problems.[4]

One notable study, conducted at Duke University Medical School, observed the level of affection and attention between eight-month-old babies and their mothers. Thirty years later, they followed up with the children and found that those who had mothers who were the most affectionate were happier, less anxious, and more resilient than those who had received less affection from their mothers. They were also less likely to report stressful social interactions, hostility, and physical manifestations of emotional distress.[5]

The researchers suggested that the availability of the hormone oxytocin may be responsible for these positive outcomes. Oxytocin is a chemical in the brain that is released when a person experiences love through emotional connection and/or physical touch. Oxytocin can act to deepen the bond between parents and children and help to create a sense of connection and trust, promote growth and healing, induce anti-stress effects, and stimulate positive social interaction.[6] No wonder this is such an important chemical to help shape the attachment styles of little ones!

Parents who foster secure attachment in their children let their children know they are loved, even when they make mistakes. They make it clear that it is the behavior that is at issue, and while they will correct the behavior, they will not make sweeping generalizations about who the child is, and they will not give a negative characterization of the child (*you are so lazy, you are so clumsy, you always make me mad*, and so on). They provide encouragement and support for the child's interests and activities and are their biggest cheerleader when they succeed and a shoulder to cry on when they don't. They help the child see any failure as an opportunity to learn but also as something to move on from, and they don't dwell on any academic or athletic losses the child experiences.

These caregivers were likely adept at tuning in to the child's emotions and understanding their needs, and generally responded to them with some level of consistency. Parents serve as a safe harbor for their children, and their children know they can come to them when they are in need. A child can, with a high level of certainty, predict how their parent will respond to them and that their parent will be willing and able to respond. Of course, no one is perfect, but in general, when parents say they are going to do something, they typically follow through. If they are unable to do something, they generally explain why they can't and apologize for not keeping their word. No one can do everything to the best of their ability all the time, but parents of securely attached children tend to be relatively consistent in their parenting approach and understand the impact of their behaviors on their children.

While they try to keep some distance between their child and their own problems, these parents are honest with their children—in an age-appropriate manner—about challenges a parent might be facing. (*Daddy is very stressed right now, and I need a few hours before we can play. Yes, Mommy is crying right now because she is sad, but it's okay to be sad, and I will feel better soon*). They show their child that it is okay to be upset or stressed but also show them the skills the parent engages in to cope with what they are experiencing (*When Mommy is stressed, she takes some deep breaths to calm down and then does something fun to take her mind off her worries*).

The Connected Explorer probably had primary caregivers in childhood who were engaged and effective at managing their own stress while also calming and soothing their child. They made their child feel safe so that they were able to venture out and explore without excessive fear that their best interests weren't being looked after. When the parent had problems, they tried not to make their child feel responsible, to expect that the child would make them feel better, or to demand that their child be on their best behavior just because the parent was having a bad day.

There is a prevailing analogy used by many mental health professionals of parents operating like a "reserve psychological bank account" for their children. Just like a financial reserve bank account, parents can provide a store of emotional resources to help their children develop, grow, and overcome challenges. When all is well with the world, the parent's influence may have no noticeable impact on the child's day-to-day activities, but just knowing that safety net is there to protect them against any threats or dangers they may encounter allows the child to explore and enjoy new horizons. If disaster strikes, the parents can then give support and assistance to their child so they can overcome the conflict or trouble they have experienced.

Fostering Secure Attachment in Your Own Children

As a parent, you want the best for your child. Even if you did not experience secure parenting behaviors in your own childhood, you can keep the following in mind when trying to develop secure attachment in your kids:

- Give your child comfort (physical and/or emotional) when they need you.
- Make them feel safe by reassuring them verbally and demonstrating consistency in your behavior.
- Ask your child what they need from you, and teach them how to communicate their needs clearly.
- Allow them to have independence and the room to explore, but also set limits and boundaries and explain why these rules are in place: for their protection.
- Help them understand their feelings and allow them to express them. Don't dismiss negative feelings or brush them aside. Give the same space to discuss both positive and negative feelings.
- Provide support and encouragement, applauding and celebrating

little achievements along the way. When they make mistakes, let them know that making mistakes is a normal part of life but use it as a teaching moment and ask what they learned and what they can do differently next time.

- Model empathic behavior toward others. Show them the importance of prosocial behaviors such as helping, cooperating, sharing, comforting, and donating.[7] Explain to your child why it's important to consider others' feelings and needs, and ask them to take on age-appropriate responsibilities.

- When you are upset with something they did, make sure to link your disappointment and any consequences or discipline to their behavior, not to who they are.

The abiding feelings that most children with secure attachment experience are trust and safety. They know it's okay if they make mistakes. They learn that if they break a rule or disobey their parents, they will still be loved and supported even when they face the consequences of their actions. The consistent response of their parents helps them come to understand that how they behave in the world makes a difference. They know that others care about them, and they are less likely to feel lonely. They can communicate their needs effectively and know that showing emotions doesn't mean they are weak and that emotions are not scary. They understand that when things aren't going well, there are ways to solve problems and manage stressful times without completely falling apart.

Remember the Strange Situation? These are the children who used their caregivers as a base of security from which to explore and learn.[8] Securely attached children tend to explore the room freely and independently when their mothers are present. They may engage with their mother from time to time, bring her a toy to look at, invite their mother to play with them, or look up at them from where they are in the room. When the stranger enters and the mother is still present, they generally display some curiosity and friendliness toward the stranger. After their mother leaves the room, they may become distressed and limit their exploring (stay with one toy or activity) and avoid or withdraw from the stranger. They may cry for a bit. But when they are reunited with their mother, they are usually delighted to see her return and, once they have been soothed, are soon ready to resume their independent exploration of the room with their mother present. Because mothers are responsive to their needs, securely attached children learn that they can depend on their mother (and, later, others) when they are under stress.[9,10]

As they grow older, young children with secure attachment can find success in many realms of life. They learn to trust themselves and their abilities, they are better able to process and manage their emotions, they can engage easily with others and work cooperatively, they do better at school, and they are able to connect with peers and successfully navigate their social environments.[11]

SECURE ATTACHMENT IN ADULTHOOD

Thanks to the consistent, responsive attention of their caregivers, securely attached children view themselves as worthy of love and others as generally trustworthy. Research shows that Connected Explorers have a stronger and more stable sense of self and higher self-esteem, which has a powerful positive influence on their self-concept.[12]

The stable and generally positive way they view themselves is evident in their relationships, career pursuits, and personal achievements—they approach new situations and their goals with realistic confidence and more excitement for what's to come rather than trepidation for the unknown. They don't fear failure because their self-worth isn't defined solely by their achievements. Secure attachment in childhood also typically causes people to have a positive assessment of themselves, including their academic and athletic abilities and general appearance.[13] They are also able to set appropriate boundaries in various relationships.

Connected Explorers feel safe, stable, and more satisfied in their close relationships than individuals with insecure (avoidant, anxious, disorganized) attachment styles. They don't fear being on their own, are comfortable depending on people they've chosen to trust, and they maintain close, meaningful relationships.

They are also likely to feel more confident in the face of stress and use more effective coping strategies than their insecurely attached counterparts.[14] Studies have shown that the securely attached also tend to have more stable mental health—particularly under stress—and are generally less anxious. This is due, in part, to their learned ability to cope with and manage their emotions. Their relationships are generally long-lasting and satisfying, and they are better equipped to resolve any conflicts with a partner. They are seldom pushed to angry behavior.[15]

Again, having a secure attachment style does not mean you're perfect or that you don't experience difficulties in your career, friendships, or romantic partnerships. The key difference is that Connected Explorers have baseline knowledge—fostered in childhood—that they have support and that they will be okay in the future. They are confident that they can get their needs met, and that gives them a foundation of safety and security to move through the world. Remember that reserve bank concept that I described? Well, as Connected Explorers grow up, they become their *own* reserve bank.

In general, Connected Explorers don't shy away from owning their mistakes and believe they will overcome their problems with some help and support. They may face challenges at work, disappointment over not reaching a goal they have set for themselves, and conflict in romantic and other interpersonal relationships. However, when faced with any challenges or setbacks, they are capable of managing their distress, engage in effective problem-solving, and emerge with their self-concept and self-esteem largely intact. With a little time and social support, any temporary losses of self-esteem are recovered.

Secure attachment lays the foundation for healthier development across your lifespan and sets up a strong, positive framework that allows you to dream big and achieve your life vision. Below are some of the most important ways secure attachment can impact you.

Secure Attachment in Romantic Relationships

Conventional wisdom suggests that the type of attachment a child forms with their parent serves as a template for the relationships that the child will have in the future—especially in the area of romantic relationships, because these are often the most intimate adult relationships for many people. For Connected Explorers, their relationship with their caregiver gives them a model of what a healthy relationship looks like and, although it is often unconscious, they can seek to emulate the trust and love they experienced as a child in their future relationships and believe that they deserve it.[16]

Research suggests that people with secure attachment are typically able to foster secure romantic attachments. They believe in their partner's love for them and assume that their needs will be met within the relationship. The attributes of having a secure attachment style—trust, communication, healthy boundaries, a strong sense of self—remain inherent to Connected Explorers, so they usually maintain their behaviors, expectations, and communication style in their relationships, even when they encounter those who do not treat them in the same manner as their original caregivers. It is possible that temporarily interacting with people who treat them in negative ways might shake their self-concept, but they're likely to recover their positive self-image and be resilient in these experiences.

No relationship is 100 percent trouble-free, and people with secure attachment can struggle from time to time with conflict with their partners; however, the Connected Explorer can generally regulate their emotions well and express empathy for a partner's feelings. They usually recognize the needs of others and not only support and respect their partner but help them feel safe and protected. In general, they can trust and be open with others. When they are with a partner, they seek emotional support and give their partner emotional support in return. They tend to desire a healthy dose of closeness and enjoy both emotional and physical intimacy. While they value being close, they do not completely lose themselves in their relationships, and when they commit to being with another person (we), they can also maintain their own sense of self (me). They are assertive communicators and are flexible and willing to adapt when needed. They can accept feedback or criticism without feeling overly attacked or controlled. They can forgive their partner's mistakes—as well as acknowledge their own. Securely attached individuals reported higher relationship satisfaction than the insecurely attached,[17] including during major transitions such as during new parenthood.[18]

Secure Attachment with Friends and Family

In the non-romantic relationships in their lives, the securely attached are good at making and keeping friends. Because they have a good model of what mutual, fulfilling relationships feel like, they can confidently connect with other people and can not only respond to overtures of friendship from others but initiate friendships as well. They can easily set boundaries for their relationships and are comfortable maintaining those boundaries. They don't become subsumed by others but will easily share and engage in mutual interests or decline if they are not interested.

They also know that they can turn to their friends for support when they need it and don't view seeking help as a sign of weakness. They trust that other people will support them and meet their needs. In return, they give support to friends and do so willingly without needing to keep score. They do not act overly needy or clingy, and they don't dismiss or avoid their friends when they are in need. Their relationships are strong and generally last for the long term. They can engage in healthy give-and-take with their friends.

The Connected Explorer generally has a positive view of others. They tend to trust people and do not feel the need to doubt others' intentions. They are able to accept displays of affection and stay connected with their loved ones at times when their loved ones express distress or upset. They are confident in their friendships and can communicate to resolve conflicts rather than act passive-aggressively or disconnect from the friend completely when upset. In her book *Platonic: How the Science of Attachment Can Help You Make—and Keep—Friends*, Dr. Marisa G. Franco explains that many people she describes as "super friends" have secure attachment. This quality these super friends have in common allows them to flourish outside their relationships as well as within them. Studies find that super friends have better mental health, are more satisfied at work, are more open to new ideas, stay calm during stressful events, and are less likely to have chronic or serious physical problems such as heart attacks, headaches, ulcers, and other health issues.[19]

A securely attached person can recognize their own value and that of their friends. Interactions with family members often bring up memories of positive childhood experiences, and there is an ease among family members in expressing emotions and connections. These connections are not broken when there is a disagreement or conflict; and whether the conflict is completely resolved or they agree to disagree, the person is confident that their family will love them (and they will love their family) despite any issues.

Secure Attachment at Work

Connected Explorers can excel at work. In fact, they report higher job satisfaction and are happier overall with their work environment.[20] They can manage high-pressure situations relatively well and seek support when needed. They can work effectively independently or in a group and take direction and constructive criticism well because they are willing to improve. Because they are confident without being narcissistic, and are willing to laugh at themselves or admit mistakes, their co-workers consider them to be good colleagues.

While they strive for success, they are not overly competitive and feel that there is room for achievement for others, and they work well in a collaborative environment. Hard workers who can self-motivate and prioritize tasks as needed, they are productive and successful at what they do and don't usually contribute to a toxic work environment. While willing to do all that is asked of them, they are not afraid to say no or push back when necessary. They can work well with their supervisors and seek out direct feedback or guidance when needed, but in the absence of positive reinforcement, they can see the worth in their own work, acknowledge it, and take pride in what they accomplish. They have the potential to be good leaders because they are empathetic, have reasonable expectations, and can be aware of the feelings and needs of others while still maintaining healthy boundaries.

They can also maintain healthy boundaries between their personal and work lives, recognize when they need help or a break to avoid burnout, and have a healthy work–life balance.

Secure Attachment in Goal Pursuits

Because they have been raised in an environment that allows them to have self-confidence, they are not afraid to reach for goals in many areas of life. While they may acknowledge the possibility of failure, they do not let that deter them from having reasonable aspirations for their health, career, and relationships. They know that achieving a particular goal—or not—does not define who they are, because their self-worth is distinct from their achievements. Their resilience and independence allow them to reevaluate goals in the face of setbacks and adjust their approach or methods. An obstacle or difficulty does not force them to abandon their goals or become discouraged. They can roll with the punches and maintain their desire and effort toward their goals. The goals they set come from their own internal drive and desires, and they do not typically pursue a goal that is based on another's perception of what they should be doing.

They can be very self-motivated and draw on their willpower to push toward goals but do not set their sights on a goal to the exclusion of all else.

They can balance relationships, obligations, and other areas of their life that require time and attention alongside the goals they are striving for.

Courtney comes from a family that has been in banking for three generations, and it was expected that she would follow in the footsteps of her great-grandfather, her grandfather, and her father, as well as her brother and sister, who all pursued careers within the banking industry. But at a young age, Courtney fell in love with music. Her favorite elementary school teacher was a musician who played in a band on weekends. She often went to her teacher's performances with her family. As she grew older, she became inspired to pursue music herself.

Although her parents seemed disappointed that she wasn't going to join the family business, they supported her dreams. She lived paycheck to paycheck for almost a decade until she found her footing as a paid musician in a city orchestra while also writing music and performing at various clubs. Although she didn't always have a clear path forward, she didn't give up on her goals or let her struggle affect her confidence in her abilities. Ultimately, she was able to live her dream and continue to create and perform music.

THE GIFTS OF SECURE ATTACHMENT

Some of the most significant gifts of secure attachment show up in the internal working models of Connected Explorers. Internal working models are like our baseline operating system, which was uploaded in our early childhood years and guides our understanding and representation of ourselves. In other words, these are the stories that inform what we think about ourselves and how we move through the world. The cognitive frameworks and self-representations of Connected Explorers tend to be optimistic yet realistic. There is a real balance in the way they think about themselves and their place in the world—but they tend to skew more positively in their views of self, others, and the world. In other words, they are more likely to see themselves as lovable and others as trustworthy, and they may feel confident in their ability to bring about good outcomes in all areas of their lives.

I have found in my research and professional experience that people who are securely attached tend to share four working models:

1. "I believe in and like myself."
2. "I can handle what comes my way."
3. "I can effect positive outcomes in my life."
4. "I can be independent and rely on others, too."

Your working models continue to evolve over the course of your life, which is great news for those looking to heal their attachment style: These working models don't only have to be aspirational. With time, and by working through the exercises in the chapters that correspond to your attachment style, you can rewrite the stories you learned in your own childhood and offer your own inner child the safety, consistency, and trust you need to adopt new ones—stories that can help make life's challenges and relationship issues more manageable, day-to-day life more rewarding, and your life vision more expansive and empowered.

"I Believe in And Like Myself"

As we've discussed, the securely attached tend to have a strong sense of self and higher self-esteem than those who are insecurely attached. They're more likely to have consistently positive feelings about themselves, their abilities, their perception of feeling accepted by others, and the overall value they place on themselves.[21] One fundamental reason for this is that people with secure attachment tend to carry less shame. Shame triggers a deep sense of personal inadequacy and unworthiness. It often keeps people in a loop of negative self-evaluation that can lower self-esteem and take away self-efficacy. Fortunately, the trust, support, and nurturing Connected Explorers received as children provide a buffer of sorts against the pervasive sense that there is something deeply flawed or fundamentally wrong with them.[22]

My client Peter is an athlete who worked very hard to receive a scholarship to play college basketball. Unfortunately, he suffered an injury a month into his fall semester that put him on the bench for the rest of the academic year. Sports was all he knew, so he felt lost and didn't know how to manage this unpredictable situation. Over and over, he replayed the accident that led to his season-ending surgery. He beat himself up about it and felt guilty, because a careless mistake and a moment of not being entirely focused led to him being injured. But as devastating as the situation was, he didn't think there was something deeply flawed with who he was as a person because of what happened. He knew he was still worthwhile beyond his ability to play basketball. He didn't feel shame over the fact that he wouldn't get to live out his vision of being one of the most productive newcomers on his college team.

It was heartbreaking not to get to hit the ground running with his college sports career. He felt like he was missing out on a lot of meaningful activities, events, and social interactions because he couldn't play. Still, because he didn't internalize the setback—he didn't let the injury mean something about him as a person—Peter was able to work through his extreme disappointment; he dug into exploring different classes and eventually decided to major in kinesiology. He also joined a few clubs and expanded his interests outside of sports to music and chess. He didn't fall into the trap that shame often brings, that prevents people who experience shame from taking action in ways that bring them out of pessimism and despair. Instead of freezing in response to this stressful situation, Peter was able to pivot and find meaning in nurturing other, equally important aspects of himself during this time.

"I Can Handle What Comes My Way"

Connected Explorers are resilient in the face of adversity and can pivot when necessary to find a solution that works even if they don't like what's happening. They are more likely to possess psychological flexibility than their insecurely attached counterparts, meaning that they can better cope with, accept, and adjust to difficult situations.[23] They're able to engage with their present circumstances "fully as a conscious human being, and to change or persist in behavior when doing so serves valued ends."[24]

What all of this amounts to is the ability to do hard things, to change course when necessary, and stay locked into activities that bring purpose and enlightenment. When you confront something in your life that feels difficult, you're able to change the way you think about it (psychologists call this "changing your script") and take action in value-driven ways, even when your thoughts and feelings might tell you to run away or pull the proverbial covers over your head.

In general, people with higher psychological flexibility report lower levels of depression, anxiety, and distress despite dealing with stressful events.[25] During difficult times, people who are psychologically flexible can persevere and continue to pursue meaningful, valued activities. They're able to shift their coping strategies and adapt to changing circumstances rather than stay stuck on solutions that don't work. They can let go of a fixation on a certain outcome and are willing to adjust as needed to find different paths toward their goals,[26,27] even during the COVID-19 pandemic, which isolated so many and was traumatic on a worldwide level.[28]

During the COVID lockdowns, Marion lived by herself in a rather isolated area. It became difficult for her to manage her depression symptoms, and she began losing interest in things she used to enjoy like running, going out to dinner with friends, and reading. Her negative self-talk increased and told her that she'd never get over her depression and was doomed to suffer alone. Rather than letting these negative thoughts and feelings take control, she was able to adapt to her changing circumstances and refocus on what was most important to her. In essence, she fully accepted reality just as it was without excessive resistance or avoidance of problems and got in touch with her most cherished values, even while experiencing difficult thoughts and emotions every day.

Even when she didn't feel like it, she laced up her running shoes and went out for a run several times a week. Sometimes the run only lasted five to ten minutes, but on other days she found the motivation to run for longer. Although there was a part of her that felt like isolating further, because one of her most cherished values was community, she made it a point to connect with her various friend groups weekly via Zoom. She enjoyed maintaining these relationships and looked forward to these calls. Additionally, she decided to pick up her old hobby of photography and spent time outside her home in nature taking photos that she posted on social media. She was further able to connect with others over her photographs, which was not only a source of joy but gave a boost to her self-esteem. As she started to feel better, she participated in some online classes, where she met new people and explored some of her areas of interest, like art history and graphic design. Although she still had days when she experienced depression symptoms, on the whole she was able to establish connections that kept her engaged during the pandemic and helped her feel less alone.

EXERCISE: YOUR PSYCHOLOGICAL FLEXIBILITY TOOLKIT

One of my favorite therapeutic approaches is acceptance and commitment therapy (ACT), and within ACT there is a concept we call *workability* that plays a big role in building psychological flexibility.

Dr. Russ Harris has a great method to decide whether a thought you're having, something that you're doing, or a situation you find yourself in is "workable." It rests on asking yourself one simple question to determine workability: "Is what you're doing working to make your life rich, full, and meaningful?"[29]

If the answer is yes, then the thought, behavior, or situation is workable, and there's no need to change it (even if it might feel difficult to tolerate the feelings that might come in the moment). But if the answer is no, then it's important to brainstorm alternatives that are workable—that help drive you to meaningful, rich, and full experiences.

To find a way to deal with a difficult situation that is workable, try these quick strategies:

- Ask yourself what you can do right now that would serve one of your top values, and do it.
- Label your negative thought(s) and detach from them. Simply add this little clause before your negative thought: "I'm having the thought that…" This helps you remember that you are the person having the thought. The thought is not having you, and the thought is not you. You are the person with the agency of having the thought, but you don't have to further interpret it or wrestle with it.
- Repeat this mantra to yourself: "I don't have to be afraid of painful feelings—I can withstand them and do what's most important and meaningful now."

More Ways to Flex Your Psychological Flexibility

If you need further support in dealing with a difficult situation in the moment, see these tools:
- Practice self-compassion by doing a lovingkindness meditation (see page 327).
- Practice radical acceptance (see page 305).
- Thank your mind (see page 322).
- Practice grounding exercises (see page 320).
- Use TIPP (see page 318).

- Practice self-as-context and visualize the chessboard metaphor (see page 297).
- Get into Flow (see page 133).

As you can see, once you've identified that a thought, behavior, or situation is unworkable, there are a lot of easy ways to pivot to a workable scenario by exercising your psychological flexibility[30]—being able to practice acceptance for whatever is going on, defusing negative thoughts, connecting with the present moment/mindfulness, accessing your self-as-context (the aspect of you that "does all the noticing and observing of one's inner and outer world," as Dr. Harris explains it[31]—for more information and applications see later in this chapter, page 92), remembering your values, and taking committed action.

"I Can Effect Positive Outcomes in My Life"

Connected Explorers have a high degree of personal empowerment. Because caregivers were consistently available, sensitive to their needs, and responsive to their emotional cues, they learned agency and felt in control of their environment from a young age. They don't tend to feel helpless in stressful situations, and they believe that they can achieve positive outcomes in their endeavors, whether it is reaching a health or fitness goal or landing a new job. They are also often successful in reaching their goals. They believe that the things that happen to them—whether good or bad—are usually the result of their own actions. They know that there are things in this world that are out of their control, certainly, but believe that, more often than not, if they put in the effort, they will be able to achieve what they put their mind to. They are less likely to dwell on what is beyond their control and are more likely to focus on what they can exert control over.

For example, Danny was recently transferred to a different department at his workplace and is having difficulties with his new supervisor. They seem to butt heads on very minor issues, and despite Danny trying to communicate as effectively as possible, they just can't get along. This made his day-to-day work very stressful, because Danny felt as if his supervisor was constantly giving him challenges to trip him up and try to make him look bad. Sometimes, just as Danny was about to leave the office for the day, his supervisor would call him into his office and give him a new project with a short turnaround time. It seemed to Danny that his supervisor was trying to set him up to fail.

Danny certainly felt he was not in control of this situation, as his supervisor outranked him and had direct oversight of his daily work. But he didn't allow this fact to get him down for long. In confidence, he spoke with a couple of good friends about what was going on and asked them to help him with ideas about how he could improve his relationship with his boss. Danny spent some time thinking about the aspects of his job that were under his control and tried to anticipate some of the challenges he might have with the supervisor before they happened and came up with plans to manage them if they did. Danny told himself that with hard work and by demonstrating his willingness to be a team player, sooner or later his relationship with this boss should improve, even if it never became an optimal situation. Sure enough, after a few months, his supervisor seemed to become more relaxed in the way he managed Danny's work. Later he shared with Danny that he felt like he had to be tough, because at his last job, people seemed to take advantage of his more relaxed style of supervision. Once he saw that Danny was willing to work with him and that he rose to the challenge each time, he knew he didn't have to be so hard on him. Over the years, they grew to have a very collegial relationship.

Locus of control is a concept that was developed by Dr. Julian Rotter.[32] It represents an individual's belief about how much control they have over what happens to them in their lives. In a sense it comes down to people believing that they can influence what happens to them (internal locus of control) or believing they are victims of outside forces (external locus of control). In Danny's case, he recognized that he had the ability to exert a positive influence on the situation with his boss and wasn't a victim of circumstance. Believing you can influence what happens to you is very important in creating a sense of stability and consistency in life—much like the stability and consistency that, ideally, your parents provided for you as a child. Additionally, people with this internal locus of control have better self-control and experience a range of better health and other life outcomes.

Securely attached individuals are adaptable and flexible in their relationships and other life situations. When they experience conflict or challenges, they have a high tolerance for frustration, can communicate effectively, and use problem-solving skills to reach a resolution—in large part because they are optimistic about their ability to solve problems, overcome obstacles, and be successful. Those with secure attachment do not cave in the face of adversity but try to determine a better or new course of action that will get them nearer to their goals, resolve relationship issues, and/or improve situations in the workplace while staying aligned with their top values and life vision.[33] They believe that the world is generally safe and predictable and that they can provide for their own safety.[34]

EXERCISE: VALUES AND COMMITTED ACTION

Living with values is a different approach than measuring success through prestige, personal wealth, and power. It is a practice of identifying what matters to you, what you stand for, and the values you have in your life. When you know what matters to you, making decisions that take you closer to your priorities and doing what aligns with your values, even when you're in the middle of a difficult time, becomes the most sensible and practical thing to do. Values-based living gives you a sense of empowerment and control over your life and will help to direct your actions toward meaningful purpose.

I love talking to people about the difference between values and goals and why both are necessary for a well-lived life. Unlike goals, values can't be checked off a list. They are at the heart of what gives meaning and purpose to our lives. They are not ethics or morals per se; rather, they are ideals that you wish to embody and to live your life by, and what you hope your life will be filled with. For example, your humor, caring, learning, or independence represent things you might like others to mention about you when you're not in the room and what you want to be remembered for when you leave this world. They are the things that bring you a deep sense of fulfillment and joy, and things that you'd fight to keep in your life at nearly any cost.

You choose your values, and you may find that your choices, or the meaning you ascribe to them, shifts at various points in life. Values are unique to every person. Even if two people choose the same value word to describe one of their top values (for example, integrity), each person will enact this value differently by their language and actions. For example, one might say that integrity is being brutally honest all the time, and another might say integrity means having an internal sense that they are being guided by their morals in all decisions. They may also live out this value differently in different spheres of life—one person committing to actions that reflect integrity at work, which includes full transparency about higher level decisions with her subordinates; whereas another person is more concerned with having integrity with their romantic partner by not cheating on them and letting them know honestly when they need time alone.

When we align with our values on a daily basis, we have more energy, feel more fulfilled, and have more motivation and willpower to achieve our goals, because we are acting based on what's important to us. Clarity about your values and recommitting to living your values every day gives you a guide for action and for your behavior during challenging times, as well as providing comfort and consistency.

This simple exercise takes only a few minutes and is an easy one to add to your evening routine. Start by naming your top three values. Examples of values include respect, authenticity, caring, health, adventure, curiosity, and knowledge. If these don't resonate with you or if you feel stuck and want to review a longer list, check out my website at https://www.drjudyho.com. For each value you choose, ask yourself: "How did I live out, embody, or move in concert with this value today?" For any of the values that you feel you did not connect with today, recommit to a values-based action for that value within the next twenty-four hours.

For example, if one of your top values is community, you can make a note to call a friend to catch up tomorrow or research a new recreational class in your neighborhood to meet some like-minded people. The key to values-based actions is that they don't have to be all encompassing or represent the best or grandest way to live this value. It's about doing something that allows you to connect with that value and keep it top of mind even during your busy days. It is equally important to recognize your values-based actions and to do them with intention. So, when you call that friend, think to yourself, "This is one of the ways I'm standing by my honored value of community." When you acknowledge what you are doing in this conscious manner, you will also get the most enjoyment, satisfaction, and fulfillment from taking that action. Instead of thinking, "I am so busy today, and now I have to call my friend," with your values front and center, you're more likely to think, "This is something I am doing because it's important to me."

Additionally, when you live your life according to your top values in a consistent way, you will feel better about yourself, you'll feel anchored to things that really matter to you, and you'll likely be helping someone else experience these values in a visceral and help-ful way. The friend you called to check on may have been needing just that exact connection to cheer them up or give them an extra motivational boost.

"I Can Be Independent and Rely on Others, Too"

We all have needs for connection *and* for self-reliance. As ever, the key is balance. We often call this interdependence.

Connected Explorers understand where they end and others begin, and in the case of more intimate or romantic relationships, where the "we" begins, without becoming subsumed. Although they enjoy connections with others, they also love their time alone—they can maintain their own inter-ests outside their intimate relationships and encourage their partners to do the same. In practice, this looks like comfort with setting boundaries, expe-riencing intimacy, and exercising autonomy. They have a strong sense of per-sonal values and will act relatively swiftly when others violate those values and communicate their disappointment or frustration assertively.

Will is in a relationship with Anna, and they have been spending a lot of time together, going out to eat or to shows or movies, attending concerts, and hanging out with mutual friends. Anna is intelligent, witty, and fun to be around, but sometimes she can become very suspicious and possessive of Will, although he hasn't done anything wrong or inappropriate. When this happens, Will reassures her that everything is fine, that he cares very much for her, and that their relationship is on track. But Anna continues to have arguments with Will. Despite this being somewhat frustrating, Will doesn't completely write Anna off. He is empathetic to her concerns but also sets strong boundaries. For example, when he feels like she is becom-ing unreasonable, he excuses himself and asks to take a little time alone. He tells her that he will reach out to her when he feels ready to connect, sometime in the next day or so (but never longer than that). He continues to express affection toward her and tells her how important she is to him.

When he needs quiet time to himself, he lets Anna know that these are his needs and they don't have anything to do with the relationship or how he feels about her. When he is taking downtime and recharging his batteries, he encourages Anna to meet up with friends or take some time of her own.

Comfortable with both intimacy and autonomy, securely attached adults generally hold a positive internalized view of themselves and a generally positive view of others' intentions toward them. Essentially, they are more likely to lead with a general belief that most people mean well rather than be overly skeptical or suspicious of others. Although they may find themselves in situations that seem to threaten these internal working models (like being in a brief relationship with an emotionally abusive person who treats them poorly), they can still objectively assess people and events, and generally recover their belief that most people can be relied upon and trusted.

Within a relationship, the Connected Explorer can exhibit appropriate independent and dependent behaviors. They can ask for help but are also comfortable handling issues on their own. Because they know how to both give and receive, they don't feel guilty about getting support from others, because they know there will be an opportunity for them to give in return. They freely express affection and don't worry that it might not come back to them; they don't avoid intimacy, nor do they desperately seek it out. They are unlikely to play games to attract someone's interest, they don't play hard to get, and they can be direct about their feelings. You know where you stand with someone who is securely attached.

They are assertive about their opinions and ask that they be listened to and valued, and they extend the same courtesy to partners. They understand that sometimes there are differences between people, and even if some things about a partner irk them, they won't try to make their partner into someone they are not. They accept the reality of disagreements and know that despite conflict they can stay connected and love each other.

Because they don't experience as much anxiety, fear, or doubt in their relationships, they can focus on being present for their loved ones. They have a good deal of empathy and not only understand their own emotions but have insight into others' experiences. However, they don't presume to know what someone else is going through. They are comfortable with being vulnerable and sharing their emotions, experiences, and fears, and likely encourage others to do the same.

Depending on the context, Connected Explorers are typically willing to open up and look for authentic connections with others instead of keeping things on a surface level, oversharing, or inappropriately divulging information about themselves. If they've built a trusting relationship, they will allow their partner access to their inner thoughts and deeper feelings. They're not afraid of close relationships and feel comfortable with the idea of commitment to good partners.

Five Types of Intimacy

Intimacy is a key element of strong, sustainable relationships. Having intimacy in a relationship means experiencing an authentic closeness and deep bond with another person—the kind that helps us feel safe, protected, secure, and loved. People often assume that intimacy only exists in the context of romantic and sexual relationships, but there are actually five types of intimacy, and all of them are essential to feeling fulfilled in our social connections and to accessing higher feelings of satisfaction, joy, and stronger mental and physical health. The five types are:

1. Physical: Includes physical touch (both sexual and nonsexual) such as intercourse, kissing, hugs, cuddling, sitting close together, or holding hands.
2. Emotional: Involves the honest sharing of your thoughts, feelings, fears, hopes, and/or dreams, and feeling heard and understood

by another person. This might include talking about your current struggles, sharing your self-development goals, or discussing something that happened in your childhood and how it shaped who you are as an adult.

3. Intellectual: Involves communicating beliefs, viewpoints, and ideas in a way that creates intellectual stimulation, curiosity, interest, and acceptance (despite possibly differing vantage points). This might include reading a book and discussing the ideas together, debating two sides of a hot topic, talking about the meaning of life, or discussing themes in a movie you both watched.

4. Experiential: Doing something together that creates a shared experience or allows teamwork toward a common goal. This might include volunteer work, training for a race together, learning a hobby, planning a trip, or playing a video game or sport.

5. Spiritual: Sharing moments that bring you a sense of awe, wonder, or acknowledgment with something bigger than yourself. This may include praying together, meditation, enjoying a natural phenomenon together (like watching a sunrise), going on a hike, or talking about meaning and purpose in each of your lives.

We need all five types of intimacy to feel fulfilled with our social connections—although it's worth noting you don't need one person to fulfill all five forms for you. You may have a favorite friend with whom you experience intellectual intimacy, while you engage in physical, emotional, and experiential intimacy with your romantic partner.

The next time you're feeling disconnected or lonely, ask yourself which type of intimacy you need the most, and connect with someone from your inner circle or another trusted person to meet this need.

An important note in this increasing virtual world and because some of your most important connections may not be local to you: Apart from the physical, you can experience all these forms of intimacy through virtual means such as a video or phone call and/or a shared experience (such as taking an online class together). It's a great way to continue to grow and deepen your relationship with people who are important to you between in-person visits, which may be few and far between for busy adults who don't live in the same area.

EXERCISE: NOURISHING INTIMACY

Intimacy, or the degree of closeness between people, requires constant work, dedicated attention, and willingness to open up to and put trust in others. The five types of intimacy, as noted above, include physical, emotional, intellectual, experiential, and spiritual. Boundaries aren't only a barrier or indicating a necessary stopping point—boundaries can be semi-permeable and are how we establish and nurture our closeness with others. This chart shows the types of intimacy and how they can be strengthened.

TYPE OF INTIMACY	HOW TO CULTIVATE IT
Physical Intimacy—body closeness and safe touch to feel close to another person.	Talking about comfort with different forms of physical touch; spending time hugging, holding hands, and kissing.
Emotional Intimacy—sharing your deep feelings, fears, thoughts, and emotions without judgment.	Using active listening and a nonjudgmental stance to explore feelings and thoughts about deeper topics, making time to take care of each other's emotional needs, communicating your emotional needs clearly.

Intellectual Intimacy—sharing your ideas, opinions, views on life, and learning new things with someone.	Having stimulating discussions about different topics and creating a safe zone to express different views, showing mutual respect for differing ideas, adopting an attitude of curiosity toward differing ideas.
Experiential Intimacy—participating in shared experiences and activities that bond you with another person, offering resources (time, financial, or skill) to those in need.	Brainstorming, planning, and doing activities of shared interest; offering a meaningful contribution to someone by asking what they need and finding a way to help them fulfill their necessities or goals.
Spiritual Intimacy—sharing beliefs, thoughts, and feelings that relate to a higher power or something greater than yourself.	Feeling close, validated, and safe sharing ideas about the meaning of life and your life purpose; praying and meditating together; learning about each other's spiritual practices and beliefs; discussing why your spiritual beliefs are important to you.

Not all relationships involve all types of intimacy, but each of your relationships in your life likely involves at least one form of intimacy. To strengthen your connections with the most important people in your life, it's helpful to consider one way in which you will build and maintain intimacy with a loved one every day.

If you feel that one of your relationships needs more TLC, over a few weeks you can choose to focus on building intimacy with that person by brainstorming one idea to strengthen a type of intimacy with them daily. Or you can rotate who you want to focus on each day, coming up with one way to strengthen intimacy with each person daily.

Look at the chart, and each day, make a commitment to strengthen one form of intimacy with a person in your life. In your journal, under the title "Building Connections," write down what you are committing to by responding to the following prompts:

- Who will I strengthen my closeness with?
- Which category of intimacy?
- What will I do?
- Degree of closeness before the activity/behavior (from 1 to 10)
- Degree of closeness after the activity/behavior (from 1 to 10)

It's helpful to rate your degree of closeness with the person before and after you take on this activity to strengthen your intimacy with them. For example, before Sarah scheduled a date night with her husband, she rated their degree of closeness as a 7 out of 10. After their date, she rated their degree of closeness as a 9 out of 10.

WHAT'S NEXT?

This chapter introduced you to the internal working models of Connected Explorers and how they tend to value themselves, express autonomy while being comfortable with closeness, and believe in their ability to bring about good things in their lives. They are resilient in the face of adversity. While they were given these gifts through the relationship with their caregivers in childhood, it is never too late: With time and effort, you can gain the benefit of these gifts in your life. No matter where you're starting, I want to say again that you *can* make these changes.

Now it's time for you to explore your own attachment style more deeply, to learn about its origins and start to heal the working models that your inner child has been holding on to. I recommend that you begin with reading about your own style, but you may want to dip into other sections as well—particularly if you have a close friend or partner who struggles with a different attachment wound than your own:

Avoidant Attachment (Fiercely Independent): See page 105.
Anxious Attachment (Worried Warriors): See page 171.
Disorganized Attachment (Surveillance Specialists): See page 233.

Remember that your attachment style didn't develop overnight, and you have likely been living with the challenges your style brings to your life for some time now. Changing your attachment won't happen instantaneously, but when you are willing to learn, do the exercises, and put your new skills into practice, I am most confident that you will make changes in your life. It's happened for my clients, and it can happen for you!

THE AVOIDANT
ATTACHMENT STYLE

CHAPTER 5

Avoidant Attachment: Fiercely Independent

L aura prides herself on being independent and has always done everything on her own. She went to boarding school as a teen, and ever
since then has made her own way. At the age of seventeen, she finished
high school a year early and moved across the country for college. A
self-identified workaholic who spends long hours at her job, she created
her own opportunities at work and quickly rose through the ranks at a
prominent marketing firm. Her social life often came second to her career
pursuits, but she socialized from time to time with a group of friends
she knows from her college years. No matter what the plans were, from a
casual lunch to a holiday party, Laura insisted on driving herself. Although
she lives close to a couple of her friends and they could carpool, she pre-
fers to drive solo. She says that she enjoys the freedom of leaving whenever
she wants to, and that she doesn't like being bound to other people's preferences or their schedules. Once, when her car broke down, rather than
getting a ride with a friend who was going to the same party, she chose
instead to take an Uber. It's not only that she doesn't want to inconvenience
someone else—although that may be what she said at the time—it's really

that she wants to be in control of the situation. Knowing that she had her options open was important. She needed to be able to leave whenever she wanted, on her own terms, and be in total control of her time and how she spends it with people.

Her staunch independence extends beyond driving. Help with a move, borrowing someone's jacket, seeking a listening ear—she didn't want to rely on anyone for anything. As the proverbial lone wolf, she keeps to herself and is reluctant to admit any vulnerability. This is what brought her to my office—her romantic partner complained that Laura was putting up walls in their relationship and refusing to take their partnership to the next level. Anytime the subject was broached, Laura would dismiss it quickly and try to turn the conversation to any other topic, and her partner had become sick of it.

At the root of Laura's fierce independence is an avoidant attachment style.

ORIGINS OF AVOIDANT ATTACHMENT

Like all attachment styles, avoidant attachment develops in early childhood in response to experiences in the early years of life, largely with parents or caregivers. The Fiercely Independent likely had primary caregivers in childhood who were somewhat disengaged, distracted, or absent-minded. These adults were not necessarily neglectful on purpose, but often were not generally emotionally or physically available to attend to the child's needs. They tended to avoid displays of emotion and intimacy and may have seemed turned off when the child reached out for reassurance and affection, and withdrew from the child, especially during times of difficulty.[1]

It is important to mention that some cultures might not value the open expression of emotions as much as other cultures—for example, some may place more emphasis on emotional restraint—and I want to be clear that this difference in outward or vocal expression of affection is *not* the same thing as withdrawing from a child's needs. Parents from these cultures may show their presence and support in other ways, and this can be just as comforting to the child. Sometimes, when a child is exposed to differing cultural values (for example, being encouraged to express emotions openly by schoolteachers but being taught to suppress vulnerable and negative emotions at home), it can cause a sense of dissonance about what to strive for. This incongruence can sometimes lead to the child developing attachment challenges when they can't make sense of the discrepancy.

What's at issue when we talk about whether a caregiver is meeting their child's needs is consistency and predictability. Children who develop an avoidant attachment style often had parents who needed them to be more self-reliant. Perhaps they were overwhelmed with work or financial obligations or struggling with a physical or mental health issue that caused them to disconnect and not engage with their child. As an infant, the child's cries and other expressions of distress may have gone unrecognized, ignored, or even discouraged, or possibly were dismissed or disdained. The caregiver might have discouraged the child from expressing emotion, whether it was joy or sorrow, fear or shame, anger or disgust. Parents may have expected the child to behave more stoically and be more reserved with their emotions, especially in public. The parents may have been overwhelmed by their child's emotions, felt they were unable to cope, thought the child was overreacting, and closed themselves off from the child. Parents themselves may also have difficulty expressing emotions, likely something they learned from their own parents in their upbringing. These children may not have received a lot of physical or emotional reassurance, and their general needs may not have been adequately met.[2]

Because a child has a deep inner need to be close to their caregiver, under these circumstances they might respond to their parents' lack of warmth by no longer seeking closeness nor expressing their emotions. They learned not to express their needs for assistance—even if they were injured or ill—and generally learned to deal with stressful events themself.

Essentially, the child was forced to distance themself from their caregivers, learn to take care of their own needs, and "grow up faster."

They were likely praised for their self-sufficiency and independence, which made them believe that they should continue to act in these ways even when they didn't feel good inside. They convinced themselves that they were perfectly fine on their own. Their behavior disguised their need for closeness while at the same time serving as their only path to connection with their caregivers, however superficial.

In Mary Ainsworth's Strange Situation experiment, infants who were classified as avoidantly attached showed no obvious signs of outward distress when separated from their caregivers. When caregivers returned, they didn't seek contact with them and showed little emotion. They also displayed other avoidant behaviors such as ignoring their caregiver, turning away from them, and/or moving past them with little acknowledgment. They didn't explore much regardless of who they were with, caregiver or stranger. They also didn't treat the stranger much differently from their own caregiver.

Ainsworth hypothesized that this seemingly unruffled exterior was actually a mask for internal distress, a hypothesis she later confirmed by studying the heart rate of avoidant infants, which showed that they experienced just as strong a reaction and as much physiological anxiety as other children when separated from parents, although their distress was not reflected in their outward behavior or expression.[3]

Infants classified as avoidantly attached had a history of being rebuffed by their parents and developed a belief that communicating their needs had no impact on the caregiver's response. The avoidant behaviors they adopted—not crying or outwardly expressing their feelings—were an attempt to become more acceptable to their caregivers and to satisfy at least one of their needs: to be physically close enough to their parents to have some protection but distant enough to avoid disparagement and rejection. Also, avoidant behaviors helped the child maintain enough control of themselves so that they wouldn't be overwhelmed with emotion and not know how to manage it on their own.[4]

Over time, all this self-suppression and distrust of their caregivers builds a behavior pattern of avoiding deep intimacy and striving for independence at all costs—even when this lack of deeper connection causes the child disappointment or sadness. Maintaining a façade of not caring continues into adulthood.

AVOIDANT ATTACHMENT IN ADULTHOOD

The Fiercely Independent seems to have it all, so much so that previous research suggested that they actually hold positive views of themselves![5] They seem happy about who they are and where they are in life. They might appear to be outgoing and social, and are a lot of fun to be around. They're often high achievers, successful by any objective standard, and seemingly able to handle anything that comes their way without missing a beat.

However, research has shown that these positive views actually seem to be a type of defense mechanism—people with avoidant attachment self-promote as a cover for their inner insecurities.[6] In more recent studies, avoidantly attached people reported more negative views of themselves compared with those with secure attachment.[7]

In fact, avoidantly attached people often have a very vulnerable sense of self,[8] based on external achievement rather than internal stability. Not having a stable and reliable environment in childhood to encourage self-exploration without major negative consequences made it more difficult for the child to understand the self and form a positive self-view. As a result, the Fiercely Independent individual developed their self-concept based less on getting validation from people and more on achieving goals. In adulthood they crave competition in every aspect of their life and create endless bucket lists in the pursuit of self-validation. Avoidantly attached individuals seek out material rewards or social praise for *what* they have accomplished, which makes them feel good about themselves, but they may doubt their self-worth when they're not achieving or doing. In other words, they may not be sure of their self-worth if they're not bringing *value* through specific actions, and they may believe others won't accept or support them for *who* they are.

When they experience disappointment in the areas of life they've chosen to invest in (usually personal and professional achievements or objects that represent status and prestige), their self-esteem plummets quickly, and they often struggle with a deeply critical inner voice. They beat themselves up with intense, self-denigrating thoughts, especially when they feel as if they should have behaved differently in a given situation. Many times, they try to use this critical inner voice to motivate themselves to be better and to strive even higher. But this inner voice is destructive to their sense of self and makes them feel worse. Still, they are unlikely to let on to anyone that they are suffering or are unhappy, and instead, they suffer alone and in silence.

The Fiercely Independent don't seem to mind being alone, but when they are, they typically don't spend their time on self-reflection because they are always busy with a project or an activity. Life that is too slow or not tightly scheduled allows too much opportunity for that critical voice to take over; they risk losing the sense of control they work so hard to cultivate. Escapist coping is a common strategy and can be beneficial in moderation (think how relaxing playing a video game is at the end of a stressful week!), but when taken to the extreme, it can open the door to process addictions or substance addictions such as gambling, overeating, overexercising, and relying on alcohol and drugs to numb or push away feelings that are hard to manage.

Workaholism is another common coping strategy. People with avoidant attachment use their work responsibilities as a buffer against emotional intimacy or to avoid engaging at home or participating in activities with family or friends. "Sorry, I can't make the (fill in the event here) because I have to work" is a constant refrain. Workaholism may seem like a "fake" or benign addiction, but it truly does interfere with relationships and connections with others. It's also an easy trap to fall into: Unlike other forms of addiction, workaholism is often easy to defend given that the person is working and making money so the family can have the things and lifestyle they enjoy as the fruits of the workaholic's labor. Add to that the cultural bias toward near-constant productivity and the cachet of being constantly busy, and it becomes even more justifiable, even admirable in some respects, for the avoidantly attached to be laser-focused on work pursuits.

Whatever their coping strategy, the Fiercely Independent are masters of pushing down their emotions. They don't typically report increased negative feelings on a day-to-day basis, but they do typically feel less happy than their securely attached peers.[9] Studies have shown that avoidant attachment is associated with higher rates of depression,[10] anxiety,[11] eating disorders,[12] and posttraumatic stress.[13] Studies have also found that avoidantly attached individuals tend to experience restricted expression of emotions, difficulties with intimacy, and social avoidance.[14]

Further, not processing highly stressful events (such as trying to repress feelings and thoughts about negative situations out of conscious awareness) is related to poorer long-term adjustment.[15] The Fiercely Independent tend to suppress distress and leave feelings unresolved, which leads them to have difficulty coping with common life stressors: loss, grief, role transitions, and interpersonal conflicts. Their difficulties are especially apparent when they have to deal with circumstances such as the chronic illness of a family member, parenting, or frequent recurrent conflicts with their spouse—prolonged, demanding, stressful experiences that require them to rely on external sources of support.[16]

No matter what they may be facing, the Fiercely Independent prefer to perceive themselves as superheroes. Research shows that avoidantly attached people are more likely to portray outward grandiosity that includes both self-praise and denial of weaknesses.[17] They think they can do it all without others' help. But unlike many superheroes, they don't easily accept help from a sidekick or a person in the wings. Part of their self-concept is built on doing things by themselves and achieving without support—which offers them a great sense of pride and a feeling of self-reliance.

Regardless of the size or shape of their support network, the Fiercely Independent tend not to identify themselves by their roles in life or their relationships with others. If this is your attachment style, you likely struggled with the self-concept wheel exercise on page 36 or noticed that you listed plenty of accomplishments but very few relationships. The Fiercely Independent often lack self-concept clarity and may struggle with describing who they are with consistency, partly because they didn't have a psychological sense of security in their formative years.[18] While they appear to be socially engaged, they rarely let anyone get close, and they make excuses to avoid true emotional connection. They roll up their sleeves to do everything themselves and rarely let their guard down. That superhero mentality can lead others to view the Fiercely Independent as aloof, hard to read, stubborn, and obsessive. Even a healthy level of interdependence can send them running, and it may be easier for them to keep a few casual acquaintances rather than maintain long-term intimate relationships.

Researchers have found that many avoidantly attached adults use "preemptive" strategies to curtail any connection so they will not become emotional. They fear being out of control and not being able to cope with what's in front of them, so they are likely to leave a relationship before that person falls out of love with them; dislike viewing artwork that taps into their emotional state (such as watching tearjerker movies); and tune out conversations that seem emotionally stressful. They may also recollect their childhood favorably and say they had a good childhood but be unable to cite specific examples of their happy younger years. Or they may mention a negative experience with a caregiver but be quick to excuse their caregiver for what they did, almost as if they are afraid of the repercussions if they told the whole truth about what happened.

Let's take a look at how these specific themes of striving for independence show up in different facets of your life and how being the proverbial lone wolf may be causing issues in relationships, work, and more.

Avoidant Attachment in Relationships

While the avoidantly attached person may have convinced themself that they don't need close relationships or connection to thrive, the truth is, all humans are hardwired for connection for emotional and physical survival. Deep down, even avoidantly attached people want close and meaningful relationships but find it hard to let their guard down enough to admit this to themselves or the important people in their lives. Even as circumstances change over time, they continue to use the same coping repertoire they developed from their younger years, even if it doesn't always serve them well.

The Fiercely Independent tend to have difficulty nurturing others. Loved ones may accuse them of being cold, callous, or inappropriately competitive. Because everything is viewed through a competitive lens, they bring this winner-takes-all attitude to relationships as well. It can sometimes feel like romantic pursuits are just another goal to check off their bucket list, another conquest to master. They are charming and persuasive in the early phase of relationships, but once the person falls for them, it all becomes too much, so they back off or disappear. This cycle can become a bit of an addiction in and of itself, because when they obtain the attention of the object of their affection, it can be extremely validating and hit those pleasure centers in the brain (cue dopamine and endorphins!).

Because they learned as young children to disconnect from their bodily needs and dismiss the importance of their own emotional life, they generally steer clear of relationships that seem too demanding or needy (but what they perceive as *neediness* is likely a healthy level of connection).

In general, they are largely disillusioned with other people and don't trust anyone enough to make a commitment to them. Intimacy on any level can be intimidating for them; they don't want to let their guard down to eventually get the rug pulled out from under them. The avoidantly attached person might feel like they are being responsible by telling their partners point-blank they aren't ready for something more serious or by backing out of obligations to signal to the person that they aren't ready for a commitment. For example, they may make excuses to not attend certain events that are important to their dating partner, like weddings, family gatherings, or work parties where they'd be officially introduced as the boyfriend or girlfriend.

My client Joshua did this constantly. In every serious relationship he would withhold in one area of intimacy, likely subconsciously, so that he wasn't giving his all to his partner. In fact, Joshua can only be intimate in one way at a time with his partner. If he feels emotionally close to her, he cannot engage in sex with regularity. But if they are having great sex, he can't be emotionally intimate, rebuffs any overtures to become more emotionally intimate, and distances himself from her outside of the bedroom.

Joshua's relationships always followed the same pattern. In the beginning, he engaged in emotionally intimate talks, planned for the future of the relationship, and easily doled out physical affection like hugging, cuddling, and kissing. Sex was also usually frequent, fun, and exciting during this phase. But as the relationship grew more serious, Joshua would have this internal sense of discomfort, like he was being stifled by his partner. This would happen even when he recognized that the partner wasn't doing anything new or different from how they had been behaving previously. He also recognized that they were usually simply responding to how he was acting toward them in the beginning—that is, enthusiastic and eager to continue the relationship.

When he started to feel this discomfort, which could begin as early as a few weeks into the dating relationship, he pulled away, stopped calling the person, even asked for a break from dating to think the situation through. Usually, he'd give the relationship another shot, but soon after, he would default to only fully participating in one form of intimacy—emotional or physical. He once had a relationship for two years where he spent almost every day with his partner. They traveled, made plans with mutual friends, and talked about the future. There was constant kissing and hugging, but no sex for over a year and a half. Whenever his partner attempted to start a sexual encounter, Joshua made an excuse about being tired and sometimes even became irritable.

Joshua was only able to give one part of himself at a time because he was afraid that by giving his all, he'd be too vulnerable to being let down and abandoned by his partner at a time when he needed them. It was clear that part of this was due to Joshua feeling overwhelmed when he found himself more deeply connected to another person. His independence, his main mode of survival, was being threatened. What if he relied on another person, and they ended up leaving? He didn't want to risk not feeling in control if he allowed himself to be vulnerable, and he worried more about how he might respond to rejection and abandonment if it were to happen. Subconsciously, Joshua didn't want to relive his earlier attachment relationship where he felt like his needs were neglected. In the process of protecting himself, he neglected his partners' needs as well as cut himself off from a potentially fulfilling and healing relationship with another person.

Like Joshua, the Fiercely Independent often send mixed messages to their partners, leaving the other person frustrated and confused. When their partners try to talk to them about their feelings or to clarify the status of their relationship, the avoidantly attached person starts to feel stifled and panicked. They may claim that their partner is overly demanding or clingy and they need their space—literally and figuratively. When push comes to shove, the avoidantly attached person will "ghost" their partner—not because they don't care about their partner's feelings but because their own psychological survival takes precedence. Exiting a situation before it becomes too intense and difficult to control is a typical coping strategy of an avoidantly attached person.

Avoidant Attachment with Friends and Family

People with avoidant attachment tend to distance themselves from relationships with friends and family, which means they are more likely to keep to themselves when stressed and use avoidant coping, such as distraction. For example, they may busy themselves with home projects rather than have a deeper conversation with a friend. They worry that reaching out might leave them feeling vulnerable to potential rejection or dismissal by the person they ask for support.

The Fiercely Independent strongly prefer being alone, even when spending time with others, for example, bouncing from group to group at a party on their own (instead of staying with a friend or two), or going back and forth between observing the action at a work function and participating in the main activity. This desire to be solo extends to times when they are on their own and have little interest in reaching out and being with others.[19]

They also tend to approach interpersonal interactions with less happiness and less positive views of their situation compared to the securely attached.[20] Feeling less cared for by others and less emotionally close to people is common, but it might be self-perpetuating (albeit subconsciously) because they are less likely to invest in relationships and usually keep people at arm's length.

They are self-reliant to a fault,[21] which provides few opportunities for other people to show up for them. Because they don't like high emotionality and may fear that they won't be able to stay in control if provoked to experience intense emotions, they often avoid gatherings like weddings or funerals—they cannot deal with the high level of emotion in these settings. They are very conflict avoidant, so if a person who will be at a gathering is someone with whom they have had issues in the past, they will pass on the event to avoid any potential confrontation. If they do attend, they will studiously avoid any contact with that person and likely take frequent breaks to get out of the crowd.

They largely operate outside their family's orbit—they don't seek advice or assistance from parents or extended family. They may be seen as being aloof but also as not needing anything from anyone. They are self-reliant to the extent that their family members typically don't reach out to them even if they haven't been in touch for some time. Family likely thinks they're doing well; after all, they tend to be lone wolves as a rule. They are perceived to be fine, successful, and not in need of being checked in on or connected with.

They can be fun and easy to be around. They can be a good friend and can be great at helping others, but only on their terms. They love it when people think they are wonderful and doing things right, but they are less thrilled with criticism and will stop helping if they feel as if they are being told what to do or that they are doing it wrong.

Avoidant Attachment at Work

The Fiercely Independent are the quintessential workaholics. They are constantly on the go, hustling, achieving, and keeping themselves occupied and distracted by projects and activities. As mentioned previously, they are also likely to use work as an excuse to avoid social gatherings. Because of their innate distrust of others, the Fiercely Independent prefer to work solo and compete with their colleagues for the highest achievements rather than connect and collaborate with them. They don't like to conform (because they don't want to think of themselves as being "part of the pack") and generally aren't shy about asserting their ideas in meetings or with higher-ups. When a deadline is approaching, they are the ones most likely to get the job done, done well, and ahead of time. Because their identity is often tied up with work achievements, they derive most of their self-esteem and self-confidence from their career.

In fact, work is so central to their identity and how they perceive themselves that while they are not jealous or concerned in a personal relationship if a partner is flirting with other people, if a new person comes to the office and gets accolades, they become incredibly jealous. They have a hard time managing at work until they can "get" their competitor and be back on top again. They can become obsessed with being the best. If you catch them in the middle of a fervent goal pursuit, they may look as though they are unempathetic to others' struggles.

They may be the overachievers that many admire, but after reaching a goal, it's hard for them to pause and enjoy the fruits of their labor. They are constantly searching for the next accolade or award they can achieve. If they hit the top in their chosen career, they won't be fully content when they reach that pinnacle. It may seem, to them, like a hollow victory.

They seem confident and secure (particularly in the work environment), but if their one attribute (an achievement or a high-profile job) in which their sense of self is tied up is taken away from them, they don't know what to do with themselves and feel awful. Sometimes, chronic burnout and its negative consequences on their ability to consistently "kill it" at work are what brings them to my office. Losing a valued position or getting fired is devastating. While another person in the same situation might view a job loss as an opportunity to seek out an even better position, reconnect with friends, or give of themselves by volunteering, the avoidantly attached can see nothing but loss. Loss of status, loss of self.

For this reason, they may also have trouble with role transitions. For example, when they retire and need to rediscover themselves, they often don't know what to do. In many cases, the anxiety and depression they've been repressing for all their life (by keeping busy, busy, busy) become recognizable for the first time. The sudden influx of emotions and their inability to manage them effectively becomes another stressor. This is the scenario they have been trying to avoid their entire life—being at the mercy of their feelings and perceiving a loss of control over their emotions and circumstances.

Avoidant Attachment in Goal Pursuits

Being able to reach their goals is one of the most important things that helps bolster the self-esteem of the Fiercely Independent. Their self-concept is firmly rooted in achievement and the pursuit of personal and professional excellence. It is dependent on whether they are able to accomplish what they set their minds to. Their motivation and perseverance are often second to none and impress others who observe all they can do.

Even their leisure activities have an element of competition and challenge to them. They're less likely to see the inherent value in quiet contemplation, preferring to fill their time with pursuits that don't involve a lot of introspection. They prefer to set their mind on goals that others might find daunting, scary, or out of reach and tend to enjoy activities that have a performative aspect to them as well as those that provide an adrenaline rush (e.g., distance running, deep sea diving, or snowboarding).

They do better with goals that are individually oriented and may not be great team players because they are so competitive. Even as they embody the team mentality for group achievement, they're contemplating how to be the best: They desire to stand out from the crowd.

This intense quest to be number one is their best distraction from dealing with their emotions. They can only celebrate their achievements for so long before they commit themselves to yet another undertaking. When they can't achieve their goals, or the ability to achieve a goal is taken away (by an injury or illness, for example) they have great difficulty managing their feelings about their perceived failures. Their thinking may go along the lines of "I'm only as good as the last accolade, promotion, or award that I have received." For these same reasons, they often have difficulty enjoying true downtime. Without a steady stream of goals and achievements, their sense of self starts to crumble.

THE *POSITIVE* SIDE OF AVOIDANT ATTACHMENT

The avoidantly attached are high achievers and motivated, ambitious people; others look up to them for these abilities. They are often very successful, set high goals for themselves, and are very often able to achieve what they set out to do. They frequently reach lofty positions in work at a young age and labor hard to keep themselves on top. Their work ethic is beyond reproach. They are often recognized and praised for being able to work independently and to deliver on all that is set out for them to do. They invest a lot of time and energy in professional growth, and they reap the rewards with accolades and positions of increasing responsibility.

They can be lots of fun to be around and are charismatic, likable, friendly, and sociable—their confidence in their abilities and themselves can be infectious. They can connect with a multitude of people, albeit on a superficial level, and are a welcome addition to any social gathering. Friends and family find them easy to be around because they do not initiate any conflict and are not likely to dump emotional issues or problems in anyone else's lap. Their independence and self-reliance are admirable, and they are not perceived as being needy.

They can pursue relationships intently, which can be flattering to their partners. When they are in a relationship, they easily take the lead and help their partners with problems and big decisions. They don't ask a lot from their partner and rarely communicate expectations that seem unreasonable or excessive. They tend to be calm in stressful situations and are able to carry out decisions with confidence.

WHAT'S NEXT?

You've learned about the origins of avoidant attachment and have become familiar with the consequences this attachment style has on the different areas of your life, from your self-concept to work and romantic relationships and goal pursuits. Having to step up to adult-size problems as a child and not knowing whether it was safe to communicate your needs led you to form the coping styles and approaches you still rely on as an adult. It makes sense that you would gravitate toward achievements and things to solidify your self-concept, and shy away from situations that would reveal your emotional vulnerability, because that is what you were rewarded for as a child.

In my experience, individuals who have avoidant attachment tend to express their attachment wounds through four major self-statements, which are representations of their internal working models. Not everyone expresses these wounds in the same way, so some of the self-statements may speak to you more than others. Or you may find that all four self-statements seem familiar to you. Whatever the case, I will teach you a variety of evidence-supported exercises that will help you to overcome the negative consequences created by the characteristics of the avoidantly attached, and to teach your inner child a different way to approach life and to build a strong self-concept that is based less in value judgments and more in unconditional acceptance.

CHAPTER 6

Healing the Avoidant Attachment Style

In the previous chapter, you learned the origins of your fierce independence and started to understand the impact it's having on you as an adult. In this chapter, it's time to put knowledge into action and gain the benefits of intimacy and healthy interdependence, emotional attunement, and a self-concept based on the essence of who you are, not what you accomplish. The façade of self-reliance you adopted to connect with your caregivers may have allowed you to cope with your environment and survive stress and turmoil in your past, but as an adult it is likely limiting your ability to achieve the life vision you have for yourself.

As I mentioned in the last chapter, the Fiercely Independent tend to exhibit certain characteristics that were first developed to cope with their challenging childhood experiences. These characteristics can be seen in your working models, which show up as self-statements that reflect how you think about yourself and the way you go about life. Initially, they may have allowed you to cope psychologically and survive stress and turmoil in your past, but over time, they may have limited your behavior and established extreme ways of dealing with life. Becoming familiar with these self-statements is an important first step for being able to make changes.

As adults we tend to assume our working models are inherently true and valid, but they are more likely to be stories that we learned in childhood, stories that our inner child carries for us today. For people with avoidant attachment, those self-statements typically sound like:

1. "I'm only as good as my last achievement."
2. "I must be in control at all times."
3. "I keep others at arm's length."
4. "When the going gets tough, I go it alone."

In this chapter, we're going to examine these statements in more detail and work to heal the unmet needs of your inner child that lie at the root of each one. The discovery exercises will invite you to dig deep, and daily workouts will provide you with activities you can engage with as often as you wish to strengthen your coping skills. While the last chapter was about understanding, this chapter is all about action. It's ideal if you go through the exercises in order, but if anything feels overwhelming or if you're short on time, you can start with the daily workout and come back to the discovery exercise at a later date, when you have the time and emotional space to process it. Use your journal to make note of your responses to the exercises and to keep an eye on your progress.

Impact Test

As you read through these self-statements, you may find that all of them apply to you to some extent. Or you may struggle with knowing whether a self-statement really impacts you or not. You might be curious about which working model to focus on healing first. By apply-

ing my impact test to each of these working models, you can determine whether they are working against you and which corresponding
exercises you should prioritize.

The impact test is simple. As you read through these self-statements and their descriptions and examples, ask yourself these four
questions, and if your answer is yes to at least one of them, it's likely
that this self-statement is something you need to address by working
through my exercises. As a bonus activity, you can reflect on them
more deeply and jot down the answers to the italicized questions in
your journal:

- **Impact on Life Domains:** Does this working model negatively affect my life in major domains (work, romantic relationships, family
  relationships, friendships, goal attainment)? *If yes, write down 1–2
  concrete examples for each of these areas.*
- **Impact on Goal Attainment:** Does this working model usually move
  me away from my goals? *If so, how?*
- **Impact on Values-Based Living:** Is this working model inconsistent
  with my values? *What are some of my top values and how does this
  working model contribute to me moving away from my values or
  not living my top values the way I want?*
- **Impact on Self-Concept:** Is this working model something that
  shakes or damages my self-concept? *If so, how?*

"I'M ONLY AS GOOD AS MY LAST ACHIEVEMENT"

If there is a gold star to be had, you know that avoidantly attached folks are
chasing it. As we discussed in the previous chapter, people with avoidant
attachment couch their self-worth in their achievements. They may also
look up to and wish to be like people who possess material rewards—a big
paycheck, a lavish lifestyle, or awards for their performance. This is not

because they are inherently superficial in any way. It's more that they've learned that achievements are a type of social currency—a way to ensure that others will appreciate them and want to be around them.

Claudia grew up as the eldest of five siblings. Her parents were busy making ends meet, so they weren't very involved in Claudia's day-to-day activities—her grandparents were her primary caregivers for most of her childhood. From a young age, Claudia took on many responsibilities, including helping care for her younger siblings. When her siblings became rebellious in their teens, Claudia remained the golden child, earning high marks in school and excelling at extracurricular activities. As a result, she garnered positive attention from her parents, who constantly praised her for her achievements and good behavior and held her up as an example to her siblings (e.g., "Why can't you be more like your sister Claudia?").

She adopted a belief that she had to continue to be this "perfect" Claudia to receive support and love from her family, and over time, this was generalized to how she felt about and behaved toward other people. She was suspicious of people who seemed to take to her right off the bat, because Claudia believed she hadn't earned their affection through her actions yet. This made it difficult for her to have deeper connections with others, and it was easier to perpetuate the belief that unless she kept doing things that were worthy of love, no one would truly love her.

Similar to Claudia's experience, when you were a child, you may have used achievements to get your parents, caregivers, and other important adults to pay attention to you and give you positive reinforcement. Over time, you likely became overly reliant on things like great grades, sports awards, promotions, accolades at work, or acquiring objects (the fastest car, the biggest house, the most expensive wardrobe) to ensure that others will gravitate toward you and value you. You may not believe that you have any importance solely by being *you* without all the bells and whistles. As a result, your self-concept is quite precarious: Rather than having a constant, internal sense of your value, you've come to believe that you're only as worthwhile as your accomplishments. Afraid to stagnate, lest everyone realize that you aren't interesting, lovable, or desirable after all, you develop an increasing drive to achieve and gather items that suggest a certain status in order to gain acceptance from others.

While this isn't a substitute for deeper connection, it is a way to keep the people you care about close to you—at least to an extent. It offers a sense of comfort even as the avoidantly attached person questions whether they'd receive the same social support if they were not the shining beacon they are in their family and their community. Over time, their self-worth becomes so entangled in what they do that they can't stop *doing*. They commit to even bigger personal and professional aspirations, often at the expense of important aspects of their lives: their health, friendships, family, and romantic relationships.

While they project a high sense of self-worth, they are viciously critical of themselves and, unfortunately, others as well. They hold others to the same impossibly high standards to which they hold themselves, and when others don't perform on their level, they become critical or dismissive. The Fiercely Independent tend to have a negative view of others' worth and judge others harshly for their actions, especially those that seemingly derail success in different areas of life. They can have a certain level of disdain for those who don't seem to have the motivation or willpower to achieve their goals, often expressing that they find these people "weak" or "lacking in admirable character." Their limited ability to value themselves beyond their achievements limits the value that they can appreciate in others. They may also look down on people who express their emotions freely and seem to make decisions based on how they're feeling. They tend to admire people who are ruled by logic and strive to be the same.

What they lose in being so driven is any form of work–life balance. They are more likely to burn the candle at both ends at work than to maintain a give-and-take in their professional and personal lives. The fuel that drives them is a lot of negative self-talk that on the one hand pushes them to get things done, but on the other leaves them with lingering doubts about their abilities—which they then try to hide by creating even more lofty goals for themselves.

In friendships and romantic relationships, they are drawn to challenging people because they believe they need to earn their time, attention, and love. The more they must work to make the connection with a person, the more they feel that proves that person's value. Their inner critic devalues those who seem to care for them quickly or without a catch—because deep down, the Fiercely Independent person does not value themselves unconditionally.

When you haven't met a goal recently, or if you didn't meet your high standards (or someone else's), you are prone to beat up on yourself with negative self-talk and, as a result, feel bad about yourself. That inner critic can push you to achieve, but it can also lead to self-sabotage and poor mental health. You can learn to rein in that self-criticism and not beat yourself up for perceived missteps and lack of achievement.

Antidote to "I'm Only as Good as My Last Achievement"

The opposite of self-criticism is self-acceptance, and that's what you're going to learn to cultivate through these exercises. By turning down the volume on that part of you that is fixated on your next goal, harshly prodding you to do more, better, and faster, you can make room to see that you are worthwhile, lovable, and deserving of care from others even without any accomplishments. Creating a positive emotional bond with yourself that is predicated on no conditions other than your being, your existence—that's how you heal your wounded inner child. By breaking free from the belief that you need to have achievements and things to deserve self-love and self-care, you can pursue your goals and dreams in all areas of life without shame and excessive anxiety. You can improve your connection and reliance on others who wish to support and nurture you—no matter what your job title is or what car you drive.

DISCOVERY EXERCISE:
UNCONDITIONAL SELF-ACCEPTANCE

When your self-worth revolves around the story that "If I do x, then I am acceptable (to myself and others)," you open yourself up to feeling terrible about yourself and engaging in self-criticism that makes you feel not only less than others around you but also as if you are not deserving of anything.

When you accept yourself without condition, you start with "I am acceptable...no matter what." This is no small feat! As Dr. Albert Ellis, the brilliant mind behind Rational Emotive Behavior Therapy, said so well, unconditional self-acceptance is rare: "[it] means accepting your life, your enjoyment, what you want to do...accepting yourself...with little approval or with no damn approval."[1]

There are no conditions required to give yourself grace, empathy, or compassion, no hoops to jump through before you can feel good about who you are. For the Fiercely Independent, divesting themselves of the armor of their achievements can feel terrifying, but it is one of the most transformational opportunities for their healing.

This exercise is designed to help you develop unconditional self-acceptance through a combination of guided meditation, inner child work, and reflective journaling. This is an opportunity to give yourself permission to let your guard down with yourself, and to become vulnerable with your inner child—and, in turn, allow your inner child to be vulnerable with you. This helps you to turn down the volume of those self-critical voices and to create a compassionate space and see that, despite your flaws (yes, *your* flaws—all people have them), you deserve to be loved and are worthy of love, support, and care.

⌒

Make yourself comfortable by sitting in a chair with your feet planted on the ground, sitting cross-legged on the floor, lying on your back with a pillow behind your head, or in any position that allows you to feel connected to the earth and in touch with your physical sensations.

Close your eyes and begin paying attention to your breath. Inhale slowly and deeply through your nose and exhale through your mouth. Take your time with each inhale and exhale, and with each breath become more aware of the present moment. If any thoughts pop into your head that distract from your breath, gently guide your attention back to your breathing and accept those thoughts without trying to judge, change, or push them away. Notice whether your body is holding any tension and focus your breath on the areas that feel stressed or tense. Imagine that with each exhale, you're breathing relaxation into that part of the body. Repeat this as many times as needed until you feel calmer and more relaxed.

Now, reflect back to the first time you remember thinking or feeling that you needed to achieve, do something productive or constructive, or perhaps take on a responsibility that a child usually doesn't take on, in order to feel safe, protected, and loved. Try to find the earliest memory that introduced this idea to you—the idea that support and caring from your loved ones was conditional on the way you behaved and what you did.

Turn your attention to the child (or younger) version of you in your memory. Your inner child needs you to teach them that their worth is not based on what they do or their achievements. Your inner child needs to know that they are supported and loved just as they are.

Imagine sitting side by side with your inner child in a favorite place. This could be your current home, a cherished vacation spot, or a landmark that has some positive significance for you. Ask your inner child how they felt having to do something to earn support and safety. Ask them to share their thoughts or feelings about what they think would happen if they didn't do these things. Would they lose the attention of their parents or feel bad about themselves? Invite your inner child to get specific about what they think the consequences would be.

Next, read the following out loud, directly to your inner child, and help them (and the current version of you) understand the important messages within.

Whatever you are feeling, my inner child, know that nothing you can do can increase or decrease your unique worthiness. You don't need to prove your worth because you have worth just by being. Your worth does not depend on your achievements or others' judgments. Your worth is not based on your degrees, titles, performance, wealth, actions, or the opinions of others. Despite your good qualities and your not-so-great qualities, you are no more or no less worthy than any other human. Your approval of yourself does not come from any external source—it comes from you. Unconditional self-acceptance means that you accept and celebrate yourself as a living human being. You can choose to accept yourself any time of the day, at any moment, and even during difficult times.

Close your eyes and bring your attention back to your breath, and feel the flow of air moving into your lungs and then back out into the world. With each exhale, release any negative self-talk, self-criticisms, and self-judgments. Let go of self-deprecation, self-loathing, and shame. With each breath, tell yourself, "I am worthy just as I am. I am worthy of being happy." When you're ready, take a few more deep breaths and then open your eyes and come back into the room.

You can return to this meditation as often as you need it, to remind yourself that you are worthwhile just as you are.

Jot down a few thoughts about what your inner child experienced during this activity. Write down the roots of the idea of needing to do in order to have worth. When did this happen, how old were you, and what self-beliefs did that create? Finally, write down one thing your adult self will do to show unconditional self-acceptance to yourself today. It can be a simple affirmation, a self-compassion exercise (see page 325), or giving yourself permission to take a break from productive tasks and engage in a hobby.

~

When Diane did this meditation, she discovered that her earliest achievements were based on her athleticism as a child. Her whole family came to her soccer games and then went out afterward, so it was a great way to spend time with her parents and siblings. But most of their support (and going out for ice cream after) was based on how well she played. She would blame herself if the team lost (regardless of her own performance).

As an adult, she is very goal-driven and pushes herself to reach goal after goal in her job, which has become a bit of a toxic cycle for her. She is never satisfied: Once an achievement is reached, she is already looking for the next. To compound this constant push to be better all the time, Diane participated in a club soccer team, and when she suffered a knee injury that put her out of physical activity for several months, her self-esteem plummeted and she became depressed. Without her achievements on the field, she didn't have much to reinforce her self-concept. Despite work success, much of how she felt about herself (which began when she first played) was tied up in her prowess on the soccer field. She was able to see, over time, that her value was about being Diane, not Diane who excels at playing soccer or Diane who is a VP at her company. She is simply valuable and has worth for being Diane.

DAILY WORKOUT: FLOW YOUR
WAY TO SELF-ACCEPTANCE

Mihaly Csikszentmihalyi is considered one of the co-founders of the positive psychology movement. He pioneered the concept of flow. We often hear athletes talk about being "in flow" and how that can help their performance. For psychologists, flow is the mental state we enter when we become so fully immersed in an activity that we lose awareness of time, space, even ourselves. Csikszentmihalyi proposed the concept of psychological flow, which is "a state of optimal experience arising from intense involvement in an activity that is enjoyable…[when] one has a sense of total control, effortlessness, and complete concentration on the immediate situation."[2]

The idea of doing something for its own sake and for pure enjoyment may be somewhat foreign to the Fiercely Independent, who are often proud workaholics, but the interesting thing about flow is that although it's not achievement-driven, through flow it's possible to achieve a high sense of satisfaction, joy, and self-worth.

If you're focused on meeting goals to boost your self-esteem, aiming for *flow* at least once a day can be extremely helpful to cultivate self-acceptance and to detach yourself from focusing on achievement to feel secure in your self-worth. Research has shown that when people are in a state of psychological flow, there is a decrease in prefrontal cortex activity,[3] which is the part of the brain that governs self-reflective consciousness. Flow may quiet your inner critic as well as foster a sense of relaxation and energization due to feeling less stress and time pressure.

Each day, commit to getting into a flow state—twenty minutes of a dedicated activity is usually enough. (I find that this is most successful first thing in the morning or when winding down in the evening.) On weekends or whenever your schedule may be more relaxed, you may choose to devote more time to a flow activity. But for now, commit to blocking out twenty minutes to knit, draw, run, sing, dance—whatever activity works for you.

It can take some trial and error to find the activities that drop you into a flow state, and that's where your journal comes in. On a new page, follow the criteria below and brainstorm a list of activities that you'd like to try to induce flow. I recommend that you start with at least seven activities so you can do one flow activity each day for a week. There is no limit to how many activities can go on your flow list, but if you try something that doesn't get you into flow, erase or cross it out and move on to those that consistently work for you. Anything that meets the following requirements is an option:

1. You enjoy doing it for the sake of the activity, and not (solely) because of an external reward (like others praising you for it);
2. You remember positive emotions related to doing the activity (when you look forward to it, during the activity, and/or after); and
3. You feel a sense of personal empowerment or see an opportunity for skill building and strengthening as you participate in it (for example, getting better at playing an instrument, learning how to knit, or doing a physical activity that makes you feel healthy and strong like a few yoga or tai chi poses, or the **power pose** described by Dr. Amy Cuddy [see page 330]).

If you lose track of time when doing this activity, for example after the activity you may have said, "I don't know where the time went," that's a good sign you were in flow.

Once you have your list, commit to doing one activity each day. If you wish, you can do the same one several times a week, but in the beginning, it's best to rotate through different activities to maintain variety (and eliminate boredom), as well as to zero in on which one(s) help you achieve a flow state more easily.

Flow State Checklist

After each activity, use this checklist to see if you've entered a flow state.

Did this activity of _____

- Hold my interest and attention?
- Allow me to be present-minded (focused on the here and now) and to disconnect from worries and negative thoughts (at least temporarily)?
- Hit that Goldilocks rule of being not too easy and not too difficult for me?
- Allow me to feel in control and empowered?
- Make me lose track of time?

My self-confidence after the activity was _____ (1–10, with 10 being the highest level of self-confidence)

My overall mood after the activity was _____ (1–10, with 10 being the most positive mood)

If you checked at least four of the first five items for the activity, and if you find that your self-confidence and mood improve after doing the activity, put a little star next to that activity in your journal so you remember which ones have been successful at inducing flow. Over time, you'll hone your list of flow state activities through evaluating them after you do the activity, and periodically add new activities

---

THE AVOIDANT ATTACHMENT STYLE

to try. The more you use the flow state to bolster your self-concept in
the absence of external rewards, the more you'll connect with an unconditional self-acceptance and self-worth that isn't tied to achievements.

"I MUST BE IN CONTROL AT ALL TIMES"

If you feel like the quintessential control freak, you're not alone. We can all dedicate our energy and brainpower to plan for, and attempt to predict, everything in our lives, to try to prevent some imagined disaster or catastrophe. But needing to be in control of everything is exhausting, and nobody knows that better than the Fiercely Independent.

Whether driven by the pressure to achieve, a never-ending quest for perfection, or a worry that if you let go, chaos will ensue and you won't ever be able to gain control again—these fears started when you were a child. You were likely asked (whether implicitly or explicitly) to take on adult responsibilities when you were young. When your parents or caregivers didn't meet your needs, you were led to believe that you had to do everything for yourself. Having to grow up too fast and shoulder too much responsibility taught you that you, and you alone, were responsible for your survival.

Because the Fiercely Independent don't trust that anyone can meet their needs (or at least meet them as well as they can), they want to have control over their plans and schedule, how they do things and when, and the pace a relationship should take, because having these routines and abilities to make decisions independently helps them to feel free. Especially when they get stressed, they don't want to answer to anyone else's agenda, needs, or desires, and they often retreat to the sanctuary of their solitude to regroup and de-stress. Being in control—or at least having the illusion of control—is how they conjure a sense of safety.

Just as importantly, people with avoidant attachment don't want others to think they're not in control and will hide any indication that they are struggling in any way. After all, as a child, they learned that struggle was unacceptable, weak, and likely to get them even less attention than if they seemed to have things under control. As adults, they project strength and competence, and appear capable enough to weather any storm—regardless of the reality of their feelings.

In relationships, they prefer to keep it all on their terms as much as they can. For example, they may frequently seek out alone time or spend time doing activities without their partner. They don't engage in give-and-take in a relationship or in making decisions about anything from when to get together (or how often) to what to have for dinner. If someone seemingly makes demands on their time or attention or expresses concern or care for them, they may feel suffocated or trapped. They are likely to brush off anyone's concerns about their health or that they're working too hard and feel as if the other person is being overbearing by caring.

They believe they're not equipped to offer deeper connections and are very wary of those who seem to want more from them. They're afraid that such requests might effectively pull them in, cause them to become interdependent with another person, and lose control of their self-sufficiency, which has been key to their childhood survival. Letting down their guard and being vulnerable with another is synonymous with relinquishing control. They don't want to give control to anyone because they expect them to either disappoint them or abuse this privilege. They fear that the person may not only exert control over them but will have an opinion about who they should be. As the alpha in the relationship, they have more "value" (at least from their own perspective) and can exert control in their personal relationships and dictate how things will go. Being in any kind of equal partnership can be scary, because there is no one in charge and there is no hierarchy to determine what is going on.

They have a lot of perfectionist tendencies, which come from a fear of failure. If they are perfect and do everything right, they believe they are okay. If they perceive that a situation has the potential not to be perfect or is a huge risk, they will not get involved. This can lead to trouble because, in interpersonal relationships, there is much that is less than perfect (conflict, disagreement) so holding relationships to a perfect ideal is unrealistic. If a relationship seems less than perfect, they will end it or disengage; likewise, if they lose the upper hand in a relationship, they run the risk of feeling vulnerable.

The avoidantly attached love solving problems but dislike conflict with others, particularly if they must share their feelings. Part of their avoidance stems from a fear that they might lose control of their emotions and behave in a way that would lift the veil on the calm, cool, and collected façade they are known for. By engaging in the conflict, they may no longer be in control of the situation or may have the potential to "lose," which is anathema to the avoidantly attached. If conflict arises and they feel emotionally provoked (signaling a potential loss of control), they will ignore the conflict and focus their attention on things they can control, like career and individual goals. If a partner expresses displeasure or initiates an argument, they will suddenly need to go to the office or do their marathon training run.

At its core, the need for control comes from a deep-seated fear of uncertainty. Their inner child learned to cope by anticipating bad situations and making a game plan in advance. They're always prepared for the worst, because they never want to be caught off guard and unable to fend for themselves; they try to minimize changes to their routines or unknown factors like other people's involvement. As a child, they may have felt that their need to control was imposed on them by others—it was less about what they wanted for themselves, but rather, how to manage their lives to be less negatively impacted by the whims of those they grew up with. They learned as a child that they couldn't fully count on others, so they now believe if they don't do something, it won't get done. The more they try to control, the more stress they experience (no one person can do it all!) and the more they lean into the belief that others can't be counted on—which only perpetuates the cycle. This need to be in control forces them to respond to situations only by taking charge and not by thinking about, or even considering, what they really want.

Antidote to "I Must Be In Control at All Times"

These exercises will allow your inner child to experience safety and comfort as they explore—because your adult self has connected with them, understands their needs, and will be there to support them to keep them healthy and safe. In essence, your adult self is acting as a wise guide or a supportive parent, to care for and lift up your inner child. Although your inner child was suppressed back then, today your inner child can find space to explore and play, and to have the experiences they were meant to have.

DISCOVERY EXERCISE: WHAT I WISH

Open your journal and create two columns. Title the left column "What I had plenty of as a child" and title the right column "What I wish I had more of as a child." Begin to free-write under each column whatever comes to mind without judging the content. After a few minutes, read what you have written. Although it may be difficult, sit with the emotions that come up. It may have been challenging to fill in one or both of these columns. Perhaps the list of what you had plenty of is not as long as what you wish you had more of, and that brings sadness and pain. Perhaps this exercise forces you to come face-to-face with things you haven't dealt with in a long time. Bringing up negative experiences from your childhood may also feel like opening the door to blaming your parents for your current troubles. But remember, this type of insight does not have to come at the expense of becoming angry with or resentful toward your parents. You can have compassion for them at the same time that you have compassion for your inner child. Our goal in this exercise is to bring to light what your reality was as a child and identify why it was particularly challenging, so that you can now give your inner child specifically what they missed out on back then.

As you read what you wrote in your journal, begin thinking about how you can give yourself the things you wish you had received in childhood. As a child, you had to rely largely on others to meet your needs, and they may not have delivered. Because of this, as an adult, you have taken things to the other extreme and decided, consciously or subconsciously, to get what you need without relying on anyone else (or, at least, relying on them as little as possible). There is a middle ground where your needs can be met through a combination of operating independently and seeking help from people who care about you and want to nurture and support you.

On a fresh page, choose one of the items from your list of "Things I wish I had more of" and under it write "What I can do for myself," and "What I can ask someone for." Now write down something you can do for yourself today to get one of those needs met, *and* write down something that you can ask of another trusted individual in order to meet that need. You can repeat this for all the items on your list.

Now look at your list of "What I had plenty of" to consider any of your strengths, skills, and innate abilities as well as any other resources—including other people in your life—that you can draw on as you consider what you can do for yourself.

If you're used to doing everything on your own, it can be difficult, but it's necessary to think about how you can reach out to others to heal your attachment. What you ask of yourself, and others, doesn't have to be mind-blowing, but it should be something that will make a difference.

Leo's parents were kind people but put a lot of pressure on Leo to get good grades so that he could go to a competitive college and embark on a successful career. They both worked out of the home in high-powered jobs and expected Leo to follow in their footsteps. In high school, Leo's dad would create extra math problems for him to do on weekends and vacations, and he was expected to take accelerated classes. In college, all his parents wanted to know was how he had done on his last test, and they discouraged him from any activities other than academics.

One of Leo's roommates was involved in art. Leo got very interested in drawing, but his parents forbade him from taking any art classes. Once he had a job and was on his own, Leo continued to work hard and received positive attention and praise from his parents for every achievement and promotion.

Doing this exercise made Leo realize that while his parents provided much for him, he was missing an opportunity to have downtime, engage in something creative, and not be striving for the next goal all the time. He decided to take a weekend art class at the local museum and went into it with the attitude of just trying it out.

DAILY WORKOUT: LETTING YOUR INNER CHILD OUT TO PLAY

If you're avoidantly attached, you likely grew up a bit too fast and were given more responsibilities than your peers. You probably had to learn to be more serious-minded or stoic than others and, at a young age, effectively deactivated the carefree, playful part of you.

This exercise can help you to discover the part of you that felt free, unabashed, and unafraid to make mistakes, fail, or lose control. You can flex your play muscles and achieve a sense of safety and security while doing so.

The key to creating that safe haven for your inner child is that the adult you—the version of you that is grown, that has learned how to adapt to different situations, is able to exert more control over your environment, and therefore is able to watch over your younger self as they attempt to recapture those precious childhood moments where life was all about new discoveries and carefree exploration. Whether you can tap back into a time you felt free when you were younger or if this is an opportunity to gift your inner child with this freedom for the first time, play is truly therapeutic. It reduces stress, releases feel-good chemicals like endorphins, and gets you to focus on the present moment (instead of ruminating about the regrets of the past or potential catastrophes of the future) quickly. When you play, you let your guard down, you let go of fear-based thinking, and that need to control everything diminishes.

When you feel free, you feel less self-conscious, you're less likely to act out of fear or avoidance, and you become more creative, adventurous, and emotionally resilient in the process.

~

Take a moment to think about the activities you enjoyed as a child (or, if that feels too out of reach, imagine what you might have liked to do, if you'd been able). Reflect on some joyful moments from your younger years and think about what you were doing. Look at old photos or talk to family members to find out what you liked doing back then. Imagine what you'd like to do if you didn't care what others thought.

Here is a list of ideas to get you started.

- Play at a nearby park
- Hopscotch, jump rope, or Hula-Hoop
- Skip down the street
- Visit a toy store
- Play a nostalgic board/video game
- Rewatch favorite childhood movies
- Work on favorite childhood crafts (coloring, Legos, Play-Doh)

- Reread favorite childhood books
- Build a fort
- Sing/dance to your favorite songs
- Visit museums/art galleries
- Go to the zoo or amusement park
- Dress up in a costume
- Complete an obstacle course
- Build a sand castle
- Blow bubbles
- Hug your stuffed animals
- Play with puppets
- Roller-skate or ride a bike
- Play laser tag
- Decorate for the holidays

Giving yourself permission to play and enjoy—without keeping score or racking up points in your head or with others—gives your inner child an opportunity to heal from being denied the pleasures of play when you were a child. You can also spend time doing different activities with your children or other younger family members and observe their wonder and awe as they discover new things. This is a wonderful gift to both your present and inner child/past self—to be able to relive the wonders and treasures of childhood and give yourself a break from daily pressures and responsibilities, many of which harbor high expectations that come from your self-critical voice.

BONUS DISCOVERY ACTIVITY:
SHOWING UP FOR A CHILD

To heal some of your own childhood attachment wounds and really explore the value of play in all aspects of your life, consider showing up for another child and helping to build secure attachment connections for them. This child could be your own, an extended family member, a friend's child, or someone in your neighborhood or larger community through a volunteer organization. Make the commitment to be there for them and show consistency and unconditional care toward them.

"I KEEP OTHERS AT ARM'S LENGTH"

Have you ever been excited in the initial phases of dating, only to feel a strong urge to pull away and keep emotional distance from your partner when they start asking for more commitment? Or have you ever been turned off, irritated, or felt uncomfortable when someone openly expresses their emotions (especially negative ones)—perhaps labeling that person in your mind as dramatic or inappropriate? Have you ever been accused of being emotionally unavailable—and when someone says this about you, you think they're being too needy or demanding? The Fiercely Independent are likely to resonate with at least one or maybe all these scenarios.

If you identify with a Fiercely Independent attachment style, it's not uncommon that you would fear intimacy and the expression of strong emotions (or seeing such expression in others). After all, at a young age you were taught that expressing strong emotions or feelings was unacceptable. If you had big feelings, you would be rejected. You may not have felt safe when you've been vulnerable in the past if people in your life responded with negative attitudes, perhaps shaming you or making you feel guilty for simply expressing yourself.

Because people with this style internalized the belief that expressing emotions is bad, they typically respond to emotionally provoking situations by retreating or pulling away. They attempt to distance themselves from situations and people that might cause them to experience intense feelings that they aren't equipped to manage. If someone else is very emotional or easily expresses emotions, they are turned off by it, because to them it indicates a loss of control. In fact, they can be dismissive of others' emotional needs and seem to have less empathy. It's not that they don't care, but they learned to take care of things themselves, so why can't everyone else?

They are guarded when there is a call for a deeper emotional connection with others and are deeply private about any worries or concerns they may have. I'll never forget the time my friend Brenda, who had been laid off suddenly from her job of ten years, waved away my concern with a brief "I'll be fine," and immediately changed the subject to her annoyance at her favorite breakfast cereal being discontinued. It's not uncommon for the Fiercely Independent to push away people who ask questions or express concern for them, or even to find it insulting. "Of course I'm okay" is their constant refrain. They believe firmly they can take care of everything themselves and don't fully trust others to help them with any worries or concerns they may have. They are likely to suppress their emotions and exhibit a stiff upper lip even in times of trouble or distress.

This is not to say that people with avoidant attachment don't want to connect on a deeper level, but over time you've learned that it's easier to ignore that need and adopt a persona of impenetrably aloof competence. When others try to connect with you, you'll only do it on your own terms so that you don't give too much of yourself and then wind up being disappointed or hurt again. You might be the life of the party and seem to have a lot of social support, but there are limits to how much you reveal about yourself, and most people don't know the whole you. These avoidant behaviors are designed to protect you, your inner child, and what makes you instinctively feel safe based on your past experiences. You might not be aware that you are keeping people at a distance (some or most of the time) because it's become automatic for you—it's what you've done to survive all these years.

In relationships, this fear of intimacy and connection prevents you from getting truly close to anyone, and if you do find yourself caring deeply, you may sabotage the relationship by picking a fight or disengaging so that the other person breaks up with you. The Fiercely Independent do not want to be beholden to anyone, and if another person is too needy, they will ghost the partner to maintain their independence. They have trouble fully committing to relationships because they avoid deep conversations, feelings, and relationship experiences. They keep it all light and on the surface, because if they get too deep, they fear they may lose control or reveal too much of themselves—making themselves vulnerable to the other person.

Also, by keeping it light and not letting anyone get close to them, they are using a defense mechanism to protect themselves from being rejected for anything they might reveal about themselves if they were to allow someone into their deeper thoughts and feelings. If their fears of imminent rejection become too great, they will be the first to get out of the relationship rather than stay and try to work through their feelings or communicate their fears to their partner. Their discomfort with emotions and their fears about the consequences of expressing them are why they prefer to focus their attention on things they can control—like their work or personal goals—and are at the heart of their feelings of loneliness.

Antidote to "I Keep Others at Arm's Length"

The following exercises are designed to help you to work through your fears around intimacy and to start opening up to safe and supportive individuals in your life who want to meet your needs. It all starts with being vulnerable with yourself first. This is what the next exercise is all about.

DISCOVERY EXERCISE:
FACING YOUR SHADOW SELF

It sounds mysterious when I talk about facing your shadow self, doesn't it? But shadow work, first developed by psychiatrist Carl Jung,[4] is a powerful way to uncover your subconscious drives and needs in a safe way that brings clarity to your life.

Your shadow is a hidden part of yourself. Some refer to it as the darker side of your personality that you try to hide away from others. Your shadow self might be made up of traits or characteristics that you think others might find undesirable, or perhaps you are the harsh self-critic who believes that these traits shouldn't be shown to others. Much of this isn't conscious, but at some point in your life, you received a message that if you show these traits to others, you'll be judged or rejected. To please others and your conscious mind, you repressed, pushed away, and rejected these parts of yourself. Over time, anything you (or others in your life) deemed faulty, bad, or unacceptable becomes a part of your shadow self. Like a program running in the background of your computer, your shadow self has an effect on you. In fact, the more you try to ignore or get away from your shadow self, the bigger and stronger its influence over you grows.

When you first come into the world, you are in many ways a blank slate. You are learning about how the world works—as well as your part in it. Over time and as you encounter experiences, you determine how to separate thoughts and behaviors into good and bad categories, including parts of who you are. You learn that when you behave in certain ways, adults around you respond warmly and give you praise. You also learn that when you do other things, adults show disdain for your actions or scold you.

Some of these lessons are good, as they help you to develop into a moral, prosocial person (for example, your parents *should* be upset with you if you steal gum from the grocery store). But some of these other lessons have nothing to do with helping you to develop compassion or an ethical compass (for example, being chastised for expressing sadness or acting upset, teaching you to suppress your emotions). These lessons aren't necessarily imparted by evil or bad people—your caregivers may have genuinely believed they were being helpful. But in the process, you learned that some things are better hidden, that there are some parts of you that are bad, and you should pretend they are not a part of who you are. They cause you to alter your authentic self, sometimes to the point that the way you show up with others isn't anything like who you really are on the inside.

For example, for as long as she could remember, Tina was told to be quiet. She had a big voice and was very expressive, but she was told she was too dramatic and to tone it down. As a result, she rarely speaks up and works hard to keep a lid on her expressions and emotions. What was a part of her personality was negatively called out by her parents and became a part of her shadow self.

Sometimes the traits that annoy you most in others are part of your shadow self. You may find yourself overreacting to these characteristics when you see them in other people, because seeing them triggers the inner critic in yourself and makes you uncomfortable. You may wonder why that individual doesn't do a better job of hiding that part of who they are.

Brian was often chastised when he was younger for being a little flaky or absent-minded. As an adult, he has worked overtime to keep this aspect of his personality under wraps. However, if anyone around him shows any flaky behavior, he hits the roof. When his son forgot to bring his lunch to school, Brian was furious and grounded his son for the whole weekend. Given that Brian himself shares these traits you might expect forgiveness and understanding toward his son, but Brian was just not having it.

Your shadow self is an integral part of your inner child. It is the child part of you that tried to solve problems with the limited resources you had at a time when you were young and reliant on those around them to care for you and to teach you effective coping skills. As a part of your inner child, your shadow self has unmet needs and craves your attention, support, and love. Your inner child wants to know that it can come out of hiding and that its existence and what it stands for are okay and acceptable.

Shadow work is helpful for healing your attachment wounds because it brings awareness to this subconscious part of yourself and helps you take steps to resolve the pain that has built up throughout the years. Affirming your shadow self and recognizing that it has many positive aspects are key to unconditional self-acceptance. You can finally understand that your worth in this world is complete without you having to strive to be loved by others (and by yourself). You are likely to find that affirming, understanding, and working with your shadow self will enhance your physical and mental well-being, clear the path for more meaningful relationships, and help you to discover parts of yourself that help you to be the best and most authentic version of you.

Shadow work takes you through three steps: bringing your shadow into the light, giving your shadow some love, and sharing the stage with your shadow. Each of these steps will allow you to acknowledge the role your shadow plays in your life and to become more comfortable with accepting this part of yourself.

1. **Spot your shadow self and bring them out into the light.** You can often spot your shadow self by paying attention to your

interactions with others. Specifically, if you find that there is a person whose behavior really irks or upsets you and sometimes causes you to overreact, think about the traits of this individual that bother you the most. For example, when you dislike something in yourself, you might point it out in others. Some classic examples are:

- A person with disordered eating restricting their child's food choices.
- A person who is impatient and talks over others gets angry at being interrupted.
- A person who is a gossip gets very mad at anyone talking about them behind their back.
- A person berates others for being late but is never on time themselves.
- A person who likes to dominate a room gets upset if someone else is the center of attention.
- A person who isn't neat and organized gets frustrated at their child and scolds them for being messy.

Now, ask yourself the following questions and jot the answers down in your journal:

- Why does this person's behavior bother me so much?
- Does this person trigger any unpleasant memories or bring up negative thoughts or feelings? If so, what are the memories, thoughts, or feelings that come up when I interact with this person?
- Are there any traits this person possesses that remind me of aspects of myself that I don't like? Why don't I like these traits in others and myself?
- What do I think will happen if I show the world some of these traits?

2. **Give your shadow self some love.** Visualize your shadow self. They may look just like you, or maybe a less-put-together version of you. They may look like a literal shadow, or they may be a bit amorphous, for example, a dark, cloud-like entity. Your shadow self might even look like a child version of you. Once you bring your shadow self into focus, affirm their presence and who they are. Some helpful affirmations include:

- I welcome you into the light.
- I accept you just as you are.
- I care about you.
- You can be yourself around me.
- I let go of shame, fear, and dislike about who you are.
- I love you.

Visualize giving your shadow self a hug as a physical form of acceptance. You can also think about watching your shadow self in action, doing the things that you felt were not positive reflections of yourself, and observing, without judgment or criticism, how they go about things. As you witness, try to understand its motivations from a place of compassion and recognize that your shadow self is a part of you.

3. **Share the stage with your shadow.** Carl Jung said, "To confront a person with his own shadow is to show him his own light."[5] It may be difficult at first, but find ways to let your shadow self out to play. This might involve any of the following:

- Take one of the traits you ascribe to your shadow self and discover its benefits. For example, if you were punished for being "too emotional," you likely hid your feelings away when things bothered you, and since then, you

151

put a smiling face out to the world even when you feel terrible inside. Ask yourself, what are some of the positive aspects of open emotional expression? Write these down. For example, emotional expression is healthy; not being afraid of your own negative emotions is a strength and helps to regulate your emotions and helps you accept yourself just as you are.

- Spend time embracing a trait of your shadow self. For example, if your shadow self delights in being loud and rambunctious, watch something funny and allow your shadow self to giggle, scream, guffaw, and express themself freely.
- Invite your shadow self out to play. If your shadow self is creative, get into crafting or sign up for a community art class. If your shadow self enjoys being messy, go paintballing with some younger family members or allow yourself to not tidy up right away from time to time.

BONUS DISCOVERY ACTIVITY:
INTRODUCING YOUR SHADOW

Introduce your shadow self to others you trust. This will be tough, but showing your shadow self to people you care about is key to giving your shadow self the affirmation that they need not to feel ignored or rejected. Start small and allow yourself to express a trait that you've denied or try to shut away with a friend. Or you can have a conversation about this part of yourself with a loved one. For example, you can tell a loved one that the reason you get so annoyed at the mutual friend who is always running late everywhere is because you also have the tendency to overbook yourself and then show up late.

DAILY WORKOUT: WHAT'S THAT EMOTION?

The Fiercely Independent tend to block, suppress, or push away uncomfortable feelings. They may be afraid of what will happen if they express their emotions. Will people truly accept them if they do? Look down on them? Will they lose control if they allow their emotions to take over? But feelings, even negative ones, serve important purposes. They help us to know when something is significant to us and, in some instances, can help us with psychological and physical survival. Feelings also help us to connect to other people, which is vital for our existence, as humans are social beings that require meaningful connections with others to thrive.

This ten-minute daily workout will help you to become more comfortable managing your challenging feelings and emotions. By calling them up in a more controlled setting, you can practice acknowledging, understanding, and expressing your feelings in a way that may feel safer. As you become more comfortable naming and moving through your feelings, you will find that it's easier to acknowledge feelings in more spontaneous settings or around other people.

⌒

To begin, choose a song or a scene from a movie that always stirs up some intense emotions for you. (My go-to is the scene in *The Lion King* when Mufasa dies. I cry every time!) Once you've selected the piece that you'll be responding to, get into a comfortable position, take a few deep breaths, and watch or listen to what you selected, trying to focus as much as possible on your sensory experience—using as many of your five senses as possible—and allowing whatever feelings come up to emerge. Once you're fully immersed in your feelings, open your journal and work through the following steps:

1. **Name your feelings.** Adopt an attitude of curiosity and see if you can name the feelings that you're experiencing. Feelings can be described with words (e.g., sadness, anger, frustration) or they can be experienced as physical sensations (e.g., quickening heartbeat, goose bumps, tears). Try not to judge whatever comes up for you. If you're stuck, grab a feelings wheel (you can find one online at feelingswheel.com) to help. If you're noticing a physical sensation, describe what you feel in your body (e.g., I feel my heartbeat speeding up and my palms are a bit sweaty). Don't be tempted to interpret what these feelings mean. Simply acknowledge their presence, describe them, and let them be.

2. **Accept and validate your feelings.** Now that you've made space to observe and acknowledge your feelings, affirm that it's okay to feel whatever feelings come up. Here are some affirmations you can repeat to yourself:
    *   It's okay to feel how I feel.
    *   I don't need to judge or make meaning of this emotion; I can just let it be.
    *   Feeling these emotions doesn't mean I have to act on them.
    *   All emotions pass, and even if I don't like this emotion, it will fade with time.

3. **Make sense of your feelings.** Still embodying an attitude of curiosity, try to make sense of your feelings. Ask yourself these questions without judgment and simply observe the answers:
    *   What does this feeling tell me about this art piece or this situation?

- Do I fear anything about this emotion, and if so, where is that coming from?
- Has there been a time when I've felt this emotion in the past? When was the most recent time?
- If it is a negative emotion (anger, grief, sadness), what is one small thing I can do now to manage this emotion so that it doesn't feel as stressful to me? What can I do to improve this moment ever so slightly?

As you bring the exercise to a close, remember that you don't need to act on your emotions in any particular way. You can sit with the feeling, acknowledge its presence, and watch it change. If there is an impulse associated with this feeling that may not be productive in this moment (for example, if your anger makes you want to throw something at the wall), you can choose to observe the impulse without acting on it. You can also decide that you want to express your emotions in some way, for example, through your own artistic endeavors (drawing, writing) or by telling someone about your emotions. Whatever you do next, it is *your* decision. Your feelings do not determine your actions or who you are.

"WHEN THE GOING GETS TOUGH, I GO IT ALONE"

By this point, it shouldn't come as much of a surprise that the Fiercely Independent tend to cope with difficult situations by themselves. Those who are avoidantly attached are the prototypical lone wolves—they maintain distance from others emotionally and physically, especially when under a lot of stress. They tend to withdraw instead of reaching out for support during challenging times. They don't reveal much about what they are thinking or feeling and tend to sulk in silence or at the most drop veiled hints about whatever is bothering them. Because they are so indirect about what they are going through or what they might need, other people (family, friends, partners) can't address their needs or help them. This leads them to feel even more alone and isolated, and only reinforces the lessons they learned from their childhood: that they can't count on others to help or meet their needs in any meaningful way.

They may either repress or avoid dealing with negative feelings head-on or act irritable and frustrated without explaining why they're being so touchy, pushing people away rather than drawing people to them, and in effect reinforcing their preexisting belief that others cannot be counted on for support and nurturance. When others seem unable to help because the Fiercely Independent haven't communicated their needs directly or made a bid for support, it further amplifies their belief that they are the only ones who can solve their problems.

Even in times of stress—a major illness of their own or of a family member, or a work crisis—they are unlikely to seek help and will retreat from others instead of engaging with them. They may brush off others' comments of concern for them, and when people ask them how they can help, they are likely to say they are fine and don't need anything.

It's not that they don't want others to care; they absolutely do. But the lessons their inner child still carries—memories of when they may have been rebuffed by caregivers for expressing their needs or when they were expected to manage things on their own—loom large and prevent them from feeling safe asking for or even accepting help. Over time, they may have equated any bid for attention, affection, or emotional support with being "needy" or, even worse, "high maintenance." The Fiercely Independent loathe being a burden to others and hate to be viewed as weak. At some point in their upbringing, they've conflated healthy interdependence with weakness, and therefore will do everything they can to handle situations on their own.

When they experience any difficulties, they are much less likely than most people to share their internal struggles, and this reluctance to communicate their challenges and needs closes them off from the opportunity to receive help from others. They try to do everything themselves, and even when their own efforts aren't getting the results they want, they're unlikely to tell someone about their disappointments—because they may see this as some kind of personal failure or worry that others will see them as a failure. They may even tell people that they are a loner or prefer solitude—but, if they are being honest with themselves, they feel twinges of loneliness, especially when they are in the middle of a particularly stressful time in their life. They may even convince themselves that they fundamentally need less connection than most people, then act in ways that bring an isolated existence to fruition.

They are happy to help others, especially if they can be perceived as the hero for doing so, but do not accept help in return, even when others honestly desire to care for and support them. They may convince themselves that others are only offering help to be polite, and that if they were to take them up on their offer, the other person would be annoyed or find their requests to be cumbersome.

Unfortunately, if things become too much, the Fiercely Independent may retreat so far that they are at risk of developing unhealthy and addictive behaviors. This can range from hours of binge-watching TV to overeating to doomscrolling on the internet or even using alcohol, drugs, sex, or gambling to avoid dealing with their problems.

It is understandable that they may not want to be overly dependent on others, but there is a happy medium: interdependence. This is a mutual reliance between people, where the interconnection between people offers support, cooperation, and working together to achieve common goals and live out shared values. In interdependent relationships, your actions, decisions, and well-being are influenced by the others with whom you're connected, but you still exercise agency and self-sufficiency, as do they. It helps to create a mutually beneficial balance between people. And while the ability to depend on others while also maintaining a strong sense of self is difficult to put into practice, it is possible for you to achieve. The more you work toward interdependence, the more you will realize that your beliefs from childhood may not apply to the people in your current environment, and you might be surprised by the meaning that a strong support network can add to your life.

Antidote to "When the Going Gets Tough, I Go It Alone"

Becoming comfortable with interdependence is a process—it requires opening up to people who deserve your trust, expressing your feelings and needs, asking for support in direct ways, and believing that none of this takes away from your independence or freedom, but rather, it helps you to achieve a stronger sense of inner security and stable self-worth.

The following exercises will help you to achieve interdependence in a safe and supportive way, beginning with an assessment of your current sources of support.

DISCOVERY EXERCISE: CLOSENESS CIRCLE

The closeness circle is used to understand the degree of connection and intimacy you have with others in your life. It is a very helpful exercise for identifying any challenging patterns in your relationships and how you can create and maintain strong connections with others, which benefits your mental and physical health. By becoming more aware of your available social support systems you can determine with whom you can be more vulnerable and intimate.

Open your journal and draw a small circle in the middle of your paper. Write your name in it, and then draw three concentric circles around it like the rings on a tree (with enough space to write in between them).

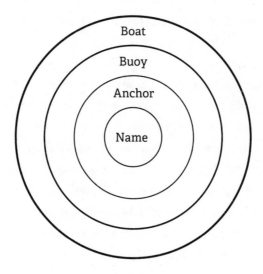

Moving outward from the circle with your name in it, the next ring is the *Anchor*. It represents the people in your life whom you trust the most and feel closest to. When you are with these people, you would consider letting your guard down and feel you can be vulnerable. Write down any names of people whom you feel fit this description. Be honest about this. Family members don't automatically go into this ring, so don't feel pressured to write down their names if that doesn't feel accurate.

The next ring is called the *Buoy*. Like a buoy floating in an ocean, these people are reliable but can move around a bit. The people who fit in this ring are important to you but may not be as secure and grounded a source of support as your *Anchors*. These are friends and colleagues with whom you are in regular contact and people you are likely to go to for advice some of the time.

The last ring is called the *Boat*. These are people who you can rely on for companionship or entertainment but may not be the first people you go to when you need to solve a problem or when you need to talk about something more personal. These people may be those with whom you spend time or share hobbies because you enjoy their company and doing so is relatively convenient (like neighbors and colleagues).

The closeness circle is a starting point in assessing the connections in your life, so you don't need to fit everyone you know into these categories. However, you should work on this for as long as you need to until you feel it captures your social interactions adequately. Once completed, it may be filled with people who are more top of mind for you and those with whom you are in more frequent contact. If you repeat this exercise a few months from now, whoever is inside each of the rings may change. Also, there may be people who don't fit into any of these categories, for example, those you are currently estranged from or in conflict with.

After you've completed the closeness circle, examine it for patterns. Jot down the answers to these questions in your journal:

- Are you leaning into your social supports when you need to? Why or why not?
- Is there anyone missing from these rings (e.g., colleagues, family and extended family, neighbors, friends)? If so, why are their names not included?
- Are there relationships that have changed with time or circumstance (for example, someone who was an anchor but is now a boat)? How do you feel about this change?
- Are there any surprises in your closeness circle?
- Is there anything you wish you can change in your closeness circle (for example, wishing you were able to place your sibling in the anchor ring but feeling that they are more in the buoy ring)?
- Are there any relationships you want to improve? Name one concrete way you can build toward this improvement.
- Looking back at the types of intimacy on page 99, notice

which relationships offer which forms of closeness. Are there any forms of intimacy that you seem to prioritize for different rings? Are there any areas of intimacy that are not represented?

- What do you like and don't like about each of the relationships you've listed in your closeness circle?

- What would you miss about each person if they weren't in your life anymore?

BONUS DISCOVERY EXERCISE: NURTURING YOUR CLOSENESS CIRCLE

If you find that you're feeling disconnected or even a bit lonely, it may be that you're not investing enough time with those who are your anchors. Or perhaps you might notice you haven't put anyone in your anchor ring. In either case, it may be helpful to think about whether there is a person in your boat circle who you might be able to enjoy a closer relationship with if you took some time to nurture that relationship, maybe by spending more quality time with them or seeking advice from them by sharing a current concern or problem. The same goes for those in your anchor ring—think about ways you can spend some one-on-one time with these individuals as a way to strengthen that connection and practice interdependence.

Sometimes the Fiercely Independent will find that their anchors are not close to them or know as much about them, because they may have difficulty letting their guard down even with this inner ring. Stephanie, for example, was surprised to find that she only put two people in her anchor ring: her best friend from high school, Susan, and her co-worker Ryan. She didn't really have anyone who fit the buoy ring and had over ten people in her boat ring—including her siblings and her parents.

Looking closer at the people in her anchor ring, she noticed that she enjoyed more intellectual intimacy with Ryan and experiential intimacy with Susan. Stephanie thought she might be able to learn to become more vulnerable with Susan and could build on their experiential intimacy to explore activities with a more spiritual or personal feeling, like taking part in a volunteer activity. Stephanie had experienced some food insecurity in her youth but never spoke about it with anyone, so she thought volunteering might give her the opportunity to speak with Susan about this topic. When it came to her family, who seem to exist outside of her support system, Stephanie thought she could ask her youngest sister to have lunch with her as they live in the same town, and try to build a connection by getting together on a regular basis.

DAILY WORKOUT: MIRROR WORK

Vulnerability requires letting your guard down, and a great, lower-stakes way to work on the discomfort that comes with increasing intimacy is mirror work. Originally developed by Louise Hay,[6] mirror work gives you a glimpse into your relationship with yourself—including your own attachment relationship to who you are. In other words, mirror work can expose the vulnerable, scared, and neglected part of your inner child.

Part of the reason you may feel uncomfortable when others express strong emotions or intense vulnerability is that their behavior becomes a mirror reflecting your own fears and insecurities. Although staring at yourself in the mirror can be uncomfortable, it is important to practice mirror work daily to continue to expose yourself to the discomfort until it doesn't feel awkward or difficult.

Mirror work can help you to let go of the fear you have about the world and how others might respond to you. The mirror can reveal your negative self-talk in startling and intense ways; at first it can feel a bit confrontational and even a little scary. But the more you practice, the more you will let go of those judgments and begin to see yourself as a being worthy of support, care, and love from others.

$$\backsim$$

To begin, sit or stand in front of a mirror where you can see your entire face clearly. Have a stopwatch or the stopwatch app on your phone handy. Take a few deep breaths and bring your attention to the present moment. If you notice other thoughts, gently bring your attention back to the task. Start the stopwatch. Look into your own eyes and gently hold that eye contact. When you feel uncomfortable to the point that you want to look away from yourself, stop the stopwatch. How long were you able to hold your own gaze in the mirror?

In my experience working with clients, most people with avoidant attachment stop the stopwatch pretty quickly. People have reported feeling unsettled, awkward, ill at ease, or emotional. Others have reported negative self-talk arising almost immediately. These reactions are all a very normal part of the process. Don't judge yourself for how quickly you hit that stop button. Instead, take an attitude of curiosity as to what this experience was like for you. Write some of your observations of this first step of the exercise in your journal.

I'd like you to set aside at least three minutes a day for mirror work. Although this exercise doesn't take much time, it's important to do this when you aren't feeling rushed. You will also want to have absolute privacy and ensure that you won't be interrupted. Have your stopwatch and your journal handy.

It will be helpful to have on hand two to three affirmations that you'll use during each mirror work session. These affirmations will help you to reduce your fear of vulnerability, affirm yourself as a worthy person, and dampen the negative self-talk that is likely to come up during mirror work sessions. You can use different affirmations depending on what you're dealing with that day or choose which ones work best for you. Some of my favorites are:

- I love you.
- I am here for you.
- I am worthwhile exactly as I am.
- It's okay for me to feel this way.
- I accept you just as you are.
- You are safe.
- You will get through this.
- Let me take your fears and hold them for you.

After each mirror work session, jot down some of the observations that came to you. I also ask my clients to rate their mood on a scale of 1 to 10 (10 being the happiest/most calm) before and after their mirror work session. As you dedicate yourself to this activity, you'll notice that you'll be able to hold your own gaze for longer and, most of the time, your mood will lift. Over time this work will translate into feeling more at ease, and being more vulnerable with trusted people, starting with those in your anchor ring. After all, you need to start trusting yourself and being vulnerable with yourself before you can start letting your guard down with those you consider closest to you.

You may also find that after doing mirror work, you learn that you haven't let the people you consider to be your anchors know very much about the true, deeper part of yourself (and this is especially true for those with avoidant attachment). Mirror work is a first step to gaining this important insight and to learning to trust yourself and those around you who deserve your trust.

Asking for Help

Although we are ultimately aiming for long-term shifts in your ability to ask for help, sometimes being able to reach out for something small in the moment can be a critical point of growth, too. The next time you're under pressure or feeling stressed, challenge yourself by asking this simple question: "Is there something I can ask someone else to do that might unburden me, just a little bit?" Most of the time, the Fiercely Independent think of ways to manage almost everything themselves. However, you can delegate a part of your emotional burden to a loved one—even if you don't technically need them to take it. Identify what that is, and then ask for help.

In making the request, I find this formula can be helpful. It's straightforward, communicates your needs effectively, and does so unapologetically but gently and warmly.

1. State your need in plain terms.
2. Make the ask by describing what you need from them.
3. Describe the impact their helpful actions will have on you.

For example, if you are feeling very stressed with work and your usual plan is to retreat to your video games when you get home, ask yourself, "What is something someone else can do that might unburden me, just a little bit?" Whatever that answer is (for example, asking my partner to sit with me and watch my favorite movie), make the request following the formula:

"I am feeling very stressed and would like to do something to decompress. Can you please sit with me and watch my favorite movie with me? That will really help me to unwind and take my mind off some things."

Try this the next time you feel stressed and could benefit from help (even if you don't technically need it). It's good to start with lower-stakes situations where someone's help isn't necessarily going to make or break the situation as you build this skill. Make the choice to resist your usual inclination to go it alone and engage someone to help you deal with the stress. This is a great example of co-regulation rather than depending all on yourself to manage issues and concerns. Over time, you'll begin to feel less vulnerable when making these requests and feel more comfortable leaning on supportive others without fear.

SELF-CONCEPT SNAPSHOT

Remember the self-concept snapshot you took in chapter 3? That was your baseline before tackling these exercises. Now that you've worked through these activities, I'd like you to take another snapshot of your self-concept and note any differences. Read the statements below and choose the option that best describes you.

1 = not true, 2 = sometimes or partially true, 3 = mostly or definitely true

- If I had the opportunity, I wouldn't change many things about myself.
- I have confidence in my decision-making.

- I don't worry excessively about what others think of me.
- I like myself even when I am in conflict with someone else.
- I value myself even when I make mistakes.
- I believe my efforts contribute to my success.
- I have control over my reactions to difficult situations.
- I like myself.
- I can start and finish projects without others' help and approval.
- I have a clear sense of who I am.
- I have positive and admirable traits.
- I can overcome challenges when I try hard.

Did your score improve after the exercises? It's helpful to do this checkup once every few weeks to see how your self-concept improves as you continue to gain insight and work through the exercises in this chapter along with any other chapters that you feel may apply to you (for example, if you feel that avoidant attachment is your predominant style but you also have a secondary attachment style).

THE JOURNEY AHEAD

Congratulations on finishing the exercises in this chapter! Attachment wounds run deep, and it takes consistent practice and awareness to heal them, but I hope that through this work, you've started to notice some shifts in your internal working models.

As you continue your journey from avoidant to secure attachment, you'll struggle less with trying to keep people at a distance as a way to protect yourself and find a balance so that you can honor your independent streak without experiencing the disconnect and isolation that many of the Fiercely Independent struggle with. You'll discover the strength in being vulnerable with select people in your life and learn to ask for help without feeling as if it reflects poorly on you. By honing the skill of identifying your emotions, you can then apply the most effective coping skill, instead of using suppression or avoidance as your go-to ways to manage difficult thoughts and feelings. Through providing emotional support and comfort to others without sacrificing too much of yourself, you'll achieve lasting, meaningful bonds with the important people in your life.

These exercises should help you find a balanced self-concept that isn't overly reliant on achievement but also honors the other equally unique and important parts of yourself.

Check your self-concept frequently to assess where your progress is at any given time, especially when you are going through challenges in a major area of life. Repeat the exercises that work best for you, and incorporate them into your weekly routines. Once your self-concept is around a score of 24 or higher, this is a great time to tap into the tips in the conclusion, "Your Resilient Self." For more self-concept boosters, see appendix C on page 329.

It is also helpful to read through the chapters on other attachment styles to gain insight into how you relate to other attachment styles. These chapters will help improve your relationships and the quality of your connection with people whose styles differ from your own.

Additionally, please refer to appendix A on page 315 for exercises that will help you to identify triggers for insecure attachment behaviors and what to do in the moment to manage the situation more effectively.

THE ANXIOUS ATTACHMENT STYLE

CHAPTER 7

Anxious Attachment:
The Worried Warrior

Whenever my friend Agnes and I get together, the subject often turns to Agnes's dating relationships. She is a serial dater, and over the past two years has had five relationships almost back-to-back. She commits very quickly to her partners and often feels insecure that they aren't quite as dedicated to the relationship as she is, especially in the beginning. When they are out of touch with her for a day or two, she begins to imagine a host of nefarious scenarios. If they return her call later than she expects, she becomes suspicious that they have been out with another woman or that they've lost interest in her. Her most recent ex-boyfriend was quite patient with her constantly seeking reassurance from him, but over time, it caused conflict, because he grew tired of her not trusting him.

A couple of weeks ago, as we were waiting for a table in a restaurant, Agnes scrolled through her phone to show me photos of Max, the man she is currently dating. She met him at a work conference, and they've been seeing each other for almost three weeks. Agnes admits that sometimes she'll text and call multiple times before hearing back from him. "It's like I can't control the compulsion to text him even though I know I should just let him get back to me." Over the course of our lunch, Agnes picked up her phone every time it beeped, hoping it was Max—and then was disappointed each time it wasn't.

Agnes is a wonderful person with so many great qualities, yet she could never really trust that anyone would genuinely care for her. No matter how well the relationship was going, she harbored doubts about the situation and believed they were going to leave her. Sometimes she would pick fights or devise tests to make sure they still cared; feeling good or confident about the relationship was short-lived, and soon Agnes was feeling insecure once again. It was clear to me that Agnes had signs of anxious attachment, and it was causing a lot of difficulty, not only in her relationships but in how she felt about herself as well.

Anxiously attached people are Worried Warriors because they're often busy with analyzing situations and people. They don't tend to feel confident on their own, so these worries tend to have themes of needing others to view them positively and ensuring they don't lose support and guidance. They're constantly looking out for signs of potential problems, which can lead to a cycle of self-doubt, relationship conflicts, and slowed progress toward goals. Studies suggest that anxiously attached people are at higher risk for anxiety and depressive disorders.[1]

ORIGINS OF ANXIOUS ATTACHMENT

Like all attachment styles, anxious attachment develops in early childhood in response to experiences in the early years of life. Often, anxious attachment style develops due to inconsistent parenting and too much unpredictability in a child's daily environment.

Parents of Worried Warriors might be nurturing and attentive some of the time, then emotionally unavailable, critical, or absorbed in their own problems at other times. They may be slow to respond to signs of distress in their child or become very distressed themselves when they are tending to their child's needs. When caregivers are present one day and unavailable the next, this can lead children to have a heightened feeling of danger and fear as they try to adapt to these inconsistencies. The child may become confused, as they can't understand what their parents' behaviors mean or decipher what behaviors they should exhibit to get a positive response from their parents.

At other times, parents may seem overly worried and preoccupied about the child's safety and well-being, even in situations where the child is quite safe and well taken care of.

For example, Ellie had been looking forward to a date night with her husband for weeks and had arranged for her mom to look after her son, Tyler. However, throughout the night she frequently texted and called to check in and see how he was doing, although he was completely safe in her parents' home. This can lead to the child becoming uncertain about how to behave as well as developing the belief that the world is a dangerous place, leading to a higher level of insecurity and fearful behaviors.

As we saw in the Strange Situation, anxiously attached children seem visibly stressed when separated from their parents or caregivers and are difficult to console when parents return.[2] These children realize they may not be able to fully trust their caregivers to meet their needs, but they also know they need to accept whatever support they can get from them—however inadequate or inconsistent—because their literal survival is predicated on adult oversight. As a result, they behave in ways that are designed to keep parents as close as possible, for example, becoming clingy or staying physically close to their parents to prevent being abandoned. A child may also conceal what they believe are undesirable qualities that might turn off their parents. When their parents become emotionally unavailable, these children try to find out why and often believe they did something to cause the disconnection.

Over time, the inconsistency they feel in their bond with their caregivers leads them to tread carefully with their parents and become chronic people pleasers. According to their logic, if the people around them are happy with them, their loved ones won't abandon them. Consequently, their own feelings, desires, and needs are often stifled or buried.

ANXIOUS ATTACHMENT IN ADULTHOOD

People with anxious attachment are often still harboring early childhood experiences that involved fear of rejection and abandonment by important adults in their lives, or the feeling that their parents' love and support were conditional on their good behavior (whether that was true or not). For this reason, even as an adult, an anxiously attached person might need constant reassurance and affection from others. The opinion of others is *the* arbiter of the Worried Warrior's self-worth, so their self-esteem and their self-concept may depend largely on how people respond to them from moment to moment or what happens to them on any given day. Casey notices this in his mood changes: He might wake up in a good mood, but if he senses even a hint of criticism from his spouse (whether that's what she intended or not), it can throw him into a more agitated and pessimistic state that colors the way he approaches the rest of his daily activities.

Because Worried Warriors depend on other people's positive reinforcement to maintain a sense of self, avoiding being alone is a common struggle. To cope, they may try to busy themselves with activities and social events, so they are not left by themselves, which is when their anxiety and insecurities surface.

They tend to fear rejection more than the average person, often have jealous feelings, and constantly compare themselves to other people and feel like they come up short. Hypersensitivity to cues of rejection or disinterest by others leads Worried Warriors to become the quintessential people pleasers, feeling overly concerned with others' happiness and putting others' needs ahead of their own. They go out of their way to get others to like them and continue supporting them.

Worried Warriors are overly concerned with earning others' approval through people-pleasing behaviors; they use people-pleasing as a way to maintain relationships, ensure support, and reduce their anxiety.[3] Because you depend on the people around you to tell you how to feel about yourself, you can't feel calm unless they're calm, or proud of yourself unless they're proud of you. Their upset is your upset, and you'd do anything to make sure that they're happy so you can be happy, too.

Worrying excessively about their support system, what others think of them, and their performance can lead Worried Warriors to thoughts of imagined rejection and plans for how to avoid being abandoned by others at all costs.[4] Many individuals with anxious attachment can find social settings more stressful than the average person. They might repeatedly mull over their previous actions and interactions with others and wonder if they should have behaved or spoken differently. They seek constant reassurance that they are good enough and that they are worthy of love and care from others. Dependent on others to form and shape their self-concept, they have a hard time holding a stable idea of who they are without positive reinforcement from their environment and those around them.

Research shows that people with anxious attachment also have lower self-perception accuracy,[5] meaning that they are more likely to draw false, and often negative, conclusions about how they are perceived by others. They tend to filter out positive information, paying special attention to negative events and believing they are to blame for bad outcomes. When things don't go their way, whether it's in relationships, friendships, career aspirations, or falling short of reaching their goals, they often blame themselves. Instead of seeing the situation with a more balanced view, they are quick to point to their own perceived mistakes or inadequacies to explain why something didn't work out. They often believe that bad things happen to them because they deserve it.[6] The Worried Warrior's deep-seated need to please others, often at their own expense, and the effect it has on their ability to believe in themselves and what they can accomplish, has impacts in all areas of their life. Let's take a closer look.

Anxious Attachment in Romantic Relationships

People with anxious attachment worry *a lot* about who they are in the world and what they mean to others. There's a reason I call this style "Worried Warriors"! They spend a lot of time thinking about how someone reacted to something they did or said and can interpret ambiguous social cues as being negative or harmful, even when that was not the other individual's intention. In intimate romantic relationships, where people tend to feel most vulnerable, these behaviors are magnified. This is because people (not just those with anxious attachment) often feel the most exposed in intimate relationships—and for many people, romantic relationships represent the most intimate and vulnerable of all their social interactions.

Becoming obsessed with their romantic partners is not uncommon—just like my friend Agnes. They commit to new relationships very quickly and often without a lot of thoughtful contemplation. They fall for people hard and fast, but they don't expect others to reciprocate, so they live in constant fear that their partner won't love them back or that once their partner learns who they *really* are, they will leave. Low self-esteem causes self-doubt and makes them question their self-worth. So they hide their needs or the parts of themselves that might be unwelcome or inconvenient. They do everything possible to stay on their partner's good side, taking their people-pleasing tendencies to an extreme; in short, they do everything they can to ensure continued positive attention and affection from their partners.[7]

They constantly seek reassurance and approval from their partners and are hypersensitive to any cues of lack of interest or rejection, like a delay in responding to a text or a call. When their partners are constantly communicating with them, complimenting them, and reassuring them, they feel comfortable and confident in the relationship. But if their partner keeps their communication short, or doesn't say something overtly complimentary (e.g., perhaps for good reason, perhaps because it's a workday and they're on a particularly busy shift), they become increasingly insecure and act in various ways to seek confirmation of their partner's affection—like Agnes did by texting multiple times when her new boyfriend did not respond to her immediately. To prove or see how much their partner cares about their relationship, they might pick a fight or display jealous or possessive behaviors to elicit signs of devotion from their partners.

Anxious Attachment with Friends and Family

Anxiously attached individuals can be very selfless in their relationships and are often the first to get to a loved one's side when they're in need. While they almost always outdo everyone else in terms of the efforts they make to help a friend or family member, they often do so to their own detriment. Helping others makes them feel good. It makes them feel needed, indispensable, and important. It's as if their inner child wants to reclaim those feelings that would have been fostered in them by their parents—if their parents had been more consistent about their attention and support. They never knew if they were on solid ground as a child, and they bring that worry into their adult interactions. At the same time, they are prone to feeling unappreciated and taken for granted by others,[8] so they can feel conflicted about extending themselves to others. This feeds into their disillusionment about how much others *really* care about them. These patterns then reinforce their already negative perceptions of themselves (for example, that no one truly cares about them and that they are unlovable).

How anxious attachment manifests can be slightly more subtle in a person's friendships. Their need for attention from a friend might be less intense, but if they don't receive the recognition they need from one friend, they are likely to seek it from another friend so that *someone* can tell them they're okay. They attach to new friendships very quickly and sometimes can become very dependent on that person's approval in a short amount of time.

Because anxious attachment usually develops from early childhood, the Worried Warrior can reenact some of these struggles in interactions with family members as an adult. The individual may find themself continually trying to seek approval from the parent who didn't affirm them as a child. They may become jealous of a sibling because the parents seem to be more attentive or loving toward them, which impacts the anxiously attached person's ability to have a positive relationship with that sibling.

Worried Warriors may seek attention through negative behaviors if positive behaviors don't seem to work, for example, creating conflict over something inconsequential to trigger the attention of family members even if the attention is negative. My client Javi was one of four kids, and he used to play devil's advocate constantly. Every Sunday, when he had dinner with his extended family, he'd pick the controversial side of the debate—even if it didn't always align with his beliefs—just to get his parents and siblings to take notice of him.

If you are a parent with an unhealed anxious attachment style, you may meet parenting demands with excessive fear of uncertainty and chronic anxiety. If your kids express any negative emotions, you likely rush to the rescue, eager to stop any sign of distress. Or you may hover a bit too close to them, afraid that they might make a mistake or experience pain—all of which are expected as a part of normal growth and development.

Anxious Attachment at Work

Our work environments are filled with social interactions, and our attachment style can affect the way we function and perform on the job just like they do any other kind of relationship. Even if you work remotely most of the time, in most jobs there is a high degree of interactivity—communicating with colleagues and supervisors by email or phone or video conference, attending meetings, and having others evaluate your work. Researchers have applied attachment theory to social dynamics in the workplace[9] and have seen that the attachment dynamics that are present in intimate and family relationships were also found in people's relationships with co-workers and bosses or managers.

Because anxiously attached individuals have low self-esteem, high inse-curity, and self-doubt, they may constantly seek approval from their col-leagues[10] and overinvest in their relationships at work. Their near-constant worries about how people perceive them mean they make an extra effort to be liked by everyone. This worry impacts their work performance because they may find it difficult to speak up in meetings and express their opinions out of fear that they might be ridiculed or their ideas might be rejected. It can also lead to them to fall into the trap of groupthink or burning them-selves out trying to impress their colleagues or supervisor. They might get hung up on little details that don't matter to try to do everything "perfectly," and base their self-esteem on whether they receive praise for their work.

If a day or two goes by without positive reinforcement, they may begin to question their own productivity, worth as an employee, or whether colleagues like them. This need for approval can cause conflicts in the workplace. Colleagues may tire of having to constantly reassure them—particularly if that colleague has an avoidant attachment style—and may over time distance themselves, provoking even more anxiety for the Worried Warrior who, in turn, doubles down on seeking reassurance. This only serves to further alienate colleagues and raises concerns with supervi-sors about their abilities and performance.

Worried Warriors might have problems starting projects or making decisions without getting others' input and approval, potentially delay-ing their progress at work and limiting their ability to grow profession-ally, take on more responsibility, and be promoted. They may risk being reprimanded because they get stuck on details, turn in their projects late, and experience trouble meeting expected benchmarks. As leaders, their people-pleasing tendencies might get in the way of making more effective decisions, because they're more concerned about how others respond to their directives than the average person. All in all, this can add up to a lot of inefficiencies in their daily life, and thoughts about others' perspectives are likely to take up a lot of precious cognitive space.

Fear of negative evaluations might keep them confined to routine actions. They are more likely to stay in their comfort zone and not venture outside the box for fear of criticism or disparagement. Over time, these behaviors limit innovation and the potential for engaging in purposeful work. Often, due to their tendency to put a negative filter on most interactions, they can feel underappreciated and dissatisfied, which can cause them to invest less in their work identity and possibly to quit jobs or give up sooner than the average person would as they progress along a career path.

Anxious Attachment in Goal Pursuits

Anxiously attached individuals tend to have a self-concept that is unstable, unclear, or rooted excessively in the roles they have. Worried Warriors might derive too much of their self-worth from the roles they occupy in life and judge themselves on whether they are seemingly making others happy and content. Because of these fleeting positive feelings, they may seek to achieve many different goals, some of which are not necessarily born out of their own interests, but they pursue them because they believe achieving these goals might garner them positive attention such as respect or admiration from others.

My client Denise struggled with her career path and often questioned her decision to pursue law. She has been passionate about fashion since she was young and had wanted to attend art school but, although her parents never directly expressed a desire for her to become a lawyer, she felt an expectation to pursue a legal career because both of her parents were attorneys. As a result, whenever she experienced challenges in her law career, she lamented her choice to pursue the field in the first place and daydreamed about how her life would be different if she had chosen another path.

Like chameleons, Worried Warriors are more likely to adopt the goals of people they are in a relationship with or those of people they look up to without careful contemplation of whether these goal pursuits are meaningful to themselves. My friend Janice used to adopt the hobbies and interests of her boyfriends, and once they broke up, she'd drop those hobbies and interests, too, and move on to those that reflected the interests of the people she was spending the most time with. Once she was in therapy, she began reflecting on who Janice was and what made her excited and happy, and she realized she hadn't asked herself those questions in a long time.

The Worried Warrior may struggle with identifying and developing their personal values and knowing their interests, because their values depend on what's happening around them at a given moment rather than on something internal and unique to them. Because their goals are not firmly rooted in their own deeper sense of purpose, they may lack the motivation to fully pursue a particular goal and persevere in their efforts when they run into obstacles or difficulties.

Anxiously attached individuals can become frustrated during goal pursuits and blame themselves for the smallest of setbacks, become so dejected that they give up on the goal completely, and use quitting as further fodder to reinforce their negative self-view. They are prone to indecisiveness in their career, in part due to their self-criticism.[11] They don't believe in their own ability to achieve goals and may think that they can't succeed without having to rely on others. As a result, they tend to be less independent in their goal striving and require frequent check-ins with other people to stay on track. They also worry more about their progress during their pursuit of a goal and look to the outside world for evidence that they're doing well. When they compare themselves to other people's progress, they're more likely to see themselves as falling short rather than appreciate any progress they have made.

THE *POSITIVE* SIDE OF ANXIOUS ATTACHMENT

Although Worried Warriors face challenges in many areas, there are also several important strengths associated with this attachment style. For one, anxiously attached individuals tend to be very considerate of others' feelings, and their hypersensitivity can be beneficial when a gentler touch is needed. They can empathize deeply, are often great listeners, and will stop at nothing to try to make a loved one feel better. They find joy in taking care of their friends and often work very hard at staying connected to the people they love. When they see someone in need, they will almost always lend a hand, even if they have too much on their plate. With their heightened attention to other people's needs, they often take the lead in organizing social events and make sure every detail is attended to and try to accommodate everyone's preferences to be sure people are happy. Others' happiness is important to them. They are great at doling out genuine compliments and can help boost morale when others are struggling. Because they don't want any criticism to come their way, they work hard at their job and can be great employees. The ultimate team player, they cooperate well with others and demonstrate a willingness to trust in others' abilities and skill sets.

WHAT'S NEXT?

You've learned the origins of anxious attachment and read about the consequences being a Worried Warrior has on the different areas of your life, from your self-concept to work and romantic relationships and goal pursuits. As a child, you were uncertain how to behave to elicit consistent, positive responses from the adults in your life, so it makes sense that you would need more reassurance than the average person that you were on the right track in what you sought to do. As an adult, you strive to avoid at all costs being abandoned or rejected, which often leads to losing sight of who you are at your core, because you're too busy worrying about other people's reactions, feelings, and needs more than your own.

In my experience, individuals who have anxious attachment tend to express their attachment wounds through four major self-statements, which are representations of their internal working models. Not everyone expresses these wounds in the same way, so some of the self-statements may speak to you more than others. Or you may find that all four self-statements seem familiar to you. Whatever the case, in the next chapter, I will teach you a variety of evidence-supported exercises that will help you to overcome the negative consequences created by these working models, and to teach your inner child how to establish, affirm, and assure yourself and guide the development of a self-concept that is rooted in your needs and what is meaningful for you.

CHAPTER 8

Healing the Anxious
Attachment Style

In the previous chapter, you learned that your anxious attachment style developed in response to your caregivers. You adapted to the inconsistency of the care you received by paying particularly close attention to the people in your environment, seeking affirmation and reassurance from them, and modulating your behavior to keep them pleased with you. These characteristics may have allowed you to cope psychologically and survive stress and turmoil in the past, but over time, all that people-pleasing and outward focus really takes a toll on your self-concept!

The characteristics you developed to cope with challenging childhood experiences can be seen in your working models, which show up as self-statements that reflect how you think about yourself and the way you go about life. Becoming familiar with these self-statements is an important first step for being able to make changes.

As adults we tend to assume our working models are inherently true and valid, but they are more likely to be stories that we learned in childhood, stories that our inner child carries for us today.

For people with anxious attachment, those self-statements typically sound like:

1. "I'm not as worthy as others."
2. "I need to rescue everyone."
3. "I fear being on my own."
4. "I have to analyze everything."

In this chapter, we're going to take a closer look at these self-statements and work to heal the unmet needs of your inner child that are at the root of each one. The discovery exercises will invite you to learn more about how these self-statements of the Worried Warrior can be countered, and there will be daily workouts that will provide you with an activity you can engage with as often as you wish to strengthen your coping skills. In the last chapter, you were engaged in understanding, and this chapter is where you take action. It's ideal to go through the exercises in order, but if something seems overwhelming or if you're short on time, you can work through them at your own pace and in the order that is comfortable for you. You can always come back to an exercise when you have the time and emotional space to process it. You'll want to have your journal on hand to make note of your responses to exercises and to keep an eye on your progress.

Impact Test

As you read through these self-statements, you may find that all of them apply to you to some extent. Or you may struggle with knowing whether a self-statement really impacts you or not. You might be curious about which working model to focus on healing first. By applying my impact test to each of these working models, you can determine whether they are working against you and which corresponding exercises you should prioritize.

The impact test is simple. As you read through these self-statements and their descriptions and examples, ask yourself these four questions, and if your answer is yes to at least one of them, it's likely that this self-statement is something you need to address by working through my exercises. As a bonus activity, you can reflect on them more deeply and jot down the answers to the italicized questions in your journal:

- **Impact on Life Domains:** Does this working model negatively affect my life in major domains (work, romantic relationships, family relationships, friendships, goal attainment)? *If yes, write down 1–2 concrete examples for each of these areas.*
- **Impact on Goal Attainment:** Does this working model usually move me away from my goals? *If so, how?*
- **Impact on Values-Based Living:** Is this working model inconsistent with my values? *What are some of my top values, and how does this working model contribute to me moving away from my values or not living my top values the way I want?*
- **Impact on Self-Concept:** Is this working model something that shakes or damages my self-concept? *If so, how?*

"I'M NOT AS WORTHY AS OTHERS"

Part of the reason people with anxious attachment have a low sense of self-worth is that they have a much higher, more universally positive view of *others'* worth.[1] As a child, they strongly desired caregiver approval and attention, and may have prioritized these desires over building a healthy and stable self-concept.

Worried Warriors tend to give others' opinions more weight than their own in forming their self-concept, which drives them to constantly seek others' approval and rely heavily on others' opinions to feel good about themselves. A low sense of self-worth can grow out of not getting consistent support and approval from important people in your life starting in early childhood, which can make you question your own worth over time. You may have developed beliefs that you are unworthy, unlovable, or incapable. Then, through selective bias, which is a largely subconscious process, you pay more attention to events and situations that might support these negative core beliefs, which causes them to strengthen in your mind over time.

If their primary caregivers were sparing or sporadic with their love and attention, this could lead people with anxious attachment to constantly seek out signs and behaviors of caring from others that "prove" they are worthy of love. Yet, even when they get validation, they seem to have trouble holding on to this feeling for long. So they seek validation again and again,[2] often from the same person who holds importance to them.

Over time, Worried Warriors' emphasis on others' thoughts, feelings, and behaviors over their own leads them to subconsciously (or consciously) form the idea that they are not as worthy as others—of love, attention, achievement. They need only look to their own behaviors to confirm this: They work so hard and so constantly to chase validation from others and put a premium on others' opinions, values, and experiences, so it must be that they are not as important as others. In trying to please others and meet their needs—often at the expense of their own—they become more self-critical and don't treat themselves with the same love and compassion as others.[3] The proverbial pat on the back from others is just a quick fix for the deeper yearning they have to validate their inner child from something less transient and grounded in who they are. Their brain starts to internalize these messages, and the belief that they are not worthwhile solidifies and drives their behaviors.

Antidote to "I'm Not as Worthy as Others"

No matter the roots of your low self-worth, the great news is that by engaging in the following exercises you can strengthen your self-concept and increase your resilience. By creating a positive emotional bond with yourself and with your inner child, you can foster a secure, nurturing, and responsive attachment style that can promote well-being, improve goal attainment, and support healing connections with others.

DISCOVERY EXERCISE: INNER CHILD WORK

Inner child work helps you to access the needs, wants, and desires of your younger self and learn the roots of working models that impact you to this day. Inner child work is especially critical for Worried Warriors because it gives you the opportunity to meet your own needs for approval and validation. Rather than seeking approval of your worth from others, or thinking that the opinions, needs, and desires of others matter more than your own, your adult self can be the parent that you didn't have as a child, and through consistency and present-mindedness toward your inner child's needs can reparent and heal the wounds of your child self, and impart a different set of lessons that are more adaptive and fitting to the current moment. This simple visualization exercise will give you an opportunity to connect with your younger self.

⌒

Get comfortable and close your eyes. Take a few deep breaths, focusing your attention on your breath as you breathe in and out. Turn your attention to your thoughts. Don't actively push away any thoughts, judge them, or analyze them. Simply observe the thoughts floating around and let them be. Now imagine yourself as a child. Try to recall a time when your inner child first encountered the idea that you were not as worthy as others. When was the first time you felt that your needs and wants were not important? Did a parent ignore you when you were in distress? When was the first time you thought you needed to take care of someone else's needs or feelings so they wouldn't leave you by yourself? Did you feel you had to avoid rocking the boat in your family so you wouldn't upset your parents?

Bring the image of your child self into sharp focus by visualizing all the details of how you looked and acted as a child. Where were you? What did your hair look like? What were you wearing?

How tall were you? What was your favorite toy? The more details you can give to the vision of your child self, the better.

Now, imagine your adult self entering the room with your child self. Visualize your adult self taking your child self by the hand and reassuring them that they are loved, they are enough, and that you will be there for them no matter what. Remind your child self that things will change and will not always be so difficult. Tell them that although your parents were imperfect, made mistakes, and were not always available, that was not your fault. Ask your inner child what they need most from you, and listen to what they say to you. Perhaps your inner child wants to tell you:

- I need to be encouraged.
- I need to be told I matter and that I am loved.
- I need to be told it is okay to make mistakes.
- I need to be guided on how to express my emotions and not be rejected for speaking out or acting out.

Listen carefully to your inner child's needs and let them know how you might help them get what they want. Reassure them that they don't always need to turn to other people to meet their needs because their adult self will always be there for them.

Express gratitude to your inner child for doing their best to cope with difficult situations when they were younger. Let them know they can call on you whenever they need you. Lastly, offer your inner child a hug. If it feels right, tell your inner child how much you love them. Then wave goodbye and let them know you are looking forward to visiting with them again very soon.

After completing this exercise, spend a few minutes journaling about how you felt during the exercise and how you feel immediately after. Write down any thoughts that come to you, and reflect on what you think about the experience of your adult self providing your child self with a secure base and a way to meet their needs.

⌒

When Theresa did this inner child visualization exercise, she became very emotional. She realized that as a child, she was often fearful of her parents' judgment because they were hypercritical and, as Theresa described them, "glass-half-empty people." She never knew if her parents truly loved her. In the eyes of her parents, her brother could do no wrong, and by comparison Theresa felt picked on. No matter how hard she tried, it seemed she was always doing the wrong thing and disappointing or upsetting her parents. She became desperate for their approval and would become down on herself when she did not receive the reactions she hoped for. This dynamic with her parents continues to this day. She admits, "Before I make a big decision, it always flickers in my mind—what will my parents think?"

Theresa's inner child needed her adult self's unconditional support. Through this exercise, Theresa was able to learn that instead of waiting for her parents to become the people she hoped they would be, she could reparent her child self and give her inner child what she needed then (and what she needs now). Theresa began incorporating inner child work into her weekly meditation routine. She also took the time to engage in deliberate self-care—as an extension of reparenting her inner child. I suggested she should honor her child self's interests and think about what she enjoyed doing when she was a child. What would make time fly by when she was young? Theresa remembered how much she enjoyed going to the park and playing on the jungle gym sets, so she started to visit different neighborhood parks on weekends. It was a fun way to engage in self-care that honored the innocent, joyful, and pure part of her psyche.

BONUS DISCOVERY EXERCISE: REDISCOVERING PLAY

Like Theresa, you may find it helpful to reflect on what you used to enjoy doing as a child to reconnect with what brings you joy, no matter what anyone else thinks. Write down a list of all those activities and make a commitment to try one or two a week. Try to embrace a childlike wonder as you do and imagine experiencing play as your inner child for the first time.

DAILY WORKOUT: ACHIEVEMENTS AND IMPROVEMENTS

A daily practice that you can build into your morning or nightly routine is something I call "Achievements and Improvements." Essentially, it's a self-esteem journal—a simple way to review your day and consciously acknowledge something that you accomplished that you feel proud of, as well as recognize something that you wish to change.

A strong sense of self and healthy self-esteem is predicated on an accurate, holistic view of self that acknowledges your weaknesses *and* celebrates your greatest qualities. Someone who feels good about themselves doesn't believe they are inherently flawless; rather, it's the idea that they can take action to shape who they are, correct mistakes, and solve problems effectively. As a Worried Warrior, you tend to focus more on the negatives—the places for improvement, the ways you feel you don't stack up against others. The more you consciously reflect on and acknowledge your strengths, the more balanced and secure your self-concept will become.

⌒

Every night for a week, I want you to take five minutes to write down one achievement from the last twenty-four hours, one area you'd like to improve, and one small way in which you can improve upon this area within the next twenty-four hours. The achievement and area for improvement do not have to be in the same domain of life (for example, one could be about work, and one could be about a friendship). Recently, my client Dobson showed me two of his daily entries in his journal:

Date: March 7
Achievement: I was able to be present for my wife when she was having a difficult time and needed to talk about how she was feeling this morning.

Improvement: Need to recommit to the goal of getting to the gym at least three times a week.

Thing to do: Schedule in calendar to go to a morning yoga class tomorrow.

Date: March 8
Achievement: I did a good job on today's presentation; my boss praised me, and I got positive feedback from my colleagues.

Improvement: Need to be better at collaborating with colleagues on upcoming projects, especially because I did everything myself and it was exhausting.

Thing to do: Set up a brief meeting with at least one colleague this week to strategize about the next presentation.

It is important to jot down ideas in a running journal entry. The benefit of writing them in the same place sequentially is that you can review your accomplishments and areas for improvement at a glance, as well as celebrate your progress and successes. Take pride in the ways you shape your life for yourself and see the immense value you bring to it. Over time, you will have a collection of wonderful reminders of the many reasons to love and be proud of yourself. You can also note how far you've come in improving in the areas you've committed to work on—particularly self-worth.

Visit these achievement entries in your journal regularly for a self-esteem boost and to fuel and support a secure self-concept that you are building, based on a strong foundation from within rather than relying on other people or situations to make you feel good about yourself.

"I NEED TO RESCUE EVERYONE"

Anxiously attached individuals have a strong desire to fix others' problems, often at their own expense. They put a premium on others' well-being and happiness over their own, and while they are busy solving others' problems, their needs are unattended, and they put their own life on hold. Although they enjoy helping others, they do so primarily because they fear that if they don't, people will abandon and reject them.

While being helpful is a wonderful trait, if you are constantly overextending yourself, it can leave you feeling emotionally drained and perpetually anxious and stressed. It's also a recipe for resentment. When you sacrifice your own happiness for others, even if you believe that your needs shouldn't come first, pushing down what you want or need in your relationships with romantic partners, family members, or friends over and over again becomes corrosive to those relationships. You're also more likely to burn out at work as you bend over backward trying to please the people you work with—your colleagues, boss, or customers. Any interaction or project is an opportunity to show what you're made of, but you take it to such extremes that it can leave you feeling fatigued and, ironically, less capable of producing your best work.

When Worried Warriors hyperfocus on others' moods, needs, and behaviors, they will do anything to make sure other people are well taken care of. If they notice someone they care about is having a tough day, they sometimes will become so immersed in that person's experience, it's as if they were the ones going through the ordeal. They will often mirror the other person's feelings, to the point that if the other person is angry, they feel angry, too. If the other person fails, they feel like they are a failure. Being tied to another's emotional experiences and behavior can cause a lot of ups and downs in their own emotional life,[4] because the way they feel is predicated on whatever happens to and around them on a given day and in the lives of the people they are in relationships with. This difficulty maintaining a healthy boundary between themselves and people they are close to leads to difficulty separating their sense of self and their individual identity from the people they are in relationships with.

This style of relating makes it difficult for people with anxious attachment to put their needs first and to take good care of themselves. One of my clients, Randy, had great difficulty asserting what he wanted even in casual social interactions. It was hard for him to speak up about his preferences even if it was simply about where to go to lunch with his co-workers. He worked so tirelessly at his job that he neglected his own well-being, letting his exercise routine and healthy eating go by the wayside. Making sacrifices like this is very common among individuals with anxious attachment. They put other people and projects ahead of themselves yet are prone to feel underappreciated and dissatisfied with all that is on their plate. They can not only burn out,[5] but their overall mental and physical health can suffer.

The sense of responsibility Worried Warriors feel for other people's happiness often leads to codependent behaviors, where they become set on "rescuing" others. As their own self-concept fluctuates, they feel the need to involve themselves in more projects and relationships to confirm that they're allowed to feel good about themselves. Sometimes they do so in ways that create unhealthy bonds or allow the person they rescue to continue with their bad behavior because the person with anxious attachment will cover for them or bail them out. The more they put others first, the more their subconscious mind tells them that they are less important than others, and the cycle continues.

Antidote to "I Need to Rescue Everyone"

The antidote to putting others' needs before your own is refocusing your attention on you and taking the time to learn about who you are, your hopes and dreams, your likes and dislikes, and what gets you excited to wake up in the morning. This refocusing isn't vain or selfish—it's necessary so that you understand what you need and value in life, and so that you can continue to give to others without forgetting or losing a part of yourself.

DISCOVERY EXERCISE: WHO YOU ARE

If you're used to putting others before yourself, it's probably been a while since you've been in touch with what you are all about. This is my version of a Japanese practice called ikigai. "Iki" in Japanese means "life," and "gai" describes value or worth. Ikigai can be understood as your "reason for being." Knowing your ikigai inspires you to get out of bed each day with enthusiasm, with joy in your heart, and to live your best life. It also helps you hold true to what's important to you and what brings you meaning, purpose, and fulfillment, while at the same time contributing to the greater good and being of service to others.

My version of ikigai focuses on a deep self-exploration of what is most important to you and what makes you unique. It asks you to focus on your values and needs, brings awareness to your positive traits, and gets you to identify your turn-offs or, at the extreme, deal-breakers. Knowing your turn-offs helps you to define and enact healthier boundaries in your relationships and gives you a sense of what to take on and when to say no.

↽

Take a look at my version of the ikigai diagram below and take some time to brainstorm about each of these areas. Draw this circle in your journal, and create the following headings, then brainstorm what fits into each of the categories and write them down.

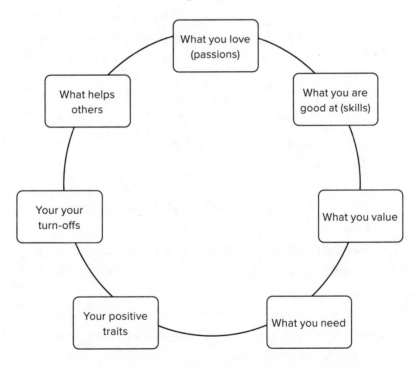

If you have trouble creating a list, below are some questions that can help to prompt your thinking.

- *What you love (passions):* What activities bring you joy and make you feel most alive and fulfilled? What activities make you lose track of time when you're doing them and make it easy to be mindful?
- *What you are good at (skills):* What are some of your skills, hobbies, or talents? What do others compliment you on?
- *What you value:* What are the most important personal qualities you choose to embody to guide your actions? What words describe the kind of person you want to be? What are your basic beliefs that guide or motivate your actions?
- *What you need:* Try assessing your needs à la Maslow's hierarchy: physiological (hunger, thirst, sleep, sex), safety (security and stability in daily life), belonging and love (feeling connected to other people), self-esteem, and self-actualization (becoming the person you have the potential of becoming and with purpose).
- *Your positive traits:* What are some of the characteristics about yourself that you cherish or are the proudest of? What do people point out to you when they tell you what's special about you?
- *Your turn-offs:* What are things that people do that cause you to feel very upset? What are deal-breakers in how others treat you?
- *What helps others:* What is something you do that helps other people, lessens their burdens, or makes them feel cared for?

After you've completed my version of the ikigai diagram to uncover who you are, by journaling your responses to the following prompts and/or taking action on these suggestions, you can begin to incorporate this self-knowledge in your everyday life.

- Take time to acknowledge your top needs each day and to pursue at least one. Make sure it is prioritized by putting it on your daily to-do list.
- Think about how you can continue to grow and nurture your positive qualities. What is something you can do to share one of your positive characteristics with others? For example, if empathy is one of your best qualities, how can you express empathy with someone you care about (without bending over backward and neglecting yourself)?
- Do at least one of the activities on your *what you love* list each day.
- How can you use one of your skills toward an important goal or to bring joy to another person?
- How can you honor your top values today? What is one thing you can do in service of your top values?
- How can you use your *turn-offs* list to set healthier boundaries with people who ask for too much from you? How can you use *your turn-offs* to know when to say no to a request so that you don't overextend yourself?
- How can you continue to help others without sacrificing what you love and your values? Brainstorm how you can serve and help others while tapping into a deeper sense of fulfillment that honors who you are, highlighted through this exercise.

The more you practice ikigai, the easier it will be to notice when your boundaries are challenged—and when to honor yourself first. After all, you must take care of yourself before you can really serve others in the way you truly want to—not to win their approval, but because doing so is meaningful and brings *you* fulfillment.

DAILY WORKOUT: SIMPLIFIED SELF-CARE

Many people say they don't have time for self-care. They will claim that it is too luxurious, too expensive, too time-consuming, and yet another thing they would have to put on their to-do list. Others say that they don't deserve self-care. They only use self-care as a reward and dole it out to themselves when they feel they've earned it. If you have people-pleasing tendencies, you are especially likely to feel as if you need to earn your self-care and to feel guilty when you're doing anything that might resemble being kind and gentle to yourself. People with anxious attachment often withhold self-care because they are constantly chasing a benchmark that is subjective and rarely met.

However, neglecting your self-care—meaning that you don't do the things that help you live well and support your physical and mental health—can lead to a cascade of negative consequences to your overall well-being, cause difficulty in goal attainment, and lead to productivity loss and substandard relationships. It is essential for you to have a self-care plan, especially if you struggle with people-pleasing and are constantly putting other people's needs ahead of your own.

You can't get water from a dry well, and no matter how much you care for the people you are in relationship with, not taking the opportunity to take care of yourself will make it harder to have positive interactions with your loved ones. There are six areas of self-care that will enhance your health, emotional well-being, and relationship with others.

- *Emotional self-care:* Activities that help you connect, process, express, and reflect on a full range of emotions. Examples include writing in a journal, creating art, playing music, dancing, working with a therapist, or watching a movie or TV show that sparks emotional reactions.

- *Social self-care:* Activities that nurture relationships and help you feel connected with others. Examples include calling a friend, having lunch with a family member, helping a neighbor with a chore, joining a club, or attending a get-together.

- *Mental self-care:* Activities that stimulate your mind or add to your skill sets. Examples include reading a book, going to a museum, solving a puzzle, learning something new, or practicing a new hobby.

- *Practical self-care:* Tasks you complete that fulfill core aspects of your life to prevent stressful situations. Examples include washing the dishes, brushing your teeth, taking a shower, creating and managing your budget, or doing your laundry.

- *Physical self-care:* Activities that improve your physical being. Examples include taking a walk, sleeping well, staying hydrated, eating a healthy diet, stretching, exercising, getting a haircut, or going to the doctor.

- *Spiritual self-care:* Activities that nurture your spirit and help you to think about things bigger than yourself. Examples include meditation, yoga, spending time in nature, going to a place of worship, practicing gratitude, or reflecting on your values.

꒦

The true benefits of self-care appear when you make time to tend to your needs every day. To that end, we're going to create an easy three-step plan to start incorporating self-care into your life. The goal is to find a set of activities that nurture all aspects of yourself that you can build into a reliable rotation. Copy the chart below into your journal, and let's get started!

THE ANXIOUS ATTACHMENT STYLE

1. Brainstorm several activities in each of the six areas of self-care—emotional, social, mental, practical, physical, spiritual—and write them down in the corresponding spaces.

2. Do one activity every day, rotating among the six areas. For example, you could do Mental Mondays, Social Tuesdays, and so on. On Sundays, select an activity from your favorite of the six areas.

3. Rate your level of enjoyment immediately after doing the activity on a scale of 1 (least enjoyable) to 5 (most enjoyable). Ditch anything lower than a 3 by crossing it off your chart, but keep everything else in rotation for your self-care tool kit. Each week, consider adding another self-care idea in each of the six domains, and repeat the process of doing the activity, rating your enjoyment, and ditching anything lower than a 3.

For example, after a few weeks, my client Mireille's list looked like this:

DAY OF WEEK	TYPE OF SELF-CARE	ACTIVITIES	ENJOYMENT (1–5)
Monday	Emotional	Writing in a journal	4
		Creating art	5
Tuesday	Social	Calling a friend	4
		Lunch with a family member	2
Wednesday	Mental	Reading a book	5
		Going to a museum	4
Thursday	Practical	Paying bills	3
		Doing laundry	3
Friday	Physical	Taking a walk	4
		Going to the doctor	3

Saturday	Spiritual	Yoga	5
		Attending place of worship	2
Sunday	Social	Brunch with friends	5

Self-care can be practical and doesn't need to take a lot of time—especially on busy days. The most important thing is that you are intentional about your self-care. Commit to a plan, follow through, and continually assess to learn what works best for you.

BONUS DAILY WORKOUT: EXERCISE YOUR "NO"

Often, people with anxious attachment say yes without thinking through the request, because they don't want to disappoint others and because they are fearful of what saying no might mean for a relationship or for what others think of them.

But time is the one thing you can't get back, and your energy is not an infinite resource. Everything you say yes to means saying no to something else—and for Worried Warriors, that "something else" is often your own well-being. To protect your time and energy for the people or opportunities you want to invest in, it's important to get in the habit of saying no. This will likely feel challenging, strange, even frightening at first, but you'll find that it gets easier with practice.

The next time you're presented with a request that will take energy and time away from your priorities, ask yourself: Will doing this thing bring me joy and fulfillment? If your response is a resounding yes, commit. If it's anything other than an immediate gut-fluttering yes, say no.

Some additional tips if you have trouble turning people down:

1. Don't overexplain and don't overapologize. Repeat after me: You have the right to say no to things you don't really want to do and still be able to maintain positive relationships and a strong and positive sense of self.
2. The goal is to communicate to the person that you understand and/or appreciate the request, then firmly (but gently) decline the request. If applicable, offer an alternative solution.
3. When in doubt, try using one of these phrases to reduce guilt and maintain healthy boundaries.
   - "Thank you for thinking of me, but my plate is full, and I won't be able to take on more at this time."
   - "I would love to help/participate, but I'm not able to right now."
   - "Hey! I won't be able to make it this time, but thanks for inviting me!"
   - "I can't do this for you today, but I will have time this weekend. Would you like me to do it then?"

"I FEAR BEING ON MY OWN"

Did you know that the fear of being alone has a name? It's called *autophobia* (or sometimes *monophobia*). Autophobia can make you feel very anxious when you are by yourself, and this can affect your relationships, social life, and career. One of my clients, Cecily, told me that she has difficulty being alone because she's afraid of "what my mind is going to cook up." She didn't want to contend with the thoughts of self-doubt or obsess about what the person she was currently dating thought of her. So she kept her social calendar packed. Even after a long day at work, nearly every day of the week she had something scheduled with co-workers or friends, just so she didn't have to spend too much time alone in her apartment.

Worried Warriors are more likely to become emotionally dependent on others than people with other attachment styles.[6] Being with people gives them access to validation, reassurance, and the physical proximity they need to feel loved and accepted. When they are left alone for long periods of time, they can feel empty, out of sorts, or insecure. In a way, they prefer to be among others to distract from self-reflection, which has the tendency to lead to negative thoughts and deprecating self-talk.

These feelings of loneliness can be exacerbated when you aren't in a romantic relationship and want a partner, if you don't have close friends nearby, if you experience conflicted relationships with family members, or if you feel like you're constantly being left out of the social circles in your work or personal life. Seeing other people in relationships can make you feel sad, or scrolling on social media and seeing other people enjoying time together can make you feel even more anxious and upset when you're on your own. Fear of missing out is a constant for the anxiously attached. As much as they long to be included in social activities, their loneliness is so pervasive that Worried Warriors can feel lonely even when they are with other people. Prolonged loneliness can harm your self-esteem, make you believe that you are inferior to others or are unworthy of love and attention. People with anxious attachment are already prone to having these negative views of themselves, and loneliness can make this worse.

Many people also experience an amplification of their worst fears when they are by themselves. They find that catastrophic thinking takes over, and they begin to imagine all the ways in which their needs may never be met by others, how they may never reach their goals, and how they will always be inferior to another family member or a close friend. Without anyone around to check their thoughts, these ideas gradually get bigger and scarier until the person feels overwhelmed and dejected. They begin to believe that their thoughts are the truth, instead of recognizing thoughts as simply mental events, little blips on the radar among the numerous mental events we all have each day. Because it can be difficult for them to find a sense of safety and calm internally, they miss out on time to notice and engage with their thoughts in more positive ways. To the Worried Warrior, being alone is the same as being abandoned. Their sense of self depends on other people's attention and acknowledgment—without others around to validate their self-knowledge, they lose sight of their sense of self. It's as if they feel that if they aren't part of the crowd, they are nothing; but even in a crowd they can feel neglected and alone.

Antidote to "I Fear Being on My Own"

Overcoming the fear of being alone lies in discovering the root of the problem. There are reasons you developed a higher dependency on others for emotional support and validating your self-esteem. The root of your fears of rejection and abandonment is likely found in early relationships you had as a child when you felt you were not consistently safe and supported. Over time, the emotional or physical absence of attachment figures led to an irrational fear you have as an adult that being away from your partner and family members means that they will neglect and forget you and fulfill the adage "out of sight, out of mind."

Your parents and other important adults in your life are not perfect. They have their flaws, their shortcomings, and their inner struggles that might have caused them to behave the way they did. To overcome your fear of being alone, you need to achieve a deeper understanding of their actions, develop further insight, and move toward some form of resolution and closure. You may be surprised to know that you can engage in this healing process without having a direct dialogue with them. This is handy because sometimes it may not be possible to talk to them directly, if your early attachment figures are either physically unavailable (e.g., deceased) or emotionally unavailable to engage in such a conversation. The first exercise, the empty chair technique, allows for a unique form of healing communication.

DISCOVERY EXERCISE: THE EMPTY CHAIR

The empty chair technique is a powerful exercise that was developed by Fritz Perls (the founder of Gestalt therapy) and Jacob L. Moreno (the founder of psychodrama). Each explains the technique a bit differently, and my version of this technique combines a bit of the theory from both.

The empty chair is designed to allow you to work through interpersonal or internal conflict, to see your situation from a different perspective, to gain insight, and to heal from past hurts and traumas. By imagining another person in an empty chair, you can converse with them as if they are present with you right now. It allows you to focus on how you are interconnected with your environment and relationships, as well as encourages you to express your thoughts and feelings in a safe and neutral environment. The emphasis is placed on the here and now, to become aware of your patterns and why you think the way you do. It also helps you to accept and value yourself just as you are, while achieving a deeper understanding of both negative and positive experiences in your life. It can help you to relieve your emotional burden and allow you to move on from the past. The exercise is rooted in self-discovery and speaking the truth, in a way that helps you to overcome some of your greatest fears and to stop avoiding uncomfortable experiences, which will help you grow as an individual.

The empty chair technique allows you to have a dialogue with a person who had an influence on your early development. In insecure attachment, this person is most likely a primary caregiver, an important family member, or an adult mentor. For this exercise, I'd like you to think about the first person in your life who caused you to feel rejection or a fear of being abandoned.

⌣

Set up two chairs facing one another. Begin by sitting in one of the chairs. Now imagine sitting across from you is the person from your childhood who, in your memory, first caused you to question your worth in any way. Perhaps it's a parent who made you wonder if they truly loved you. Maybe it's another family member who you thought you could always count on, but they disappointed or abandoned you in some way. Maybe it's a mentor or caregiver who made you feel rejected or made you feel like you had to prove yourself to earn their love and support.

Once you bring this person to mind, I want you to speak to them as if they are in the chair opposite you. I want you to say out loud whatever occurs to you. This is your chance to express yourself freely with this person, without being afraid that they might interrupt you, put you down, stonewall you, avoid talking about certain topics, or be emotionally unavailable to you in some other way. You may have been too afraid to speak your mind with this person in the past or currently (if they are still in your life), but in this exercise, you can say what you want without fear of judgment.

If you feel uncertain where to begin, start by explaining what you're feeling and why you feel that way. Get in touch with the emotions that surface when you think about and interact with this person, and name those emotions. Talk about the range of their impact on you—tell them why they are important to you and what positive influences they have had on you, as well as where they've disappointed, hurt, or upset you. Ask them any questions you want.

Give yourself a bit of time to talk about what's been on your mind and pay special attention to how your relationship with this person might have led to fears of being on your own or by yourself.

After a few minutes, move to the other chair and embody the person you've been speaking to. Try to think about their mannerisms, the way they position their body, and the way they speak: inflection, pace, and tone. Imagine that this person has been carefully listening to you, tried their best to be open-minded about what you have to say, and attempted to put themselves in your shoes and to have empathy for how you feel. Although they are far from perfect, they are going to try to tell you some things that might explain why they acted the way they did, why they were flawed in how they dealt with you, and to answer at least some of the pointed questions you posed to them. Now allow this person to say out loud what is on their mind. Try to speak from their perspective as much as possible, and if this is difficult, simply give your gut reaction response based on what you think they might say if they heard what you communicated to them.

It's fine if your imagined response for them is realistic and in keeping with your understanding of who they are and how they behave. It's possible that this person may be somewhat uncooperative or combative, but try to imagine what this person might say if they were able to self-reflect to any degree. This might mean that they are still defensive but able to admit that they caused you pain and hurt and can take some responsibility for why your relationship has been problematic. It may mean that they own a mistake they made but still blame you for some of the conflicts at the same time. In any case, you are trying to bring the version of them into the room that is actively attending to you and at least trying to understand your needs to some extent.

When you reach a natural pause in the conversation, switch back to your original chair, take a deep breath, and resume the experience as yourself. As you consider what they've shared, check in with yourself and how you are feeling. Have your emotions changed from when you first started this exercise? Have they expressed something that has made you feel a bit more comforted? Did they say something that raised more questions, or brought up additional negative feelings or thoughts that you want to be sure to express? Don't hold back. Say what you want in response to their dialogue with you, and ask more questions if you'd like.

Once again, switch chairs and take a moment to embody the person so you can continue the conversation. Respond as if you are that person, just like before, being as authentic as possible and speaking from a place of honesty, transparency, fairness, and empathy. They may have some questions they'd like to ask you as well. Allow that to be part of the dialogue if it comes up.

Switch back and forth a couple of times until you feel like you've reached a good stopping point. You'll know it's time if you feel that you have run out of questions (at least for now), if you feel you've gained some new insight into your experiences with this person, or if you feel a shift in your emotions from the start of this exercise (for example, from higher intensity to lower intensity, or from a more negatively charged place to one that feels more relaxed). Know that you can always return to this exercise to conduct a dialogue with this person, to create more understanding about past experiences, and to learn more about yourself.

By doing this exercise, letting your guard down, and being in a vulnerable place, you are in fact alone and on your own. If you can engage in such a deep exploration of your thoughts and feelings by yourself, and if you return to this exercise (see below for additional empty chair exercise ideas), you will gradually build your confidence in doing other things on your own with less trepidation and concern about rejection and abandonment.

BONUS DISCOVERY EXERCISE: ADDITIONAL EMPTY CHAIR PROMPTS

The more you can foster inner dialogue, the more secure you will feel in your own company, as well as in your thoughts, feelings, and relationships. As you get more practiced with chair work, consider using one of these prompts to go deeper:

- Have a dialogue with a person you are in conflict with to try to find mutual ground and understanding. Use this experience to practice what you will actually say to the person when you talk to them.

- Talk with a part of yourself that is repeating certain patterns that intensify your anxious attachment (for example, the part that fears being alone so much that you end up participating in activities you dislike).

- Do the exercise with a person who has had a positive influence on your self-concept, perhaps someone who has always been supportive of you and told you they believed in you. Ask them for advice on how to tackle a difficult situation in your life.

- Conduct a dialogue with the part of yourself that needs a pep talk before taking on something challenging. Assume the role of someone who cares about you, and hear what they have to say and their tips for how to succeed in this situation.

DAILY WORKOUT: SPENDING QUALITY TIME WITH YOURSELF

Fears grow when you don't confront them, because the imagined catastrophes in your mind have no limit. By confronting your fear, you learn through experience that what you were so afraid of doesn't turn out to be so scary after all. Most important, you learn that you've survived the feared situation, leaving you with increased confidence in your own abilities.

By spending time on your own, you will learn to value yourself just as you are and begin to be comfortable with your thoughts and feelings when you are not around others. As you practice this skill, you will learn to become more comfortable with yourself and make peace with your circumstances and your flaws (we all have them). It's like working out and building a muscle so that it strengthens over time. You will learn to cherish and enjoy your time alone, and this will also help you to enact healthier boundaries with others, particularly those to whom you may have felt tethered, although spending time with them didn't make you feel better about yourself or more connected. A huge advantage of being comfortable on your own is that during this time, your thoughts, feelings, and actions are influenced only by you and not by others. You can truly do what you'd like and think what you'd like without having to consider what others might expect or want of you.

Make a list of things in your journal that you enjoy doing or write down some new hobbies or skills you've wondered about but haven't set aside the time to learn. At least once a week, commit to challenging yourself to do something alone that you usually would do with someone else, or explore something new. Start small and build up to larger and more extended activities. For example, start by grabbing a cup of coffee at your favorite coffee shop and sitting on your own at a table without distractions like your phone or a book. Simply sit, people watch, and enjoy your coffee mindfully. Eventually, consider treating yourself to dinner on your own without distractions or showing up at a community meeting or industry mixer event by yourself.

At first, when you engage in these activities without distractions or without another person, you may fear the judgment of others. You might wonder, "What are they thinking of me having dinner on my own?" When you notice thoughts like these, take a few deep breaths to steady your nerves and send the message to your brain that all is good and there is no reason to engage the fight-or-flight response. Then, challenge your thoughts. Remind yourself that 99 percent of the time, people are only thinking about themselves and what's going on in their lives. Even if they briefly notice that you are by yourself, they may have no opinion about it, and even if they do it is likely to be a quick flash in their mind, and in the next moment they are already on to another thought.

You can repeat mantras to yourself that help you to solidify your resolve to do more things on your own. Some helpful ones include:

- I am doing this to become more confident and comfortable with myself.
- I am learning to enjoy and cherish time on my own and getting to know myself a bit better.
- This will help me to have healthier relationships and to reach other goals I have in life.
- I am more comfortable today being alone than I was yesterday, and every day I will feel better about spending time on my own.

If you notice discomfort while on your own, it's also helpful to take out your journal and write down your thoughts and feelings. This is another mindful activity that you can do to understand the underlying fears that you have about being alone, and as you gain more understanding, you'll be able to move toward more ways to resolve the fears that come up and to confront those fears with behavioral experiments such as these.

BONUS DAILY WORKOUT: SELF-SOOTHE AND DE-STRESS ON YOUR OWN

As you venture out on your own more and more, you'll gain more confidence in your ability to tackle things alone and even grow to enjoy these periods of solitude. But as you're practicing and growing, there will still be times when you'll experience discomfort or anxiety because of old working models, especially when you're in a new environment or if you're under a lot of stress. The fear you experience is rooted in worries that you can't meet your own needs as well as someone else might be able to. This is why self-soothing practices are so crucial. As you see these techniques work for you, you'll be more assured that you can, in fact, take care of yourself well. Here are some of my favorite ones. Make space to practice at least one of these daily and then, in a pinch, you'll be able to use them to calm your fears and experience relaxation even in high-stress moments when you're by yourself.

- **Self-soothing touch:** The impact of this simple strategy is shown by decreases in the stress hormone cortisol for those who practice it![7] Use your own body to comfort, calm, or provide relief from emotional distress or physical discomfort. Try placing your hand over your heart or hugging yourself gently, lightly stroking your arm and hand with your fingertips, stroking your hair or scalp, gently massaging your temples, jawline, or forehead, or applying gentle pressure to pressure points such as the space between your thumb and forefinger or the center of your palm.

- **Emotional Freedom Techniques (EFT):** This evidence-supported technique combines elements of acupressure, psychology, and exposure therapy to alleviate emotional stress and reduce negative emotions.[8] You can find a detailed walkthrough on the EFT International website: https://eftinternational.org/wp-content /uploads/EFT-International-Free-Tapping-Manual.pdf.
- **The Voo Sound:** This technique is used by somatic experiencing (SE) therapists to help regulate body responses and emotional reactions. Because of the proximity of vocal cords to the vagus nerve, making vocal sounds and vibrations—like "voo"—can help relax you during or after an upsetting event.[9]
- **Sensory Distraction:** Engage your senses by focusing on something pleasant. Enjoy a soothing cup of tea, smell a calming essential oil, or touch a soft object.
- **Quick Visualization:** Close your eyes and visualize a calming scene or situation, like a serene beach or peaceful forest. Imagine yourself there, fully immersed in the soothing environment.
- **Fresh Perspective:** Spend time in nature or simply step outside for a breath of fresh air. Connecting with the natural world, even briefly, can have a calming and rejuvenating effect.

"I HAVE TO ANALYZE EVERYTHING"

We constantly analyze information we receive, which helps us to make decisions, plan, and navigate the world in a way that ensures our survival. However, anxious attachment might cause you to overthink and overanalyze to an unhealthy degree, turning an adaptive human trait into one that can be self-sabotaging and zap you of your motivation and drive.

Worried Warriors often become obsessive about their relationships, particularly intimate relationships. They become preoccupied with overanalyzing situations to the point of exhaustion. They are often uncertain and anxious about whether their needs will be met, or whether their feelings and actions will be reciprocated, so they try to predict how others might respond to them, as well as how they might respond in turn to try to obtain the outcomes they want from or with that person.

Extensive and perpetual overthinking leads to exhaustion, and many times, this "mind reading" isn't effective. It's not uncommon that your interpretation of what's happening in a relationship or a situation could be completely wrong, and your subsequent actions, based on your misinterpretation of the situation, might result in creating the very situation you feared in the first place: rejection by a partner, disconnection from a family member, or disappointment or lack of success at work.

My client Carmen often talks about how she constantly tries to "mind read" what her boss wants. She had just started a new job, and her boss was someone she really looked up to. Carmen felt that her boss seemed to be very no-nonsense, so Carmen didn't want to ask too many questions. Her boss articulated what she wanted but spoke very quickly, and because Carmen didn't want to give the impression she might not have been listening carefully or appear to need a lot of reassurance, she didn't ask for any clarification about what was wanted. After each meeting with her boss, Carmen spent time obsessing over what she *thought* her boss expected and putting projects together essentially in the dark that she hoped would make a good impression. Unfortunately, because she tried to predict what her boss wanted instead of coming out and asking her what she expected, Carmen's work didn't quite hit the mark. Eventually she received a subpar performance evaluation, with her boss noting that Carmen seemed to have difficulty following instructions.

Worried Warriors have a deep preoccupation with acceptance from others and an overwhelming desire for interpersonal closeness. This causes them to overinvest in social relationships and to obsess over little details of interactions they had with others as a form of self-evaluation. They're often trying to figure out whether they behaved in a way that will make others like them and are hypersensitive to cues that they may have turned someone off. This type of intense scrutiny of one's behavior makes it hard to be spontaneous and relaxed in social settings, especially where the anxiously attached person hasn't quite figured out how to best fit in yet, or situations in which it is hard for the anxiously attached person to read or predict what other people want and expect of them.

When you're anxiously attached, the fear of embarrassment or rejection is significant. As a result, you are constantly scanning your environment for cues that your worst fears might be realized.[10] This leads you to obsessively ruminate over the last conversation you had with your boss, what your romantic partner's facial expression meant right before they left the house this morning, and what your friend really intended when they made that offhand comment about your choice of career. You'll likely take the worst interpretation of whatever occurred and then run with that, basing your own reactions and further actions on this inaccurate assessment. This can cause a cascade of events that lead to a self-fulfilling prophecy and your worst fears being realized.

The underlying driver for this heightened preoccupation with people, details, and situations is the baseline anxiety that a lot of Worried Warriors experience. To try to quell doubts or fears, they engage in excessive analysis and constant worrying as an ineffective form of problem-solving. These misdirected efforts make it more difficult for the anxiously attached person to solve problems effectively and take them further away from feeling like they are on equal footing with the people with whom they are in relationships. They may be left feeling like they are putting much more into the relationship than the other person, which further drives down their self-concept and makes them feel insecure. It makes it more difficult to build genuine connections with people and may even push people away when some of these obsessive thoughts and preoccupations show themselves in unhealthy ways, such as resentful, jealous, or possessive behavior.

Worried Warriors may obsess over the details of goal pursuits to the point that they miss the big picture. They may spend a lot of time planning out exactly how they will execute the steps of a goal but then run out of steam to do the steps. Or they might spend a lot of time working on what-if contingency plans that are rooted in catastrophic thinking to the point that they scare themselves out of taking any step forward at all. This stems from a fear of not having the skills, motivation, or willpower to achieve what they set their minds to.

When they have a setback or encounter a challenge, they may give up on the goal, which then reinforces the negative self-belief that they aren't capable or worthy of experiencing good outcomes or success in their lives.

Antidote to "I Have to Analyze Everything"

The exercises on the following pages will help you to accept the part of you that overthinks and overanalyzes. Essentially, it's not a bad quality; it's just one that has likely become excessive, all in the name of trying to protect you. You'll learn to stop looking for hidden messages and to change your thinking in a way that aligns with what's happening, so that your subsequent decisions will be better informed and specific to the situations you're dealing with.

DISCOVERY EXERCISE: WHAT'S THE REALITY? REWRITING YOUR SCRIPT

Ben came to see me at my private practice because he was having a tough time thriving at work. He had just started a new job—a position he was very excited about—and found himself going all in to please everyone at work. As a way to ingratiate himself with his new

colleagues, he organized team lunches and volunteered for commit-
tees he didn't have time for because he wanted to be seen as a team
player and not be left out of *anything*.

Although his first performance review went quite well, to ensure
he doesn't get on his boss's bad side, Ben obsesses about the details
of his work to the point where he is missing the forest for the trees.
This hyperfocus on details, many of which don't matter in the grand
scheme of things, led him to reach several important deadlines just
under the gun. "It wasn't procrastination," he said. "I just end up
spending too much time obsessing about everything because I want
to make sure my boss is happy. There are a lot of people vying for my
position, and I just don't want her to regret her decision."

Ben's mind was constantly filled with worries about how people
perceived him and whether his performance was up to par. When he
came to see me, Ben felt like he was on the verge of quitting because
he couldn't handle the pressure. This was quite a change from when
Ben first learned he got the job—he was ecstatic that he had landed
a position with a great company doing work that he was truly passionate about and he believed he was good at.

Ben's biggest fear was that people would discover he didn't
deserve his position and he would be replaced. Despite this, he
acknowledged that the initial reactions of his colleagues and his
boss were complimentary, but he worried it was simply because
they were being nice and they didn't really value his abilities.

Ben and I had been talking about his anxious attachment style
for some time in our sessions. He had worked through some anxious attachment issues in his romantic relationship, and now it was
showing up at his job, which made a lot of sense to me: After all, Ben
was in a brand-new environment with a new set of people who might
have different opinions and expectations of him that he wasn't
accustomed to. You too may find that your anxious attachment can

flare up under unfamiliar circumstances or when you find yourself faced with challenges.

In new situations, Worried Warriors become more insecure than usual. Their fight-or-flight responses are triggered because they don't know what the formula is for getting the approval they need, so they sometimes grasp at straws trying to do everything they can to get what they need to feel better. Any information they gather that might be a tad ambiguous and hard to decipher causes great anxiety, and because Worried Warriors see the world through a negative lens and sometimes selectively filter in pessimistic information while ignoring or downplaying the positive aspects of a situation, they're likely to see something nefarious within innocuous social interactions. You recall this is what happened to my friend Agnes, who perceived that not hearing from her new boyfriend, Max, meant he had lost interest in her. She took one unanswered text and spun it into being abandoned and never being able to find and keep a boyfriend.

Once they perceive potentially threatening information, Worried Warriors begin to utilize misshapen coping strategies to try to obtain the reassurance they need to settle their nervous system. They bend over backward to please others, overcommit, and struggle with saying no even when they know they should push back. They spend excessive amounts of time trying to make sure they don't do anything that might elicit a negative response. This can be very distracting and take away from the focus and motivation that is needed to succeed. It's difficult to be productive when your emotions are constantly thrown into flux by the smallest potential provocations, many of which don't carry any significant meaning.

The following technique of rewriting your script works well because it combines the benefits of role-playing a challenging scenario in advance with the proven benefits of visualization and mental imagery[11] to give your mind an opportunity to practice a skill in advance and imagine yourself achieving the desired outcome.

Rewriting your script allows your conscious mind to process a different outcome than what your preexisting pessimistic expectations tell you is going to happen. Over time, rewriting your script will start to chip away at your negative beliefs, making way for new and more balanced beliefs to replace them.

Research shows that if you have rehearsed a situation, when faced with a similar scenario, you are much more likely to be able to do what you had imagined. It's like practicing your tennis stroke before you play in a match so that you are comfortable with hitting the ball accurately. You are likely to be more confident in your actions and believe that your actions will lead to a better outcome. So, next time you're facing a moment of ambiguity and you notice that you're starting to over-analyze, pause and try this rewriting exercise.

To start, open your journal, and recall a recent situation that you've spent a great deal of time mulling over. Perhaps you weren't satisfied with what you said to your friend over lunch or you didn't like an outcome with a family member, which led to second-guessing your decisions and wondering whether you should have done something differently. Write down some of the details of this event. Next, write down a different version of the event, one in which you emerge feeling good about yourself and how you communicated and behaved. Imagine in detail what you might think and feel during this version of the event, and write that down, too.

On a scale of 1 to 10, with 10 being the highest level of confidence that you could carry out this alternate scenario, rate this reimagined scenario. Generally, if you can write a version of a scenario for which you have a confidence level of 6 or higher, chances are, you'll be able to carry it out with a little prep work and some encouragement.

~

Let's see how this exercise worked for my client Ben. In one of our sessions together, Ben shared that after a recent conversation with his boss, he started to panic. She had popped by his desk to ask when Ben would have a project ready for her review. Although she didn't seem upset, Ben immediately started to worry that she was getting impatient with his progress. In his head he analyzed their interaction over and over again and wondered why she'd make a special stop at his desk to casually inquire about the project's progress. Ben then beelined to his boss's office, overpromised, and told her he'd have it completed immediately, but now he is extremely stressed because he doesn't think he will have time to turn in his best work. He spent the better part of the afternoon thinking about what she would think of his subpar product and how he might explain it in a way that wouldn't give her a bad impression of him—beating himself up over a self-imposed deadline!

Ben and I talked about this pattern—he would overanalyze a situation, shoot himself in the foot by acting impulsively based on what he thought was happening, and did it all without any additional input or feedback from the other person. I asked Ben to write down a different version of this event, one in which he could emerge feeling good about himself, how he communicated with his boss, and the deadline. I asked him to imagine in detail what he was thinking and feeling during this version of the event and to write that down, too. This is what Ben wrote:

My boss comes to my office and asks when the project outline will be delivered. Although it made me nervous because I wasn't sure if it meant she was already upset with me for not having it done already, I asked her when she would like to receive the outline. She said, "How about next Monday? Does that give you enough time to put it together?" Although it sounded reasonable, I knew that I had another deadline over the weekend and really wanted to be able to put my full focus on the outline. Although it made me feel slightly uncomfortable to propose a slightly later deadline, I knew it would be for the best. So I said, "I am working on the team report over the weekend. If I can have until Tuesday, I think I'll do a much better job at getting the project outline to a place we can both feel great about." My boss agreed that Tuesday will work well. I breathed a sigh of relief as it seemed my boss was fine with my suggestion. I also knew that I could do a much better job now that I had more time.

I asked how Ben felt as he read over this reimagined version of the event, and he shared that he not only felt better but in fact wished this version of events were what had actually happened. I then asked him on a scale of 1 to 10, with 10 denoting the highest level of confidence that he could carry out such a conversation in real life the way he had written it, what rating he would give to this reimagined scenario. Ben said he felt that he had a confidence level of 7.

By writing out this scenario, Ben could imagine how to respond more productively to a situation rather than defaulting to his old attachment habit of overanalyzing, overpromising, and putting himself in a tight spot. In writing out a better response, he is retraining himself to deal with challenges at work from a better perspective—not making assumptions about what his boss wants and getting clarity on the expectations she has for him.

DAILY WORKOUT: BEHAVIORAL EXPERIMENTS TO HEAL ANXIOUS ATTACHMENT

Worried Warriors overanalyze because of their heightened fear of abandonment and rejection. The constant monitoring of relationships and scenarios is a coping mechanism that helps them to combat fear with a false sense of control. They are typically hypersensitive to subtle cues and signals in relationships, reading too much into things even when there's no concrete evidence to support impending rejection or embarrassment. Often, behavioral rules grow out of this overanalysis, and Worried Warriors determine that there are certain ways things should be done to avoid potential abandonment or harsh judgment.

For example, my client Jacob had a rule never to ask for favors because he thought others would find him to be a burden. To avoid the potential no that he might hear if he asked, he'd rather not ask at all. This was not very practical, because he worked at an advertising firm where group projects were the norm. In the rare times he asked for favors, he found himself overanalyzing exactly how he would ask and then what would happen once he asked. Would the person find him annoying, respect him less, make an excuse not to do it? These worries filled his head, and it was hard to stop the chatter.

I asked Jacob to devise a scenario in which his belief that others would not do him a favor without some kind of negative repercussion could be directly challenged. To do so meant he would have to ask someone for a favor and see how that person responded and take that response at face value without overanalyzing what he thought they really meant.

I asked Jacob to first write down his rule regarding favors. He wrote:

I shouldn't ask people for favors because they might find it annoying and then distance themselves from me and/or make an excuse not to do the favor for me.

I then asked him to think about a favor he could ask of someone at work: something that isn't so small that it would not require much effort from the person he asked, but also something that is not so significant that it would be difficult for someone to say yes even if they genuinely wanted to help. After pondering this, Jacob wrote down the following:

I'll ask my co-worker Jenna if she can make copies of my presentation tomorrow and distribute them on my behalf because I'll be busy with another deadline.

I then asked him to write down what he thought would happen as a prediction ahead of time. You can see the overanalysis in his thought pattern. Jacob wrote:

I think Jenna will probably say yes but only because she feels like she has to. Deep down she will likely be annoyed with me, and she'll probably start avoiding me more at work. Or Jenna might make an excuse about why she can't do it, because she really doesn't want to go to the trouble and doesn't care enough about me to help me.

The next step was for Jacob to ask Jenna for help and observe her reactions. Jacob asked Jenna before the end of the workday whether she could make copies and distribute them for the meeting. Jenna agreed and made the copies. I asked Jacob to try his best to refrain from trying to imagine how Jenna might respond, or what Jenna might be thinking, and focus instead on her actual behaviors, writing them down in his journal if he needed help to remember them accurately. Over the next few days, I asked Jacob to observe his interactions with Jenna. Were there any changes to how she reacted to him? Did she say hi to him less in the hallway or stop asking him to go to lunch?

When I next saw Jacob, we went over the results of his experiment. Jacob shared that although he was a little uncomfortable asking her for help, he was glad he did it. He also noted that he didn't see any changes in Jenna's behavior toward him following his request for help. She talked to him just as much as usual, and they went to lunch several times as well.

I then told Jacob that it was very important that he write down in his notebook what happened and compare it with his prediction. Once he compared notes, I asked him what he thought of the discrepancy. Jacob noticed that when he first wrote down the prediction, he was sure that it was going to be the version of events that happened, but his fears didn't come to fruition. I then asked him to rewrite his existing rule to make room for this new observation. His existing rule was not to ask for any favors because people would find him bothersome. After this experiment, he rewrote his new rule as "I can ask for reasonable favors, and people will likely be okay with that."

These behavioral experiments are very powerful because you can see in real life how things unfold when you challenge your existing rules one at a time. You can see how your existing rules might be fueled by overanalysis. Then you can return to your rules and edit them according to what actually happened, and not feel trapped in your mind, overanalyzing the what-ifs based on what you fear might or might not happen. Experience teaches you that overanalyzing isn't the real problem-solving technique, but observation and paying attention to objective information are.

Over time, this exercise will help you to rid yourself of unreasonable rules based on fear and to become more flexible in your core beliefs, so that you aren't holding on to globally negative ideas that don't bear out in your day-to-day interactions.

You can devise your own behavioral experiment by following these steps:

- Write down a rule that you've adopted in order to cope with fear of rejection, uncertainty, or negative judgment from others.

- Write down a situation where you can challenge yourself to go against this rule you've devised for yourself, and write down a prediction of what you believe might happen.
- Next, perform this challenge and refocus your attention from internal analysis to the observable aspects of the outcome. Write down what actually happened, and note whether it lined up with your initial prediction.

Continue to come up with more ways to challenge your existing rules by devising other behavioral experiments. Consider challenging yourself progressively, so that each challenge is slightly more difficult (but will then also have more of an impact on changing your negative core beliefs).

SELF-CONCEPT SNAPSHOT

Remember the self-concept snapshot you took in chapter 3? That was your baseline before tackling these exercises. Now that you've worked through these activities, I'd like you to take another snapshot of your self-concept and note any differences. Read the statements below and choose the option that best describes you.

1 = not true, 2 = sometimes or partially true, 3 = mostly or definitely true

- If I had the opportunity, I wouldn't change many things about myself.
- I have confidence in my decision-making.
- I don't worry excessively about what others think of me.
- I like myself even when I am in conflict with someone else.
- I value myself even when I make mistakes.
- I believe my efforts contribute to my success.
- I have control over my reactions to difficult situations.

- I like myself.
- I can start and finish projects without others' help and approval.
- I have a clear sense of who I am.
- I have positive and admirable traits.
- I can overcome challenges when I try hard.

Did your score improve after the exercises? It's helpful to do this checkup once every few weeks to see how your self-concept improves as you continue to gain insight and work through the exercises in this chapter along with any other chapters that you feel may apply to you (for example, if you feel that anxious attachment is your predominant style but you also have a secondary attachment style).

THE JOURNEY AHEAD

Congratulations on finishing all the exercises in this chapter! You've learned to work on all the different aspects of your anxious attachment style through these discovery and coping strategies. Attachment wounds go way back, so it will take consistent practice and awareness to heal them. These exercises will set you on a path that will allow you to wrestle less with people-pleasing and become more confident in your own decision-making. Gradually, you'll learn to embrace and honor your own needs and not lose yourself in trying to save others. By now, hopefully you're learning about your inherent value. Through these exercises, you'll come to love your alone time, trusting that you are more than enough and that you don't need another person to validate your worth. The work you've already done should help cut through the analysis paralysis that you experience and help you to manage overwhelming and stressful situations with greater mastery.

As you continue this journey, you'll learn to balance your strong needs for intimacy and connection with self-reliance and to self-soothe when loved ones aren't readily available to care for you. With more time and focused attention, you'll find your way to a resilient self-concept that isn't overly reliant on what others think or what happens to you on a given day, but one that can remain steadfast even as things change around you.

Check your self-concept frequently to assess where your progress is at any given time, especially when you are going through challenges in a major area of life. Repeat the exercises that work best for you, and incorporate them into your weekly routines. Once your self-concept is around a score of 24 or higher, this is a great time to tap into the tips in the conclusion, "Your Resilient Self." For more self-concept boosters, see appendix C on page 329.

It is also helpful to read through the chapters on other attachment styles to gain insight into how you relate to other attachment styles. These chapters will help improve your relationships and the quality of your connection with people whose styles differ from your own.

Additionally, please refer to appendix A for exercises that will help you to identify triggers for insecure attachment behaviors and what to do in the moment to manage the situation more effectively.

THE DISORGANIZED
ATTACHMENT STYLE

CHAPTER 9

Disorganized Attachment:
Surveillance Specialists

Of all the attachment styles, disorganized attachment is perhaps the most misunderstood. For one thing, people often assume that it's just a mix of the anxious and avoidant attachment styles when, in fact, it's a style rooted in its own unique attachment wounds—largely due to trauma and neglect. Because of its complex and contradictory nature, there is an assumption that people with this attachment style are unpredictable and dramatic, and many believe that it's impossible to heal. These inaccurate ideas and stereotypes can be stigmatizing and probably make it difficult for people who identify with this attachment style to feel they can make positive changes. While it is true that disorganized attachment can be challenging to overcome, you can absolutely do it—I've seen myriad success stories in my own practice and those of my colleagues.

The sad truth is that the majority of people who develop disorganized attachment do so because they've had a difficult and even traumatic childhood. When children grow up in a family where unpredictability, neglect, and trauma are the norm, they become fearful of their environments. It's a normal, even adaptive reaction, but that fear leads to mistrust and vigilance about everything and everyone around you. You become, in essence, a Surveillance Specialist.

My client Todd, for example, spots threats everywhere. While some people might operate on a "trust, but verify" basis, his motto was "distrust, distrust, and never really trust." At work, if someone compliments him on a project or his contribution to a meeting, he can't take the compliment without wondering not only if they really mean it, but also if they have some ulterior motive. He wonders if they are complimenting him to get something out of him or put something over on him. If someone does something nice for him, he immediately starts speculating about what they might want in return—it's never about what's been done for him but what it will ultimately cost. Rather than enjoying the nice gesture, he almost always acts as if he's been handed something that's going to bite him back.

It doesn't matter who the kindness comes from—a romantic interest, his dearest friends—Todd's fear leads him to push people away with criticism of the gift or gesture and ends up making him look unappreciative or suspicious. Sometimes, in the face of a compliment or kind gesture, he will freeze and have little or no reaction at all. Over time, people are less likely to extend themselves to him because of these reactions. Todd is working very hard to resolve these trust issues and is successfully coping with things at work. He's taking one arena of his life at a time.

Surveillance Specialists can engage in a range of self-sabotaging behaviors and find themselves jumping from job to job, relationship to relationship. They may say that it doesn't matter if they leave one job for another—it's just another job. Without long-term objectives and with a tendency to create chaos, they often find themselves unsettled and even aimless, without a strong purpose and a lack of clarity about who they are or what they want. In essence, their self-concept, or sense of self, seems to be missing or can shift rapidly from one scenario to another. They may take on different temporary personas depending on who they're spending time with and find themselves going back and forth on their goals and aspirations, not being able to make a long-term commitment to any single objective. This lack of self-concept clarity can also be associated with a feeling of emptiness that is painful and difficult to describe to people who haven't felt the same way.

Seeking Additional Support

While any of the attachment styles can benefit from the added insight of working with a professional, I especially recommend that people healing from disorganized attachment find additional support. Because many people with disorganized attachments have experienced some degree of trauma, your nervous system is carrying a heavier load, and it can be more challenging to make consistent progress on your own. If you find this is true, don't despair—you will be able to overcome these attachment wounds with a little more help. An experienced attachment-based therapist can help you work on the thoughts, feelings, communications, behaviors, and interpersonal exchanges that you have either suppressed or amplified due to your early experiences with your caregivers. Developing a secure attachment with your therapist can itself be a healing model of connection for many people.

If any of the information in this chapter becomes overwhelming or confusing, I recommend that you work through the exercises with a mental health care professional who can assist you in discovering more about yourself and give you more intensive support as you move toward healing.

If finances are a barrier to receiving professional treatment, I urge you to investigate low-cost, sliding-fee community centers in your area. Many clinicians offer a sliding scale in their private practice, and you might also work with local universities with student clinics where you can work with therapists in training (all of whom are supervised by licensed psychotherapists).

ORIGINS OF DISORGANIZED ATTACHMENT

Like all attachment styles, disorganized attachment develops in early childhood in response to experiences from the early years of life. Unfortunately, in the case of disorganized attachment, those experiences were persistently stressful or traumatic.

The child might have been neglected or largely ignored by the caregiver, or caregivers may not have protected the child from circumstances that led them to fear for their physical and psychological safety. Caregivers likely didn't provide the child with helpful or effective coping strategies for managing stress and didn't model effective coping strategies when they were going through their own difficult times.

In times of need, the child may have been exposed to a negative response from their parents—for example, a baby's cries might have been ignored or met with anger, yelling, or exasperation. In some instances, the trauma was inflicted upon the child by the caregivers themselves, in the form of physical, emotional, or sexual abuse, or extreme neglect.

Sometimes, the neglect or abuse the child experienced is a result of the caregiver struggling with their own problems like marital conflict, alcohol or drug misuse, or untreated medical or psychological illnesses. Parents may have done the best they could given their own circumstances and resources but nevertheless created traumatic experiences for their children.

Some parents suffered trauma themselves in their childhood and/or had several adverse childhood experiences (ACEs)[1] that were unresolved or untreated. In her research, Dr. Mary Main and her husband, Dr. Erik

Hesse,[2] found that unresolved trauma and loss in a parent's life is the best predictor of disorganized attachment between a parent and child. The parent's own experiences of abuse, neglect, or unresolved trauma early in life can have lasting influence and leave them prone to being flooded by emotions in times of stress between themself and their child. In essence, that unresolved trauma impacts the parent's ability to notice and respond to the child's needs in a sensitive and responsive manner.[3]

This is often the dynamic we're talking about when we talk about how intergenerational trauma is perpetuated: Disorganized attachment can be passed from generation to generation, because parents who struggle with unresolved trauma and are not able to regulate their own emotions may have trouble tolerating a range of emotions in their child. Their own inability to make sense of what happened to them during their own childhood influences how they parent, and they are likely to engage in confusing and inconsistent behavior with their child.

For example, they may react to their kids with fear or other primal emotions (such as anger, sadness, and disgust) that surface in moments of stress. At these moments, the parent may act out or engage in destructive behavior and not be fully aware of how they are behaving. They may lash out at the child and inappropriately take out their anger on them, saying things like "I wish you were never born," or "You're the reason I drink." After an outburst like this, parents may be overly contrite, becoming extremely emotionally needy with their child and begging for forgiveness, or lean in even further on their wrath for the child, punishing them harshly for small mistakes or showing indifference to the fact that they hurt the child's feelings. In general, this leads to parents responding to their child's needs without any definable pattern. Crying may be met with either comfort or punishment; being still and quiet may be met with being praised or being ignored.

Over time, the parent becomes a scary, unapproachable figure, and the child is less likely to seek help from them. Because the parent is so volatile in their emotional responses and can blow up at the drop of a hat (particularly if a child needs something from them), the child does not learn emotional regulation—they don't understand how to respond with an appropriate emotional response to a given situation. They begin to recognize that how they attempt to interact with their parent or to reach out to the parent is not met with a consistent response or that response is largely negative. They begin to adopt learned helplessness—feeling powerless to make changes in their life as well as being unable to connect with their parent.

Learned Helplessness and the Still Face Study

Early in our lives we learn, through experience, about other people's reactions to us and how our behavior can affect others. Having a parent be non-responsive in short doses is not a problem; however, as Dr. Edward Tronick discovered, if it occurs frequently over longer periods, it can have a detrimental impact on the baby's development. Dr. Edward Tronick[4] described a phenomenon in which an infant, after three minutes of attempted interaction with a non-responsive, expressionless mother, "rapidly sobers and grows wary." In his original Still Face study, mothers were directed to interact with the child as usual, then become expressionless and unresponsive for three minutes before resuming their usual play with the child. When the mother is expressionless as directed by the researcher, babies look confused and attempt to use all their abilities to initiate a response from her.

As their attempts to connect continue to be ignored by the mother, babies begin to show distress and frustration. Eventually, they begin crying, which escalates to screeching. The central nervous system of babies in this experiment can become so overwhelmed that they can physically collapse. A baby may even bite their own hand to self-soothe. As the baby dissolves emotionally, it can be uncomfortable to watch their distress. Toward the end of the experiment the baby becomes withdrawn, hopeless, and no longer attempts to engage with the mother or to try to get the mother's attention.

This experiment was also conducted using fathers, and the videos of these interactions clearly show that babies react just as strongly to their father's still face as they do to their mother's. Babies then demonstrate the same behaviors to attempt to connect with their fathers as they do with their mothers, and then eventually give up and show behavioral signs of learned helplessness. This demonstrates that fathers' influence is critical in children's development and life.

I want to acknowledge that not all disorganized attachment styles stem from abuse or neglect. Sometimes, it is a result of consistently broken trust. The caregiver may have made promises, big and small, and then didn't follow up. A string of broken promises and frequent lies will erode a child's trust in the parent. A parent's struggle with substance abuse can also greatly influence the attachment style of the child. In fact, a child who grows up with an alcoholic parent is four times as likely to display disorganized attachment as an adult.[5]

Regardless of the specific behavior or reason, parents of children with disorganized attachment may have behaved in ways that created unhealthy boundaries by making the child feel responsible for the parents' emotional and physical safety. A child may be punished or threatened when they seek out comfort from the parent or caregiver when they are in distress—for example, "Grow up! You don't need me to help you!" or "Stop crying or I'll give you something to *really* cry about!"

An unbalanced relationship may develop that is characterized by emotional and physical withdrawal, unresponsiveness, and hostile or intrusive behaviors, which can lead the child to develop an extreme fear of the parent.[6,7]

Parents of disorganized children may have verbalized regret about having a child or made the child feel responsible for the parents' feelings, particularly when they were upset—yelling at the child, "You make me so mad!" When their parents' behavior is unpredictable—they may overreact to a situation, dismiss a child's fears or concerns, or simply not be available to the child—the child never learns how they can get their needs met or if they can get their needs met at all. The parents may have created a chaotic and unpredictable environment in the home, which may have been frightening or traumatizing, that created this constant sense of precariousness in the child's world. Amid this chaos the child can't figure out a stable way of dealing with the world. They may experience great difficulty in developing an organized strategy to deal with stress and conflict that allows them to feel safe.

DISORGANIZED ATTACHMENT AND THE STRANGE SITUATION

Infants in the Strange Situation (see page 5) who were classified as disorganized exhibited behaviors that suggested a conflict over simultaneously wanting to connect with the caregiver and run from the caregiver. In the Strange Situation, disorganized infants made up about 19 percent of those studied. When they were reconnected with their parent after the time away, they acted scared, conflicted, and in unexpected ways with their parent or caregiver.[8] When a frightened child seeks comfort, they will naturally turn to their attachment figure as a source of safety. However, in situations where the attachment figure becomes a source of distress or alarm, the child may experience conflicting signals. They may grapple with the inclination to move closer for comfort while simultaneously feeling a pull to move away from the attachment figure.[9]

This pathway would produce, Main hypothesized, "an irresolvable and ultimately self-perpetuating conflict situation" between approach and withdrawal.[10] The behaviors of the infants that were identified as disorganized included:

- acting fearful of the caregiver,
- contradictory behaviors or displays of emotion occurring simultaneously or quickly in sequence,
- odd physical movements, and/or
- freezing and apparent dissociation (seemingly disconnecting from the world around them and minimally responsive to environmental stimulation).[11]

While many children who were categorized with disorganized attachment style had likely suffered abuse or neglect, it is important to note that, as Solomon and George[12] have documented, lacking a safe and secure environment can predict disorganized infant behavior in the Strange Situation Procedure. For example, a child who is separated from a parent for a lengthy period—through a divorce proceeding, for example—but who isn't being maltreated in any way is increasingly likely to develop disorganized attachment.

In general, the researchers noted that these behaviors occur only briefly before the infant then returns to one of the other attachment styles. In the study, all infants who were determined to be disorganized were also given a secondary attachment classification. This may mean that if you have disorganized attachment, you will also frequently identify with the feelings and behaviors of either anxious or avoidant attachment. If this is you, it's possible that during times of stress, you may first experience a phase of overwhelm and disorganization, and then, as the dust settles, you may find yourself additionally adopting some of the forms of coping associated with one of the other insecure attachment styles. This means that some of the information from one of the other insecure attachment chapters might resonate with you, and doing the exercises from that chapter in addition to the exercises for disorganized attachment will help heal your attachment wounds more completely.

〜

The primary theme driving the behaviors of most individuals with disorganized attachment is a deep fear that they don't deserve love or closeness from others, and that they don't deserve to have good things happen to them. There is a constant fear of being discovered for who they really are (even if they are unsure of who that is) and being ridiculed, reprimanded, or abandoned. They can feel as if they are constantly walking on a tightrope and at any minute they will lose their balance. No wonder people with this attachment style become Surveillance Specialists: They're used to feeling afraid, threatened, and constantly on edge, particularly at the hands of the people who are supposed to care for them.

The fundamental lesson that children with disorganized attachment learn is that love can be unpredictable and confusing. The erratic behaviors of their primary caregivers lead them to adopt a range of complex and contradictory ways to cope with their environment, and there is no coherent or consistent message about how to attain emotional safety or who they are in the world. Without emotional safety, it's much harder to focus on goal attainment, self-actualization, or enacting healthy boundaries.

DISORGANIZED ATTACHMENT AND BOUNDARIES

Boundaries are certainly a hot topic in therapy, and even in colloquial discussions, but it is an especially crucial concept for the health of Surveillance Specialists. Their early experiences did not afford them opportunities to learn about and enact healthy boundaries, and the inconsistent experiences with caregivers were likely very confusing to them, which made it hard to know and express what they needed from others while still maintaining integrity and respect for themselves.

Boundaries are psychological demarcations that protect the integrity of a person and help the individual set realistic, healthy limits on how they interact with others.[13] Strong boundaries allow you to define a safe space for yourself and respect your own needs, yet are flexible enough to allow you to provide support to others, rely on others, and form meaningful connections. The ability to understand, request, and respect boundaries is predicated on establishing a firm self-concept, which gives you a clear sense of where you end and where others begin. This is likely not something Surveillance Specialists learned from caregivers. Their chaotic upbringing taught them that mistreatment and/or neglect was the norm, so it's hard to recognize these events as boundary violations when they happen. That's why this next exercise serves a very important role: It helps you to learn the various forms of boundaries and shines a light on what you need in order to feel safe.

Completing this inventory will help you to clarify what you need and expect in five areas of life: physical, emotional, intellectual, experiential, and spiritual. You may not feel ready to enforce your boundaries right away, and that's okay. Starting to notice where you end, where others begin, and when your boundaries are being pushed by others (or even by your own thoughts and self-judgments!) is itself a vital skill. As you feel more secure, you'll find that you're more comfortable communicating about your boundaries.

I recommend doing this inventory once every few months, because you may find that your boundaries shift in different situations or relationships. Sometimes the shifts are healthy, while at other times, changes might signify that some important aspects of your boundaries are being trespassed. Checking in can bring to light what's crucial for you to maintain your mental and physical well-being. The more you do this boundaries assessment, the more you will start to understand what you need to feel safe, strong, and secure.

EXERCISE: BOUNDARIES INVENTORY

In your journal, list each of the five types of boundaries found below, and for each one, write down some of your expectations or guidelines. The questions are provided to guide you in discerning your boundaries in each of these areas.

Physical: boundaries you set about your body, touch, physical personal space, what you eat and drink.

- How comfortable am I being touched by others, and in what ways (hugs, handshakes, fist bumps, and so on)?
- Who am I comfortable being touched by? How do I verbally and nonverbally express consent to be touched?
- How do I like to communicate when I am sexually intimate? What am I comfortable doing in these situations?
- Am I comfortable inviting others into my personal space (home, work office, and so on)?
- What foods and drinks do I not want to have?
- How do I prioritize my physical health needs (eating well, getting enough sleep, time for exercise, and so on)?

Emotional: boundaries regarding what you're comfortable sharing with others, how emotionally available you are to others, and how much time and energy you spend on yourself emotionally versus others.

- Who do I turn to when I need to discuss something personal?
- Who am I not comfortable sharing emotionally charged information with?
- When do I make time for my own self-care?
- How much can I give to someone who needs more support from me than I can offer?

- How do I process my own emotions?
- What emotional coping strategies do I use and when do I need to use them?

Intellectual: boundaries about your own thoughts, values, opinions, and interests.
- What topics do I feel comfortable discussing?
- Which topics are off-limits?
- When do I need to walk away from a discussion?
- What do I need to feel respected in a conversation or disagreement?

Experiential: boundaries about how much time you spend with people and in certain activities, and how much of your resources you wish to share (such as how you manage money and lend/give materially).
- What types of activities take priority when I am busy?
- How do I like to spend my free time (in solitary activities as well as with others)?
- When and for which activities will I make space to do things other people want to do?
- What types of projects and activities do I have to respectfully say no to?
- What are my needs and limits around spending (or saving) money?
- What am I willing to share in terms of financial resources and material goods with friends, family, and those in need?

Spiritual: boundaries that have to do with your right to believe in what you want, explore and practice spiritual activities that are of value to you, and to communicate and share your ideas about the meaningfulness of life and belief in a higher power or something bigger than yourself.

- What spiritual or religious practices are important to me?
- When do I make time for spiritual or religious practices?
- In what ways do I need or want to communicate these ideas to others who may differ from me in their worldview?
- Under what circumstances am I able to listen to the beliefs of others?

BONUS EXERCISE: ONE THING TODAY FOR HEALTHIER BOUNDARIES

After completing this boundary assessment, ask yourself, "What is one thing I can do to honor my boundary in any of these areas?" Commit to doing it in the next twenty-four hours, whether it involves communicating your boundary to another person or acting in a way that is consistent with one of your boundary preferences.

DISORGANIZED ATTACHMENT IN ADULTHOOD

Disorganized attachment tends to have the most negative impact on self-concept. Surveillance Specialists have a difficult time holding on to a stable self-concept, and as a result, they often have trouble achieving their goals in more than one area of life, from romantic relationships to work to personal health goals. As adults, they do not have a clear sense of who they are, what they believe, the meaning behind their thoughts and actions, and they have lower self-esteem.

Because they don't have a solid sense of who they are, like a chameleon, they adapt to the thoughts, feelings, and behaviors of those around them. Doing so leaves them feeling at odds with themselves and not sure who they are on the inside, which leads to feelings of instability and inconsistency, like the feelings they experienced when they were children.

Because the mental representations disorganized people have about their self-identity and worth (and expectations of other people's reactions to them) are not well established, there tends to be a persistent blurring of boundaries between themselves and others. These beliefs and behaviors, which were formed from interactions with their caregivers and guide future behaviors and expectations, tend to involve themes of threat and fear, provoking them to react with a fight-or-flight response. For example, they may feel very defensive or want to completely avoid a situation or any form of confrontation. As a result, their relationships with others and the world in general can feel frightening and unsafe for them. They have deep distrust of other people and may find close relationships confusing and threatening to their well-being, because they fear having to lean on people who they expect will eventually disappoint, hurt, or even abuse them. Their confusion may lead them to experience severe swings of love and hate for another person or partner—often the result of a subconscious projection of their anger and frustration toward their caregivers that were never dealt with or directly expressed. Because they are not able to connect with others easily, they cannot share their pain or concerns and often suffer in secret and isolation over any of the negative outcomes they continue to experience in their lives.

Negativity is a constant theme. Their view of themselves is largely pessimistic, and they often feel defeated before they begin, because they don't trust themselves to achieve any level of success. Their view of others is also primarily negative. They don't feel that they can trust others to follow through on what they say or do. And even when someone is nice to them or does something nice for them, they are wary of the gesture and offer of connection. All of this contributes to their worldview, which generally assumes that all is hopeless. Nothing will work out for the best, and even if something looks good for a time, it will never be sustainable and last—jobs, friendships, or relationships. Because of this expectation of failure, they often set themselves up to lose and do so by self-sabotaging and engaging in negative self-fulfilling prophecies: They believe it will never work, and they do things (often unconsciously) to ensure that it does not work. They are then proved right that nothing ever works out. Someone with a disorganized attachment style may never have had the opportunity to learn how to self-soothe with any consistency. (If you'd like some ideas on how to learn this skill now, see page 214.) If they developed a strategy that seemed to help in a time of stress, their caregiver likely introduced a new stressful situation or conflict into their life, causing the child to feel out of control and unable to cope.

My client Desmond explained that when he was a child and witnessed his parents' constant fighting, he would run to his room and bury his head under his pillow and covers to drown out the noise and find some semblance of peace. One time his father barged into his room and asked him why he was being "a little girl," and said that he should "see what kind of woman your mother really is." Since that day, whenever his parents got into a heated argument, Desmond felt pressured to stay in the vicinity of the conflict and was forced to watch, quite helplessly, as his father berated his mother and sometimes threw things at her. His father's actions took away the one small way that Desmond had found to cope—removing himself from the stressful situation. Desmond then developed a new way to cope—dissociating from what was happening and going into a fantasy land in his mind where he could be happy and at peace. As an adult, when in very stressful situations, Desmond continues to dissociate, disconnecting his conscious mind from the conflict in front of him. Sometimes he has trouble remembering exactly what happened during a stressful encounter, or he struggles to think clearly, especially when he feels under pressure.

These themes and self-beliefs have an impact on all areas of your life, from romantic relationships to achieving your goals. Let's take a closer look at how they are influencing you.

Disorganized Attachment in Romantic Relationships

Disorganized attachment helps people to protect themselves from rejection and pain. They will reject first to avoid getting hurt or will not engage, connect, or commit to ensure that they do not experience loss or hurt if things don't work out. Relationships can be difficult for Surveillance Specialists because, to put it simply, they didn't learn how to connect and can't maintain a consistent way of reaching out and developing relationships.

While they may crave meaningful and deep relationships, they feel unworthy of love, are terrified of getting hurt, and tend to push people away if they seem as if they are getting too close or if the person with disorganized attachment feels as if they are beginning to depend on the other person too much. What is familiar to them—even if it is negative—feels comfortable. They resist being close to another person because it feels unfamiliar and, therefore, risky. From their perspective, it is better not to engage at all rather than get hurt once again. They may appear very self-sufficient, but it's all because they are hiding their fear of being hurt.

Surveillance Specialists have likely been through much interpersonal trauma, and the legacy of that trauma on their emotional dysregulation can cause obstacles in creating connections and relationships with others. Sometimes people attempt to reenact past traumas in a (usually subconscious) effort to heal from and overcome the past situation. It's a little like living in a time loop and trying to find your way out of it with little success. They enter into a similar situation in the present, hoping to have a better outcome. For this reason, they may subconsciously find themselves drawn to partners who are aloof, dismissive, and neglectful (just like their parents) and find themselves being extremely hurt by their actions, but they nevertheless try to seek their attention, support, and love.

They may go to extreme lengths to engage someone at a deeper level, then push them away without warning. They may make offhand caustic statements about themselves and other people, but at the same time seem to have unrealistic expectations of their romantic partners and others with whom they are in close relationships. Sometimes they can engage in "trauma bonding" and find other people who have had similar trauma to theirs. In the beginning, it can feel as if they have found someone who understands them, but eventually it blows up because they constantly trigger each other's deepest struggles, leading to recurrent, extreme emotion dysregulation and feelings of rejection and abandonment.

Generally speaking, their comfort with emotional dysregulation can lead people with disorganized attachment to frequently find themselves in unhealthy or unstable relationships that involve emotionally, physically, or sexually abusive partners. However, Surveillance Specialists may have difficulty leaving unhealthy relationships, because their own boundaries and sense of what is normal or acceptable between two people have been distorted by their experiences with their first caregivers.

This isn't to say that people with disorganized attachment are always victims. As partners, they can be insensitive, selfish, controlling, and untrusting. The intensity of these feelings can lead to them being explosive or potentially abusive. The partner isn't the only one who is looked at in a very critical light—the Surveillance Specialist is on high alert for *everyone* and can be just as hard on themselves as they are on others. As a result, they may swing through the emotions of love and hate for their partner and be very inconsistent in how they interact with them and express affection or care.

Unconsciously, they may create various tests for the people in their life so that others can prove they are worthy of their attention. For example, Susan will pick fights with her husband and then leave the house in a huff, waiting with bated breath to see if he'll come after her to try to fix whatever made her so upset. Over time this has caused her husband to feel frustrated. He believed she was playing games or creating drama for no reason, which ultimately caused friction and dissatisfaction in their relationship. Just as importantly, the threshold for his passing grade was ever-changing and didn't seem to be based on logic. For example, Susan used to be satisfied if her husband came after her immediately as she was leaving the house, but over time, she wanted him to apologize as well, even when he didn't do anything to make her upset in the first place.

Part of what characterizes disorganized attachment is having difficulty remaining fully present in the moment with feelings and needs. People with this attachment style can look to past relationships and idealize them, and this fantasy ex-partner becomes very difficult for their present partner to live up to. Frankly, they are likely to have partners throughout their lives who are very similar to one another, so the favorable comparison and the placement of an ex on a pedestal is only a creation in their own mind. They may put all their eggs in the same relationship basket and become disillusioned when their partner does not end up being the savior they were hoping for.

When it comes to intimacy in relationships, the Surveillance Specialists have difficulty giving all of themselves. They may engage in casual sex, exhibit signs of sexual addiction, or abstain from sex altogether—and may even switch rapidly from one extreme to the other. When people retreat or distance themselves, the person with disorganized attachment vacillates between being overly conciliatory and trying to repair the situation or becoming angry or aggressive with the other person. This is what would happen between Susan and her husband. When he felt fed up and needed space, she would chase after him to apologize over and over again, being extremely self-deprecating in the process. At other times, she would become irate with him for giving up on her so quickly and not understanding what she needed in that moment. In extreme cases, Surveillance Specialists may engage in avoidant coping mechanisms such as using alcohol or drugs, or possibly replicate abusive patterns they were exposed to as a child by treating someone the way their parents treated them.

Because relationships can be intimidating, they may seek out safer low-stakes relationships. For example, a Surveillance Specialist may engage in "harmless flirting" with the local barista without intending to start an intimate relationship. They may attempt to get their more intimate connection needs met through online courtships that are unlikely to ever have the prospect of in-person meet-ups (for example, with someone who lives overseas). They may prefer to fantasize about relationships rather than actually pursuing them (like developing a crush on a married friend) or over-romanticize what they see on TV and in movies while at the same time lamenting that they don't have a similar relationship in their life. In fact, Surveillance Specialists might find it more comfortable to connect with animals or fictional characters, idealizing the relationships they see in books, movies, or TV, rather than investing time and energy into people in their lives.

Disorganized Attachment with Friends and Family

The Surveillance Specialist's family relationships can be fraught with conflict because they can shift between idealizing certain members of their family and feeling demoralized that their family does not provide them with connection, understanding, and support. In some cases, they may become estranged from family members, particularly if their early experiences involved severe neglect, abuse, or trauma. This may be a way of protecting themselves from further harm or a coping strategy to get away from toxic family dynamics. Sometimes, their behaviors can change abruptly from one day to the next. They may lash out at their loved ones for perceived slights or insults, and their reaction may be out of proportion to the situation.

Because of the stress and trauma Surveillance Specialists have experienced in their lives, their stress or trauma response can be triggered by nearly anything—even something that may seem benign. For example, my client Darren was visiting a childhood friend for the weekend when

Darren's friend was unexpectedly called by his boss to take care of something urgent at the office. He told Darren that he'd be back as soon as possible and to make himself comfortable until his return. Although his friend was gone for only a couple of hours, Darren felt abandoned, didn't wait for his friend, and took an earlier flight home. Although he recognized intellectually that his friend was doing his job and his leaving had nothing to do with him, Darren couldn't fight the feeling of being unimportant to his friend, and as he sat in his friend's home alone with his thoughts, the distress became too much for him, so he escaped.

If you're a Surveillance Specialist, you are probably capable of great emotional depths in friendships and other relationships but can feel overwhelmed by them. It's a double-edged sword, as you can be perceived as being overwhelming yourself—people may have told you that you're "too intense," and this rejection can leave you feeling lonely, isolated, and ashamed.

Although you have a desire and need to connect with other people, you don't want to burden others with your problems, but feeling unable to share your inner thoughts, feelings, and fears leaves you feeling confused about what your true needs are in relationships with others. If you cannot truly connect with others, then what is the point of the relationships in the first place? Also, it can be scary and intimidating to be vulnerable with another person, and this fear of intimacy can lead to not seeking out support in moments of stress or distress. When opening up to people even slightly, you can feel very vulnerable and scared if the person doesn't give you the kind of attention you need to feel safe.

When friends or family are in distress, you are less likely to support them because your attachment behaviors can be inconsistent, which may cause you to want to distance yourself from them physically or emotionally.[14,15]

Extending empathy toward others also likely reminds you of when parents did not help you when you were in pain or distress—and out of self-protection, you may seem less empathetic than the average person. You may not know how to effectively comfort another person in their time of need (because you never received such comfort), and it may appear that you don't care, but you simply don't know how to react or what to say to them to ease their discomfort.[16]

One of the things that might get in the way of connecting with others is a tendency toward black-and-white thinking—thinking in extremes with no nuance: everything is either all good or all bad; you consider another person to be either a genius or a fool. As a result, you have a tendency toward becoming a polarizing provocateur in a community or being very judgmental of others. The all-or-nothing perception that comes with black-and-white thinking can lead to someone being your best friend and savior one minute and your enemy the next. Sometimes the smallest perceived slights can set off the evaluation of this person to flip from the best to the worst. This behavior is essentially a coping mechanism for protecting yourself in case that person ends up being truly unreliable and not a source of genuine support—you've written them off before they can reject you. Conversely, there's a part of you that is hoping for the best in people, to prove yourself wrong and to give you another outlook on life, which may result in you flipping your perception of a person from negative to positive even at a minor hopeful sign that they could be someone worthy of your time. These wild swings can be emotionally exhausting for you—and confusing and frustrating for your loved one.

If someone becomes a parent without having worked through their own attachment trauma, they tend to pass on their disorganized attachment style to their children. They can be emotionally unaccepting of their children's stresses, ignore their needs (partially because they can't identify them clearly or are at a loss for how to help), or act confused when their children are upset, leading their own children to have difficulty forming consistent ways to manage their emotional distress. (Remember that cycle of intergenerational trauma we talked about on page 237?) In general, people who have unhealed disorganized attachment tend to find parenting more stressful, less rewarding, and less meaningful than others.[17] They also feel less emotionally attached to their children.[18]

Disorganized Attachment at Work

For the disorganized attached, work can be challenging, particularly in relationships with colleagues. Remember, the function of disorganized attachment behaviors is to protect you from rejection and pain, and although they want to connect, hypersensitivity to any signs of perceived rejection often creates a self-fulfilling prophecy. The Surveillance Specialists decide they aren't considered part of the team, or that their boss doesn't value their work, or that people probably don't believe in their ability in the first place, and then set about (often unconsciously) self-sabotaging their employment situation.

Surveillance Specialists may have a hard time relying on others at work and subsequently prefer to work independently. At the same time, they feel isolated and left out from connecting with co-workers as well as feeling unfairly burdened by the amount of work they have taken on. They may easily abandon work relationships to avoid further pain and potential rejection of any kind. Their interactions with colleagues can be somewhat inconsistent, at times intently seeking validation for their work (and worth) and at others giving a cold shoulder and maintaining distance from others.

They can see their position on the job as being precarious and are always on the lookout for threats and danger to their continued employment and whatever status they receive from their job. They are constantly waiting for the other shoe to drop and sometimes see threats where they don't exist. The boss's closed door means that she is talking about you, and you are about to get fired. The colleague who doesn't immediately respond to your email is angling to take your job. These fears may be overwhelming and debilitating—so much so that you develop a new fear about the work piling up that you were worrying about completing in the first place.

Disorganized Attachment in Goal Pursuits

Surveillance Specialists tend to rely on something called escapist coping, which comes from a need to avoid unpleasant feelings and to evade the problems of the real world by looking for security and peace in a fantasy world. You may numb your feelings (using alcohol and substances, emotional eating, and physical self-harm such as cutting), distract from real-world responsibilities (by playing video games, procrastinating, or doing activities that take you away from productivity), or retreat to a fantasyland in your mind (by imagining a scenario where your desires come to fruition with little or no effort) rather than taking active steps to solve the problem. Along with relying on escapism and fantasy to cope can come disillusionment when things don't work out the way you fantasized in your head.

Long-term goals—both setting them and achieving them—can be a challenge for the disorganized attached. They are plagued by feelings of emptiness that fuel despair about the future in and of itself, let alone any positive future achievements. A lack of self-concept formation, and not truly knowing who they are, can interfere with deciding how to pursue who they want to be in the future. At work and when trying to reach other goals, they can engage in self-sabotage, destroying their accomplishments and any good fortune that comes their way, largely because internally they're not sure if they deserve it. In fact, those with disorganized attachment have a hard time conceptualizing the future at all, so long-term goals are difficult to perceive and set.

This lack of hope about the future is exemplified by my client Angie. Angie had tried to set goals in the past about her health—losing weight, eating better, exercising more—but was never able to reach any of her intended goals and decided it wasn't worth trying. Why should she care about herself when no one else did? Even when she had a health scare, she couldn't bring herself to take action. Instead of being empowered to make positive changes, she believed that she didn't deserve to recover and was doomed to die early. She had nightmares about dying and found herself fantasizing about her death, imagining that she would not live for another year and that hardly anyone would attend her funeral.

Not reaching goals in the past combined with Angie's chronically low self-esteem caused her to shut down and give up. She didn't have confidence in a more positive future—or any kind of future at all. That lack of faith in the future is common among people with disorganized attachment. When faced with anything that involves looking forward or planning for the future, Surveillance Specialists tend to give up before they start because they have learned from past experiences that it's not worth the bother. It won't work out anyway.

THE *POSITIVE* SIDE OF DISORGANIZED ATTACHMENT

I know that so far it sounds like a rough road for people who are Surveillance Specialists, but there are also several important strengths associated with this attachment style. For one thing, when they attach to people, they have the capacity for deep loyalty. They don't give up easily on a loved one. When they become aware of their own hot-and-cold behavior, they sometimes try very hard to shield people they care about from it. They tend to worry about everyone else around them and are hypervigilant about anything that feels wrong. They may feel very intensely and have more highs and lows than the average person, and at times are able to communicate this through productive and awe-inspiring undertakings such as creative pursuits. When they feel safe, they can be very empathetic toward others as they are sensitive to human emotions. In fact, many Surveillance Specialists have a soft spot for people who have been mistreated and abused and will be more vulnerable with (and protective of) these individuals.

On an individual level, they don't trust easily, so they are not likely to get duped or taken advantage of. To others they may appear to be daring and adventurous and seem to have no fear in certain situations. They can be very artistic, either in their own innovative endeavors or they can react viscerally to art and be easily moved to tears by a wonderful performance. Their artistry can extend to rich inner lives, including a propensity for fantastical thinking and a rich imagination. They can be well-liked by children because of their imaginative interactions with them.

WHAT'S NEXT?

You've learned the origins of disorganized attachment, and discovered the consequences this attachment style has in the different areas of your life, from your self-concept to work and romantic relationships and goal pursuits. Trying to make sense of who you are and how the world works when you grew up in an environment with persistent chaos, unpredictability, and trauma is hard, to say the least. As an adult, this can lead to a deep-seated fear of other attachment figures, and it's no wonder that you might sometimes feel or do things that are highly contradictory and try on different coping strategies for size to get some semblance of safety. But these conflicting coping strategies can lead to more struggles in forming stable relationships and cause confusion and turmoil in your understanding of self and your vision for your life.

In my experience, individuals who have disorganized attachment tend to express their attachment wounds through four major self-statements, which are representations of their internal working models. Not everyone expresses these wounds in the same way, so some of the self-statements may speak to you more than others. Or you may find that all four self-statements seem familiar to you. Whatever the case, I will teach you a variety of evidence-supported exercises that will help you overcome the negative consequences created by disorganized attachment, and teach your inner child that you can heal from trauma, learn to self-regulate, and achieve consistency and healthy boundaries in your everyday life.

CHAPTER 10

Healing the Disorganized
Attachment Style

In the previous chapter, you gained a deeper understanding of how you've developed your disorganized attachment style and learned how it impacts your life in the present. Now you're ready to start getting in touch with your inner child and begin to build a new, secure attachment with yourself.

As discussed, the road to healing disorganized attachment is long and has unique challenges because of the unresolved trauma you may carry with you. Even so, as you learn to recognize the characteristics of disorganized attachment, as well as when or how these behaviors can be triggered, you'll encounter new solutions for these attitudes and behaviors.

The characteristics you developed to cope with challenging childhood experiences can be seen in your working models, which show up as self-statements that reflect how you think about yourself and the way you go about life. Becoming familiar with these self-statements is an important first step for being able to make changes.

As adults we tend to assume our working models are inherently true and valid, but they are more likely to be stories that we learned in childhood, stories that our inner child carries for us today.

For people with disorganized attachment, those self-statements typically sound like:

1. "I hate you, don't leave me."
2. "I deserve to suffer."
3. "I can't control my emotions."
4. "My life is in constant chaos."

There is no judgment about any of these working models or how you embody them as you start your journey. These are the natural outcomes of how you needed to seek love and belonging, and how you tried to meet your needs as a child. That said, these are the stories that I see keeping my clients stuck, but when they can be turned around, they hold the most potential for your healing.

In the pages ahead, I'll give you a set of exercises tailored to each self-statement that are designed to help you overcome the negative impact your upbringing had on your inner child as well as your self-concept and reframe the assumptions you have made about yourself, your relationships, and your ability to achieve goals. A discovery exercise will invite you to dig deep, and daily workouts will provide you with an activity you can engage in as often as you wish to strengthen your coping skills. It's ideal if you work through the exercises in order, but if something seems overwhelming or if you're short on time, you can go to the next exercise and at a later date circle back to anything left undone. You'll want to have your journal on hand to make note of your responses to the exercises and to allow you to keep an eye on your progress.

Also, as I mentioned in the previous chapter, you may wish to seek professional support as you work through these exercises. If anything feels too daunting to complete on your own, visit with a therapist or another trusted mental health professional with expertise in attachment trauma to further your self-development work. It's okay to ask for help.

HEALING THE DISORGANIZED ATTACHMENT STYLE

Impact Test

As you read through these self-statements, you may find that all of them apply to you to some extent. Or you may struggle with knowing whether a self-statement really impacts you or not. You might be curious about which working model to focus on healing first. By applying my impact test to each of these working models, you can determine whether they are working against you and which corresponding exercises you should prioritize.

The impact test is simple. As you read through these self-statements and their descriptions and examples, ask yourself these four questions, and if your answer is yes to at least one of them, it's likely that this self-statement is something you need to address by working through my exercises. As a bonus activity, you can reflect on them more deeply and jot down the answers to the italicized questions in your journal:

- **Impact on Life Domains**: Does this working model negatively affect my life in major domains (work, romantic relationships, family relationships, friendships, goal attainment)? *If yes, write down 1–2 concrete examples for each of these areas.*
- **Impact on Goal Attainment**: Does this working model usually move me away from my goals? *If so, how?*
- **Impact on Values-Based Living**: Is this working model inconsistent with my values? *What are some of my top values, and how does this working model contribute to me moving away from my values or not living my top values the way I want?*
- **Impact on Self-Concept**: Is this working model something that shakes or damages my self-concept? *If so, how?*

"I HATE YOU, DON'T LEAVE ME"

People who have disorganized attachment often show extreme push-pull behaviors. Their relationship and interactions with their caregivers caused them to simultaneously desire closeness and be fearful of it. As a result, they have deep-seated trust issues and don't believe that others will be there for them when they really need them.

Frankly, these intense push-pull behaviors can be exhausting for Surveillance Specialists. Vacillating constantly between connection and disconnection erodes your ability to feel stability and peace in your life and can diminish your opportunities to authentically connect with others. This behavior can be very confusing for loved ones because Surveillance Specialists can seem to want to reject and connect in the same breath.

Bill thinks that people who desire to be close to him for either platonic or romantic reasons must have some kind of ulterior motive—something they need from him—rather than just genuinely wanting to befriend him or spend time with him. This perpetual fight-or-flight response toward others makes it very hard for him to maintain closeness in his relationships. At the same time, his fluctuating self-esteem makes it hard to believe that others might be interested in him or that he is worthy of their attention and care, and he has persistent negative beliefs about ending up alone and never finding people who will love him through thick and thin. This results in a self-fulfilling prophecy where he pushes people away but then sees their distance from him (which he created) as proof that no one will truly care for him, which further cements his belief that he isn't worthy of meaningful connection.

The push-pull dynamic really boils down to two needs: on one hand, a powerful desire to avoid the pain of abandonment and, on the other, a strong motivation to connect with others and have negative expectations about people proved wrong. Because you fear that people will not be constant or caring, you may set up tests over and over again to see if others (romantic partners, friends, or colleagues) will pass and prove you wrong. Unfortunately, the distress that often comes with waiting for them to respond is so great that you may disengage before they can connect with you, which then reinforces your preexisting idea that others won't love and care for you the way you want or need.

If they *do* pass, you will come up with an excuse to explain away their loving actions and dismiss them, which also reinforces your preexisting negative beliefs about yourself and whether or not others can care for you. If the person you are testing responds to you negatively, shows frustration, or is upset by your push-pull behaviors, you may then engage in over-apologizing and trying to ingratiate yourself with them to win their approval and affection once more, setting the stage for a seemingly never-ending cycle of being fearful and worrying about connecting, sometimes disengaging, and then strongly pursuing a connection.

This dance of wanting closeness but not being able to tolerate it also happens when those with the disorganized attachment style open up to someone. Much as they crave it, vulnerability with another person feels so scary that they will back away or act out to create distance. That might be more passive, like ghosting, or they may actively push away from someone, especially when they fear that the person they're becoming closer to will reject, hurt, or ridicule them. Even if these fears are unfounded and the person has shown no signs of untrustworthiness, their earlier ideas about attachment figures might trigger them to push someone they care about away with such forcefulness (e.g., insulting the person's character or doing something like cheating or lying about something major) that they end up creating the very scenario they feared would happen.

Antidote to "I Hate You, Don't Leave Me"

Although this behavior pattern may sound difficult to overcome, you can learn how to promote a sense of internalized security and calm. Try to give yourself grace and compassion (for tips, see page 325) in the process. It will take some time, but with dedicated work, you can break this pattern. The first step in the healing process is to create a coherent narrative of your particularly stressful experiences.

DISCOVERY EXERCISE: CREATING
A COHERENT NARRATIVE

Remember when you did the timeline exercise in chapter 3? You might have felt that was an especially challenging assignment, and there's a perfectly good reason for that. Surveillance Specialists tend to struggle with a coherent picture of their life's story.

When people try to recall details from stressful or traumatic times, or if they are currently experiencing stress, they often say that it is difficult to talk about what's happened in a logical and meaningful way. They might say that they're too overwhelmed or feel "all over the place." My patients who have been diagnosed with PTSD often tell me that parts of their memory about the trauma they experienced are missing or can't be accessed. They know something terrible happened, and can recall some details with excruciating clarity but can't quite put the whole story together. They describe periods of dissociation or feeling disjointed or lost when trying to recall their childhood experiences. This can lead to extreme emotional dysregulation, resulting in push-pull behaviors, because they don't know quite what they need in the moment and are grasping at straws to make something work to calm their nervous system. It's a bit like the fight-or-flight response except that instead of fighting, the Surveillance Specialists desperately want to connect but they don't trust the connection, so they flee and get caught in a cycle of pushing people away and at the same time wishing they could pull them closer.

If a majority of your stressful or traumatic experiences happened in early childhood—as is often the case for Surveillance Specialists—it can be especially hard to form coherent narratives, because these events occurred at a time when you were beginning to learn about yourself and the world around you, and you lacked the ability to describe what happened in sequence. Your language skills were just emerging, so you may not have had the vocabulary to recount your story in a logical, meaningful way.

For example, you may feel alone, scared, or sad, but do not know how to name what you are feeling, tell others about it, or ask for what you need. You may blame yourself for the negative events happening around you, because you haven't yet mastered the idea that other people have their own thoughts and motivations that have nothing to do with you, but rather, are based on their own past experiences, wounds, and ineffective coping strategies. As a child, you may have felt that whatever happened was your fault. (Let me assure you, it was not.)

In my work with clients, I have found that forming a coherent narrative helps them to fully process the meaning of stressful events (including their thoughts, feelings, and behaviors related to those events) and puts them in the driver's seat. Creating a coherent narrative helps people to understand the root causes of their push-pull behaviors and mood swings by reflecting on life experiences, identifying patterns, and making sense of their coping strategies as well as why they react in the ways they do. Through developing and reviewing their narratives, they can identify specific triggers that lead to their push-pull behaviors and learn to manage these triggers and respond to them more effectively. By understanding your story, you will be able to connect your past experiences to current emotional responses, so that you can develop healthier ways to manage intense feelings and mood swings. Each time you explore one of your memories, you'll develop more trust in your ability to make sense of what's happened to you and to transform challenging experiences into opportunities for self-discovery and personal growth.

As a reminder, if the trauma you have experienced feels overwhelming to process on your own, please connect with a mental health professional to do some of this work. They will also be able to help extend your learning by introducing you to other trauma-focused therapeutic techniques. As a stopgap, you can also use the grounding exercises in appendix A on page 320 to come back to feelings of safety.

⌒

Grab your journal, a pen, and a timer and get into a comfortable position. You can cozy up in your favorite chair, snuggle up with a weighted blanket, sit cross-legged on a couch or floor, or lie down in your bed—whatever brings you to a place of relaxation and ease.

What happened? Take a few deep breaths and close your eyes. Recall an event or period in your life that has caused you difficulty every time you try to bring it to mind. Perhaps this event is tied to your continued struggles in some area of your life (e.g., romantic relationships, work, friendships, family relationships). Maybe each time you think about this event, you find it hard to trust people who are currently in your life, even with seemingly the smallest tasks (like having them run a routine errand for you when you're busy).

Once you have something in mind, open your eyes and set your timer for twenty minutes. Begin writing an account of the event from start to finish in the third person (referring to yourself by your name or preferred pronoun). Write about the event in the past tense; this is essential to help you notice that this is something that happened in the past (and is not happening to you right now). The idea is to tell this story from a narrator's point of view—like you are watching the plot of a movie unfold. Without including any emotional interpretations (yet), write down, one step at a time, what you remember to have happened. Describe your thoughts, feelings, and behaviors at the time. Invoke sense memories or bodily experiences whenever they are applicable. For example, "Jake remembers the air smelling crisp and fresh, the way it smells after the rain." Or, "Carly remembers her hands feeling cold and clammy, even though it was a hot day."

This is an accounting of what happened to you, so it's okay to write what you believe happened and what feels true to you even if it is not logical or you aren't 100 percent sure how things transpired. Don't forget that some of our early memories are not clear and well-defined.

Leave some space between the lines for the second part of this exercise (if you are using lined paper, write on every other line). Don't judge yourself about how quickly you write. If something doesn't come to you immediately, take a few deep breaths and allow the pauses in your writing to happen. When you think about a stressful time, it is natural that it might take a little effort and patience. Be gentle with yourself.

Why did it happen that way? Once you are comfortable with the narrative you've generated and feel that it is a relatively complete accounting (or once your timer goes off), read what you wrote, and as you do so, ask yourself "Why?" about incidents or other people's behaviors throughout your narrative. For example, if you wrote, "Taylor's mother was very angry and made her feel like she wasn't important to her." Ask yourself, "Why might she have acted this way?" Jot down a few words that capture your responses in the spaces you have left in what you wrote. For example, Taylor might realize that her mother probably acted this way because she was angry at herself and angry at what was happening in her life—because her marriage was breaking down and she probably didn't know what to do. So, on the line (or space) below what she wrote about her mom, Taylor would write: "She was angry at self, situation, marital issues."

What are the connections between past and present? After asking yourself why throughout the narrative and inserting additional information about your interpretations of why things happened the way they did, the final part of this exercise is to write about how the past influences your present behaviors and experiences. This part of the exercise will help you make connections to how the stressful event or time period in the past may influence how you act in certain situations or with specific people in your life in the present. For example:

As she grew up, Taylor believed that she wouldn't be important to others, and this anger and frustration caused her to lash out toward people who tried to show kindness to her. She would sometimes go out of her way to make these people feel unimportant because it somehow made her feel safer to keep her distance from people and to avoid being let down. But she was hurting these people, just as her mom had hurt her when she was a child.

As you write about what has happened in the present, you may notice some things that you don't like about the way you react or respond, or you may notice strong negative feelings such as guilt, sadness, anger, or shame. When negative self-talk arises, try to adopt an attitude of compassion. We all have baggage we're contending with, and no one's response to every situation—particularly a stressful one—is perfect. Especially without a coherent narrative about what you were experiencing or why you might have been feeling the way you were, you can't be expected to respond to triggers or stressors in an optimal way.

Reread your story. Make a commitment to read this narrative once a week for a month. Put a reminder in your calendar or on your phone to make sure you come back to this. Each time you reread it, add anything else you feel is important to your story. It is quite likely that more details will arise as your narrative grows more linear and more coherent with each read—this is a sign of progress and healing. Continue to add to and edit your narrative as new thoughts or memories surface. This will help you continue to make sense of your story and add clarity to your understanding of what happened and how it has impacted you.

Rewrite your story. At the end of the month (four rereads), change the third-person references to first person so that you can begin to integrate the experience into your life story. You can start by simply crossing out the third-person references and inserting the words "I" or "me," but sometimes people find it very powerful to completely rewrite the narrative from the perspective of owning this story as their own and seeing what details might change or how they might capture certain events and situations a bit differently. Either approach is a great way to move forward in this process, so do what feels most natural and helpful to you.

At this point, you may start to feel more comfortable with the process of recalling this specific part of your personal story as well as with the process of doing this exercise. This coherent narrative might bring new meaning, some additional insight, and differing perspectives to help you understand what you've experienced. Remember, this process of developing a coherent narrative was initiated by you, and the narrative of this stressful and even traumatic event or events in your life was developed, created, and reviewed by you. Each time you decide to think about what happened, you are doing so on your own terms. The trauma is a part of your personal history, but it does not have to be who you are.

Return to this narrative whenever you feel it's helpful to revisit this part of your past to make sense of your behavior patterns. Every month, challenge yourself to repeat this exercise with a new difficult memory. Over time, this discovery practice will help you to achieve a feeling of inner stability and strength that will lessen the likelihood of you defaulting to push-pull behaviors in your important relationships.

Sharing Your Narrative

Some people find it helpful to share their narrative with supportive people in their lives, like a trusted friend or their therapist. Talking over your narrative with another person can help to support discerning meaning and making sense of your story. This is especially helpful because many people who have been through trauma feel incredibly isolated. When you feel connected with someone else, it may allow you to process your trauma in a safe place where you can rely on supportive others to help you deal with emotions the experience brings up (such as aiding you with grounding if you feel like recalling certain aspects of your story is too stressful).

DAILY WORKOUT: IDENTIFYING AND MEETING YOUR EMOTIONAL NEEDS

We all have emotional needs. Needs that are fundamental, necessary, and nonnegotiable are different from wants (things you desire but that may not be necessary). When your needs are not routinely met, this can impact the development of your self-concept and cause persistent emotional dysregulation. This internal chaotic feeling and a loss of control over how to manage it is at the root of those push-pull tendencies.

You've likely heard of Maslow's hierarchy of needs, but you may not be familiar with Dr. Scott Barry Kaufman's work. What I like about his model is that it is a reframe to envision one's life journey as a sailboat in a vast ocean that represents life's opportunities for "meaning and discovery but also danger and uncertainty." In choppy surf, a

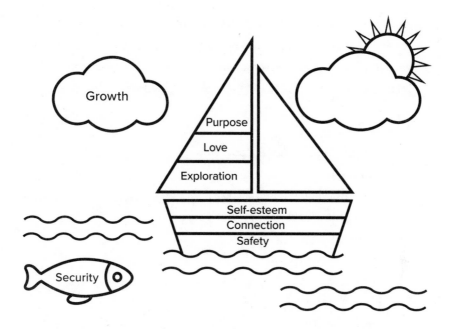

sailboat is a helpful metaphor because the key to satisfaction and ful-fillment is not which level you reach, but the "harmonious integration you have within yourself, and how that interacts with the world."[1]

Dr. Kaufman compares the boat to security needs such as safety, human connection, and self-esteem because "with holes in your boat, you can't go anywhere."[2] Once we are in a place of stability (our boat is sound), we can then focus on self-actualization and developing our potential, the growth needs that are represented by the sail.

Your daily workout is to identify your most pertinent need each day, define what that need looks like for you, and name one spe-cific way of getting that need met—partially or fully—on that day. To extend Dr. Kaufman's metaphor, there will be days when you find yourself focused more on stabilizing your boat—the security needs. On other days, you will find that there is space to focus on your sail—which allows for vulnerability, creativity, exploration, and self-actualization. Only you can decide your true needs on a given day.

To help get you started, take a look at this list of security and growth needs. I've highlighted here many of our essential human needs, as well as some of the most common needs I hear from my patients. This is by no means an exhaustive list, so feel free to add your own![3]

Security Needs
- Physical safety (shelter, food, water)
- Being able to express yourself honestly
- Feeling accepted for who you are
- Feeling confident
- Feeling in control
- Feeling needed by someone
- Feeling protected
- Feeling reassured
- Feeling worthy
- Being appreciated/valued by someone
- Feeling heard and understood
- Feeling emotionally supported
- Being respected
- Accomplishing something
- Feeling capable and competent
- Connecting with a person
- Connecting with a community

Growth Needs
- Feeling admired by someone
- Being desired by someone
- Taking on something challenging
- Being creative
- Doing something that helps you to grow (emotionally, intellectually)

- Doing something interesting
- Doing something independently
- Exploring something new
- Contributing to a greater good
- Feeling purposeful
- Doing something meaningful
- Feeling proud
- Feeling valued
- Feeling optimistic
- Feeling fulfilled
- Feeling empowered
- Feeling helpful to someone else
- Being knowledgeable
- Being recognized
- Feeling successful
- Feeling important

Each morning, start a short journal entry with the date followed by the words "Core Need Today." Reflect on which need is most crucial to you today, and write it down in your journal. Write what this need means to you, for example, "I need to feel accomplished today because I've been struggling to be productive recently." Then, write down one way you can meet this need today (either by yourself or with the help of someone else). For example, "I will spend an hour working on my presentation for work next week," or "I will ask my friend Sara to help me with a home improvement project for an hour today."

Over time, you'll start to notice that the more you can state your most important needs, define what they mean to you, and work to meet them (either on your own or with someone's help), the less inclined you'll feel toward push-pull behaviors, because your needs are being addressed consistently and you are spending less time in emotional dysregulation. You'll also feel better equipped to manage intense emotions even when they do come up (and they'll likely come up a lot less because your needs are being regularly expressed and tended to). In essence, you are giving yourself and others the opportunity to provide you with what you desire, which can then influence your beliefs about your own capabilities and the intentions of others toward you. You'll feel less compelled to push people away because you will begin to trust certain relationships.

Better still, by asking for help clearly and directly rather than setting up tests for others to prove their support, you are setting the stage for healthier interactions based on assertive communication rather than approaching each interpersonal relationship as a covert operation where your goal is to sniff out those who wish to do you harm (rather than finding out who might actually be on your side).

Doing this exercise routinely will help you develop more balanced, realistic thoughts about yourself and the people around you, and reduce the push-pull dynamic between your fears of abandonment and your need for deeper connection. You will find that your thoughts about yourself and other people won't be quite as extreme, and you'll discover that middle ground of healthy self-protection along with a cautious but genuine openness toward positive relationships.

Asking for Help

If you are not accustomed to asking for help, it may be difficult to ask someone directly for their assistance in meeting your need. Here's a simple formula to help you to communicate clearly with gratitude.

State the concrete and observable action you'd like the person to do to help meet your need. For example, "I'd like you to spend a few minutes after dinner today with me so that we can go over our weekend plans."

Tell them what their action will mean to you. For example, "It will help me to feel calmer and more organized, because right now I feel overwhelmed with all that I have to do this week."

Express gratitude. For example, "Thanks so much for considering this."

If the person says no to your request, it may be challenging to process this as thoughts such as "this is why I never ask for help!" might come into your mind. Remember that their "no" does not mean they don't care about you or don't want to help—people often have their own reasons for politely declining (and this is a good reminder for you that you also don't have to say yes to every request that comes your way). Have compassion for yourself if these thoughts come up (see page 325 for self-compassion strategies), and then take the following two courses of action: 1) ask another person who might be able to fulfill part or all of your request, and 2) make a mental note to try asking this person for something else again in the future (rather than completely shying away from asking them for help because they said no once).

"I DESERVE TO SUFFER"

Surveillance Specialists tend to experience intense loneliness and repeated feelings of shame, which are highly distressing feelings that lead to emotional suffering. Although suffering almost always refers to some form of mental anguish, emotional and/or physical pain, or threat of self-concept destruction (termed "intactness of person" by physician E. J. Cassell),[4] suffering is an incredibly complex human experience that is deeply personal and can manifest differently in different people. Because these feelings of loneliness and suffering are a constant for Surveillance Specialists, they are apt to believe that they deserve what's happening to them, especially because they already possess low self-worth and may doubt they deserve better. This persistent suffering also erodes the already fragile self-concept that Surveillance Specialists possess.

Loneliness has profound emotional, psychological, and physical impacts on individuals, which increases the severity of suffering over time. You may have heard that chronic loneliness is harmful to our health. After the onset of the pandemic in 2020, loneliness has become an even bigger problem. Thirty-six percent of Americans felt "serious loneliness," according to Harvard research.[5] Recent studies have shown that social isolation increases a person's risk of premature death from various causes, especially as we grow older. Loneliness is associated with a 50 percent increase in dementia, a 29 percent increased risk of heart disease, and a 32 percent increased risk of stroke.[6] It is also associated with higher rates of depression and anxiety. People who reported the highest loneliness scores were fourteen times more likely to have major depressive disorder and eleven times more likely to have generalized anxiety disorder. This association was especially pronounced in men and younger people.[7]

When Surveillance Specialists were young, they thought that their parents' erratic behaviors were their fault. When you can't figure out what behaviors will (or will not) keep your caregivers happy, the story you come to believe becomes less that you *did* something wrong but that *you* are wrong. Carrying that sense of wrongness eventually grows into pervasive feelings of shame which, when unaddressed, are held on to by our inner child all the way into adulthood.

Shame is the uncomfortable feeling in the pit of the stomach that happens when it seems there is no safety from the judgment of others. It is a disdain for who you are fundamentally and is not based on your actions. When you experience constant shame, you come to believe that there is something wrong with you; you can feel inadequate, unworthy, in pain, distrustful, and disconnected. Shame tends to result in self-sabotaging, self-destructive behaviors when these irrational frustrations are turned inward, and the person can feel anger or vengeance toward themself. You may find that you punish yourself, believing you don't deserve better.

Underneath the Surveillance Specialist's painful feelings of shame and loneliness is a struggle to believe that they are worthy beings—people deserving of love, compassion, and support. They may find it especially difficult to feel self-love and compassion, and that makes it difficult to accept love and acceptance from others or believe in others' genuine desire to care for them in this way. Because they struggle with self-compassion, they distrust others who want to connect with them, because deep down, they don't believe they deserve good things. If others react to them neutrally or they cannot easily read their social cues, Surveillance Specialists might interpret these behaviors as threatening due to their lack of trust in the basic goodness of human beings.

What's more challenging is that a lack of trust in others perpetuates loneliness and a lack of connectedness. A study from 2017 suggested that lonely people may focus more attention on potentially threatening social stimuli (for example, entering a room where you don't know anyone and being hypervigilant to any signs of disapproval, like a side-eye glance that might suggest a dislike for you), expect social rejection, and evaluate themselves and others more negatively.[8]

A recent study conducted at Bonn University in Germany examined the connection between trust and loneliness.[9] During the study, brain function was monitored via imaging while people responded to social interactions. Results showed that there may be actual brain differences between those who reported high levels of loneliness and those who did not. Those with a high level of loneliness were found to have reduced oxytocin (the feel-good hormone) response during positive social interactions (e.g., a pleasant conversation with a stranger) and experience less activity in social and emotional brain regions during a trust task.

This difficulty with trust and connection might lead people who have disorganized attachment to feel lonelier after certain kinds of social interactions. They may enthusiastically approach and then rapidly retreat from an individual or social situation, and when called out on their hot-and-cold behavior, they will feel shame and isolate themselves from others, further increasing their loneliness. This makes complete sense when we think about what they've been through with important caregivers during a time in their lives when they had to rely on others to survive. If this is your style, remember: You have worth, just as you are, and you deserve the goodness of life just like everyone else.

Antidote to "I Deserve to Suffer"

These next exercises will help you to appreciate and believe in your self-worth, as well as to reduce suffering caused by persistent loneliness and shame. By connecting with people who are likely to provide positive experiences and by giving your inner child the validation that they need to know their inherent worth by just *being*, you'll build your sense of self and create avenues for aligning with a greater purpose and meaning for your life.

DISCOVERY EXERCISE: CONNECTING WITH YOUR INNER CIRCLE

Because humans are, by definition, social beings, we all need an inner circle to support us. No matter how independent you are, no one in the world does anything major by themselves with no help, no support, and no interaction with others. We all need to feel like we belong to something bigger than ourselves to feel both physically and psychologically safe. And having that deeper, meaningful connection is a sure way to reduce loneliness and emotional suffering.

This exercise will help you identify and connect with people in your inner circle to reduce feelings of loneliness. It is also very helpful for letting go of shame, as people in your inner circle are the ones who are most likely to hold similar values as you and to accept you as you are.

There are many definitions for what constitutes an inner circle, but to me, it represents a small group of people who:

- accept you as you are without judgment or qualification
- are honest with you and hold you accountable (even if it doesn't feel comfortable sometimes)
- motivate you to be a better person
- cheer you on as you reach for your goals
- aren't competitive with you and are happy for you when you succeed
- offer different perspectives, opportunities, and life experiences
- are those with whom you are most able to let down your guard to share your dreams, vulnerabilities, and strengths
- share similar or overlapping core values with you
- offer a natural give-and-take dynamic to your relationship (rather than a one-sided relationship in which one person is doing all the hard work)

Do you have anyone in your life that meets all (or most) of these criteria? If so, on a new page in your journal, write "Inner Circle" at the top and then write their names in a list on this page. Bookmark this page, because you will come back to review who is in your inner circle and to edit and add to this list as needed.

Apart from this exercise, this is a good list of people to reach out to for support when you are having a particularly difficult time. You may find that certain people in your inner circle are most helpful with certain types of problems (for example, relationship-based or career-based), and you may find that you value different types of intimacy and closeness with different individuals on this list (check out the Five Types of Intimacy on page 97 and the Nourishing Intimacy exercise on page 99). Therefore, to grow and deepen your relationship with each person, you may wish to set aside time to participate in different activities with each of them.

Someone who has disorganized attachment might find it hard to identify an inner circle whom they feel they can trust and count on all the time. Your childhood experiences may have led you to have some trouble identifying or creating mutually beneficial relationships. You may have some difficulty setting healthy boundaries because that wasn't modeled for you when you were little. Or you may find yourself engaging with people who cause you a lot of stress or possibly trigger your trauma response. If you find individuals who deserve your time and attention, you may have difficulty connecting with them without engaging in the push-pull dynamic, or you may struggle with believing that they will truly be there for you, especially when things get messy or difficult.

Your inner circle may only consist of one or two people to start. It's also possible that the only people in your inner circle at this moment are your mental health providers. That's perfectly okay, and there is absolutely no judgment on how many people should be in your inner circle or how you know or interact with them. The quality of those connections is far more important than the quantity. In fact, I believe most people have five or fewer people that they count as part of their inner circle. Maintaining high-quality, deep connections takes time, effort, and sacrifice, and most people can't dedicate this type of attention to more than a handful of people at a time.

As you learn more about what represent healthy sources of connection, you'll be able to recognize and know whom to count among your most trusted. Also, over time, you may decide that more people are making their way into your inner circle. If you want to expand your inner circle, I'd suggest you do some or all the activities below with people who you think might be trustworthy and potential inner circle additions to try a deeper level of connection with them. After a few weeks, you can go back to the definition above (on page 279) to assess whether they seem to fit the criteria of others who are in your inner circle.

Each day for one week, I'd like you to check in with at least one person in your inner circle and do something to strengthen or deepen your relationship. You can check in with a friend for an eight-minute phone call,[10] walk, coffee date, or virtual meeting. This connection can be used to touch base on the goals you're working on and give mutual support. In a longer conversation, you can help each other problem-solve and brainstorm solutions. The connection doesn't have to be goal oriented; you can use your time with someone to reminisce about a shared experience that you enjoyed and to plan for future adventures. You can also join a person in your inner circle to explore a new hobby, attend a lecture, or view an exhibit at a museum.

Make these actions intentional, and do them with the goal of fostering healthy, meaningful connections that will help you feel safe and cared for, and therefore create space for you to explore new experiences, develop insight, and be your true self.

DAILY WORKOUT:
SELF-WORTH VISUALIZATION

In order to overcome the belief that you deserve to suffer, we need to help you get in touch with your inherent worthiness, one that does not need to be earned but is your birthright. Get comfortable wherever you are (sitting, lying down, indoors, or outside) and close your eyes. Take a few deep, cleansing breaths and release your stress and fears. With each inhale, breathe in calm and peace, and with each exhale, release your stress and fears by saying to yourself, "I release and let go of my fears and stress that are holding me back from a meaningful, fulfilled life."

It's not necessary to clear your mind, but allow yourself to become curious and act as an observer of your thoughts. Whatever thoughts pop up, simply acknowledge them by saying to yourself, "I see you," but don't engage or wrestle with any particular one. It may help to envision each thought that arises like a cloud in the sky and then let each one gently drift outside your field of vision.

Place both of your hands over your heart and continue to take deep breaths. Feel the warmth of your hands over this area, as this is the location that symbolizes where you experience feelings of love for others as well as for yourself.

Now imagine a bright and warm white light enveloping your entire body, flowing through all the different parts of your body from your head to your toes, giving you vitality, warmth, strength, and love. Imagine the source of this white light as something bigger than yourself, whether that's God, the universe, the world, or your community. Imagine that this source that is bigger than yourself cherishes who you are, just as you are. You don't have to do anything to deserve love. You don't have to act in any specific way to have worth. You, like all human beings in the world, have inherent worth. Nothing and no one can take that worth away from you.

Now turn your attention to your breath. With each inhale, press both of your hands gently over your heart to receive self-love and self-compassion and say, "I am worthy." With each exhale, open your hands outward, extending them from your chest into the space in front of you, releasing anything that causes you to feel self-loathing or self-rejection, and say, "I accept myself." Repeat this at least ten times, or more if you'd like. (One inhale and one exhale counts as one time.)

Now imagine yourself being surrounded by the loving, supportive people in your life. These people are not necessarily those who are perfect at showing you love and compassion (and who really is?), but they seem to have the right intentions and want to be there for you. It's okay if it's a small number of people—one or two people who you feel have a desire to support and love you is plenty. It's also okay to include people whom you've lost, like a loving grandparent or a deceased friend.

The people you envision may be from your family of origin, your current family, your friends, co-workers, or a mental or physical health professional. Imagine them laying their hands on you, each of them activating another stream of bright and warm white light as they make contact with you, causing even more of the white light to flow throughout your body. Bask in this warm, loving feeling and allow yourself to believe that there are those who want to care for and heal you. Sit with this for as long as you'd like while focusing on your breathing.

Next, imagine other people in your life or in the world who might need that same healing. Now visualize the entire earth and how many people feel loneliness and shame—you are not alone in your experience. Imagine yourself giving this warm, white light to someone else who needs it. In doing this, remind yourself that we are all connected, and you are never alone.

When you're ready, take a few more deep breaths, gently open your eyes, and allow your attention to come back into the room or wherever you started.

Take a few moments to journal about your reactions to this experience, including any thoughts or feelings that came up. To conclude this journal entry, answer this question: What can I do to treat myself with compassion today? This could be something simple like "drinking more water," or "getting one extra hour of sleep," or it could be bigger, like "forgive myself for yelling at my mom yesterday—for the third time this week." If you're at a loss, start by practicing some of the techniques for self-compassion and emotion regulation found in appendix B on page 325.

I suggest that you come back to this practice often to create self-worth and self-love whenever you are feeling low in self-esteem or need some extra self-assurance. This exercise will help you let go of feelings of shame and loneliness and embrace yourself just as you are right now.

"I CAN'T CONTROL MY EMOTIONS"

Sarah has been struggling with constant emotional dysregulation for most of her life and frequently experiences intense mood swings. This emotional roller coaster leaves her feeling overwhelmed and exhausted and makes it challenging to maintain stable relationships or hold down a job. She can wake up in the morning feeling energized, happy, and excited about the day's possibilities, but by the afternoon, a minor inconvenience like a traffic jam or missed phone call can trigger overwhelming feelings of frustration, anger, and sadness. Her emotional reactions are often disproportionate or seemingly out of sync with what's happening. For example, when her supervisor gives her well-intentioned constructive feedback, Sarah interprets it as a personal attack, becomes defensive, and holds grudges against her boss for making the small suggestion for improvement. This tendency to be touchy and unpredictable has led to conflicts with colleagues and supervisors, jeopardizing her career trajectory.

In her personal relationships, Sarah struggles to maintain stable connections, because she vacillates between idealizing new friends and partners and devaluing them as soon as she perceives the slightest hint of rejection or criticism. Her instinct is to cut ties with them before they do it to her—usually unceremoniously and without warning. Sarah doesn't feel good about the way she responds to these situations, and her inner dialogue is filled with self-doubt and intense self-critique. She berates herself for her decisions and beats herself up for her mistakes, leading to further feelings of loneliness, shame, and suffering.

Like Sarah, most Surveillance Specialists have trouble regulating their emotions. Emotion regulation refers to the ability to understand your emotions and manage your emotional responses in a helpful, soothing, and/or goal-oriented way, even (and perhaps especially) in stressful situations. While all people experience a loss of control over their emotions at one time or another, people who have disorganized attachment may find that their emotions seem to spin out of control more often than for those who are securely attached. Emotional dysregulation can lead to a cascade of events that makes us feel shame and prompts us to act in ways that we regret later—those "heat of the moment" responses that we wish we could take back when cooler heads prevail.

The nervous system plays a crucial role in emotion regulation because it is responsible for processing and responding to emotional stimuli and signals in the body. Ideally, our parents teach us as children to self-regulate through physical affection and emotional presence; their nervous system quite literally soothes their infant child's. For example, research shows that parental hugging can lead to a decrease in cortisol (dubbed the stress hormone) levels in preterm infants,[11] and maternal physical affection was associated with better emotional regulation in preschool-aged children.[12]

When they were children, those with disorganized attachment didn't learn a standardized or effective response to fear or distress. Their ability to develop healthy co-regulation may have been derailed by experiencing trauma or abuse at the hands of their caregiver. Moreover, those experiences of trauma or consistent stressors constantly activate their nervous system's distress responses—fight-flight-freeze. As adults, they may respond to intense situations by acting out and picking fights with others (fight) or running away from an emotionally intense situation (flight), though that often backfires: When they go into full retreat, loved ones can feel abandoned and as if the person with disorganized attachment doesn't care about them, especially during times of duress. Sometimes they will not react at all (freeze). When asked about their non-responsiveness, they will report that when this happens, they feel empty inside or have an overwhelming sense of numbness. They may show no outward expression of how they feel while internally they're in turmoil.

Not having been taught how to engage with or manage emotions, those with disorganized attachment see emotions as scary and uncontrollable. To cope with an emotional experience, they are more likely to try to regulate their emotions through their environment, sometimes in unhealthy ways (like addictive behaviors). Many of my patients have described their first pull into addictive behaviors as motivated by trying to numb, block, or ease the emotional pain they experience. As one patient told me, "My mind is so full of these self-deprecating and depressing thoughts that the only way to get away from them at least for a brief period of time is to drink until I pass out."

Surveillance Specialists also frequently dissociate from their negative emotions to try to dampen their trauma or stress response. The problem is that, over time, it's not just negative emotions that get dampened: You begin to numb yourself to *all* emotions. Joy feels just as unnerving and unsafe as fear or sadness. The good news is that emotional regulation is a skill that we can learn at any age. Let's explore how.

Antidote to "I Can't Control My Emotions"

Although parents played a crucial role in the development of emotion regulation when you were young, it's not too late—you can teach yourself this skill even if you didn't learn it before. In fact, it's one of the most sought-after and helpful skills in psychotherapy. Being able to regulate your emotions consistently and effectively builds your confidence and self-efficacy (belief in yourself and what you can do), as well as strengthens your self-concept and belief that you can create positive change in your life. Learning to regulate your emotions and address the unmet needs of your inner child takes a lot of time and practice. Go slowly, and be gentle with yourself. The exercises in the next few pages are aimed at helping you teach your inner child new ways to view yourself and the way you interface with your social world. These are long-term changes, and as you work toward healing it's likely that you will still encounter moments of emotional dysregulation. To help you support yourself in the moment, you can find a list of quick and dirty tips to self-regulate in the Style Triggers and Timely Tips appendix on page 315. These quick tips are especially useful as they offer in-the-moment practice, and the more you work at them, the more easily you'll be able to regain control and deescalate future situations that trigger a dysregulation response.

DISCOVERY EXERCISE: CHILD MODE AND IMAGERY RESCRIPTING

After years of studying adults struggling with emotional dysregulation, psychologist Dr. Jeffrey Young proposed that our unhelpful coping responses to distressing emotions are motivated by basic needs that were not adequately met during childhood (for example, physical

THE DISORGANIZED ATTACHMENT STYLE

and emotional safety, connecting and belonging, self-esteem and validation, intimacy, and affection). He noticed that there were patterns in the ways that people tried to cope, which he called maladaptive child modes,[13] and each mode is characterized by specific dysregulated emotions. By determining what mode someone is in at a certain time in response to a certain situation, we can understand what needs are crucial. The person would then be able to learn more effective ways to cope that would enable them to meet these crucial needs.

There are nuances to the different child modes, but the three major categories[14] are:

Vulnerable Child Mode: Emotions including sadness, shame, and anguish characterize this mode. It includes subcategories such as the lonely child (where the person feels lonely, unworthy of love, and unaccepted, and is associated with sadness), abandoned/abused child (the person feels scared and alone, and feels pain and fear related to their previous experiences of abandonment and/or abuse, and is associated with anguish), and inferior child (the person feels incapable, with poor autonomy and self-sufficiency, and is associated with shame).

Angry Child Mode: Dysregulated anger is the hallmark of this mode, and subcategories include the angry child (person who feels frustrated and impatient because their needs have not been satisfied—and may therefore make pretentious, flawed, or unreasonable demands) and enraged child (person feels stronger levels of anger that may lead to anger outbursts—associated with feeling furious).

Impulsive Child Mode: When this inner child is active, the person discharges all locked emotions immediately and directly to meet needs, without being able to postpone gratification or predict the consequences of their actions. A related category is the undisciplined child (an extremely frustrated person who is unable to make efforts to fulfill routine responsibilities and consequently easily gives up).

Different modes can show up in different situations in response to specific triggers, and are often associated with specific coping strategies. The vulnerable child may retreat, isolate, and avoid. The angry child might act out toward others through an emotional outburst or verbal tirade. The impulsive child might do something that seems self-destructive and act on a whim.

Some examples of these unhelpful coping strategies can include prolonged escape strategies (such as playing video games for hours, drinking too much alcohol, or overeating to numb or nurse hurt feelings), suppression of negative feelings, denial of basic needs (telling yourself that you don't need connection or affection from others, for example), or taking out your frustrations on other people (lashing out at a friend who was only checking in to see if they can help) or even on yourself (through increasingly self-critical thoughts and depriving yourself of experiences because you don't think you deserve them—like spending time with friends or good self-care and hygiene). These coping strategies might lead to temporary relief of distressing feelings, but in the long run they cause more suffering and further emotional dysregulation, which is then likely to lead the person to feel out of control.

Rachel often gets into conflicts with others because she seems to make outrageous demands on other people's time and efforts while not giving back in kind. It's not because she is devoid of empathy or doesn't care about others. Because she felt like her needs were never met in childhood, as an adult she feels she must exaggerate her requests to make sure that people pay attention to her, and that by making bigger demands, she increases her chances of having at least some of her needs partially met. She realized that especially when she felt like people were neglecting her or not considering her, her angry child was being activated. With this insight, she was able to move forward with the following imagery rescripting exercise to get her needs met in more consistent ways that didn't put stress on her existing relationships and cause her to feel more distressed.

Review the list above and think about which child mode—vulnerable, angry, impulsive—represents you most when you feel emotionally dysregulated. Your child mode is sometimes activated through other unpleasant memories or events that remind you of the past trauma. Certain people and situations may also trigger your child mode and activate negative feelings. Make a note of which child mode you think comes up most often for you before moving on to the next step of this exercise, in which you will visualize your adult self learning the needs behind your child mode(s) and offering to hold and take care of these needs for your inner child.

Take a few deep breaths and get into a comfortable position, either sitting or lying down. Call to mind a situation when you were a child and experienced a similar feeling to the predominant negative emotion of your child mode (lonely, angry, impulsive, and so on). What memory comes to mind? It may be recalled in images, words, or both. Describe your environment. What do you see? What do you feel, smell, taste, and touch? Who else is in this scene with you? Imagine what happened as if it were a movie playing in front of you, so that you can observe the child version of you behaving, interacting, and reacting with the events unfolding as they do when you watch a film. Some stressful feelings may arise as you replay these memories. To maintain control of this visualization and how you decide to recall this memory, imagine that you are holding a remote control in your hand. You can choose to pause the movie at any time and take a break, rewind, or fast-forward.

Now stand up from where you are sitting or lying down, and picture yourself entering the scene you have created for your child self as the adult you are now. What do you feel, seeing what the child version of you has experienced?

Imagine the child version of you looking up at the adult you. Ask the child, "What needs do you have?" Pause and allow the child to respond to you, then acknowledge and affirm what they have said. You can tell the child, "I hear you and I affirm that you need [state the need they have expressed]. I will do my best to help you to meet this need and to protect you."

As you continue looking at the child, imagine what you want to say or do now to take care of the child. How might you, as the empowered adult that you are, be able to help? How can you help the child make sense of what has happened to them? Say out loud what you think you can do, or go ahead and act on what comes to mind. How is the child reacting to your words or actions? Is the child looking more comforted, relieved, or less scared?

Once more, assume the vantage point of the child. Imagine yourself as you were in your younger years, looking up at your adult self, experiencing the support and kindness from your adult self. How has the adult you helped you learn about this experience? Is there a different way to understand and make sense of what happened to you and how you reacted? Is there a way that you can learn to feel protected, knowing that your adult self wants to be there to take care of you?

Imagine the adult you taking your child self's hand. What feelings come up for you? Name them out loud if you can or describe out loud the physical sensations you experience. Note how this is similar or different from the primary emotions of your child mode. Imagine your adult self leading you to a happy and safe place where you can recharge and escape the stresses of daily life. This could be a real place that you associate with positive memories, or it could be an imaginary location. Visualize your adult self leading you here so that you can heal and grow. Your adult self will continue to help you meet your child self's needs and teach your child self ways to deal with any stress or difficult situation that is to come.

Spend a little time in this happy place, where your adult self and your child self are connected. Remember that you can come back to this happy place any time so that your adult and child self can connect, and so your adult self can teach your child self and remind them how much they are cared for.

As you come out of the visualization, take a few more deep breaths and bring your attention back into the room. How do you feel? How are your feelings different now after this exercise compared to before the exercise? In your journal, write down the needs that your inner child expressed, and what your inner child mode looks like when triggered. Write down what actions or affirmations from your adult self helped to meet these needs.

BONUS EXERCISE: ONGOING AFFIRMATION

It is helpful if you can practice meeting your inner child's needs on a regular basis. When you notice your inner child mode expressing itself (which you identified in the journal follow-up to the above exercise), do one of the actions or use an affirmation or two. You can also fold a couple of these affirmations or actions into your daily self-care routine as a way to anticipate the needs of your inner child and give them the security and comfort they're looking for before they need to be addressed through a child mode.

DAILY WORKOUT: VAGUS NERVE STIMULATION

Your emotional states, which comprise subjective, internal experiences along with bodily sensations, are connected to your autonomic nervous system, which has two branches. Emotional dysregulation is usually related to the sympathetic nervous system, often referred to as the fight-flight-freeze system. When you feel physically or psychologically in danger, your sympathetic nervous system gears up for a crisis and gets ready to take extreme action. Conversely, when you want to relax, reduce the intensity of difficult emotions, and achieve calm and peace, your parasympathetic nervous system takes over.

The vagus nerve plays an important role in relaxation. It is the longest cranial nerve in the body, connecting the brainstem to your internal organs. It helps you to remain calm even when under duress as well as helping you know when to relax when you aren't in actual danger. The vagus nerve is related to stress management, and developing vagal tone (or the activity and responsiveness of the vagus nerve over physiological processes that include relaxation) can help you to become more resilient and to consistently manage difficult emotional experiences.[15] The ability to successfully regulate responses to emotionally triggering events is related to increased vagal activity and higher levels of well-being.[16]

In some ways, we can train and strengthen the vagus nerve as if it were a muscle. When the vagal tone is high, the vagus nerve can quickly and effectively counteract the fight-or-flight response initiated by your sympathetic nervous system during stressful situations and help restore calm and balance to the body. People with higher vagal tone also tend to recover more quickly from emotional dysregulation and experience greater overall well-being and higher resilience. As you can see, working toward higher vagal tone and strengthening the vagus nerve's influences over the body's physiological responses has many rewards!

~

Commit a few minutes each day to stimulating your vagus nerve and improving your stress response. Here are some of my favorite techniques:

1. Cold water immersion: A change in temperature can help make the switch from the sympathetic nervous system to the parasympathetic system. Try dunking your face in a bowl of ice water for a few seconds, putting an ice pack on your neck, switching the temperature to cold for the last sixty seconds of your shower, or taking a cold bath.

2. Humming or singing: Your vagus nerve is connected to your vocal cords, so humming, singing along to your favorite tunes, or making a "voo" sound positively impacts your vagal tone. As a bonus, singing increases oxytocin (regardless of whether or not you're a good singer).

3. Lovingkindness meditation: Research has shown that the positive feelings you experience during lovingkindness meditation help to create a healthy vagal tone (see page 327 for more information).[17,18]

4. Diaphragmatic breathing: Deep, slow, conscious breaths, roughly an equal amount of time inhaling and exhaling,

stimulate the vagus nerve, helping to lower blood pressure and heart rate and calm feelings of overwhelm.[19,20] Place one hand on your tummy and the other on your chest. Take a deep breath in and feel your stomach expand. As you exhale, feel your stomach flatten. Repeat ten times.

5. Massage: The vagus nerve can also be stimulated by massaging specific areas of the body. Research shows that a ten-minute massage applied to the head and neck increased both self-reported and physiological measures of relaxation (measured by heart rate variability).[21]

    You can do a simple self-massage whenever you need it: Start at your collarbone, gently massaging in an upward motion along the left side of your neck. Repeat on the right side. Then gently rub behind your earlobes.[22] Finish by rubbing your temples in a circular motion with the tips of your second, third, and fourth fingers for one to two minutes.

"MY LIFE IS IN CONSTANT CHAOS"

Surveillance Specialists are likely to find themselves drawn to chaos, or they may inadvertently create chaos around them. Growing up in a world that was chaotic and disorganized might cause them to be unconsciously attracted to chaos as an adult because chaos feels familiar. The familiar, even if it is turbulent and unsettling, always feels safer than the unknown. So, when there is too much order, or things are going smoothly, alarm bells go off and they think something must be wrong. When there is no drama, they aren't sure what to do because they're used to dealing with dysfunction and disorganization. For better or worse, Surveillance Specialists have strategies to cope with chaos (even if they are not effective, emotionally healthy ones) and will sometimes feel more at home in chaos. They may pick a fight or engage in negative behavior to break the calm and create a bit of chaos, because they are accustomed to managing chaotic situations.

Surveillance Specialists are likely to unconsciously re-create the extreme stress or trauma they experienced in their early years—their patterns of relating to others are ingrained, and the default is trauma (remember the discussion of trauma bonding in chapter 9?). Repeating patterns or situations that remind you of past trauma may occur because there is a part of you that wants to find a way to fix what happened, achieve closure, or achieve a different, more positive outcome. Additionally, you have likely adopted a belief that life will always be chaotic, disorganized, and unpredictable. People who find themselves in the cycle of repetition compulsion have difficulty believing that change is possible and may feel hopeless about their future. They may also not believe they deserve calm or peace, or because they may not have experienced true calm or peace for an extended length of time, it feels unfamiliar and uncomfortable.

As you continue to heal your attachment wounds, you can find and maintain a comfort level with calm and peace. By understanding that the chaos that feels so familiar and comfortable is generated from within, you can learn to overcome it and reduce your tendency to stir up chaos in your life.

Antidote to "My Life Is in Constant Chaos"

The bottom line is nobody thrives in chaos. You may have come to believe that you do because it's what feels normal to you. But in the long run, living in a constantly activated state will erode your physical, mental, and relationship well-being. These exercises will help to reprogram your mind and body to let go of the part of you that has integrated chaos and trauma into your working scripts. It allows you to access a transcendent part of yourself, the wise being that was always a part of you, in your everyday activities, and particularly when you are struggling with moments on the precipice of trauma re-creation. When you do find yourself in the middle of a chaotic situation, these exercises will also help you to learn effective coping skills to weather the storm until it passes.

DISCOVERY EXERCISE: SELF-AS-CONTEXT

Hard to believe, but we are not our thoughts and feelings. In reality, we have access to so many more perspectives and points of view on our own experience. Our thoughts and feelings are both inherently transient, so when we rely on them to tell us who we are or to inform our self-worth, our self-concept becomes equally unstable and inconsistent.

Self-as-context, borrowed from the principles of ACT (acceptance commitment therapy), is a helpful way to maintain a sense of self that isn't easily drawn into whatever stressful situation you might be dealing with—and the thoughts and feelings generated from that experience. There are a lot of synonyms for self-as-context, including the observing self, the transcendent sense of self, the core self, or being your own watcher. What they share is a sense of detached perspective. As Dr. Russ Harris, a pioneer in ACT, describes it, this is the self that "does all the noticing and observing of one's inner and outer world."[23]

Your observational self has seen it all…the good, the bad, and every moment in between. Yet, despite all these ups and downs, it remains constant and isn't overly attached to any one memory or experience. It knows that, as Dr. Russ Harris says, "there is more to you than your body, thoughts, feelings and memories; more to you than the roles you play and the actions you take; that all these things are continually changing throughout your life, but the aspect of you that notices them is unchanging and always available."[24]

When I describe the idea of self-as-context to my patients, I often use the analogy of a chessboard. I want you to visualize one clearly in your mind's eye: the checkered pattern, the different colored pieces. On one side, the chess pieces represent your positive feelings, thoughts, and memories. The chess pieces on the other side hold your negative feelings, thoughts, and memories.

On this chessboard, many games will be played. You will have internal struggles in your mind, with your self-deprecating thoughts battling it out with your hopes for a more positive outcome and a better future. Or you may try to push back unpleasant and distressing thoughts and feelings, but try as you might, those chess pieces always find their way back to the board somehow, and another game ensues.

If you assume the perspective of the chess pieces, then each battle feels significant and wrought with stress and pressure. If you're caught up in the identity of an individual chess piece, then you've taken a side in every battle you're a part of. Your objective is to defeat the other chess pieces at all costs, and you're deeply, personally invested in the outcome of each match. In the middle of a fast and furious chess game, everything can feel chaotic and disorganized, like you're swept up in a whirlwind. You may think this is the only way to be, because it's all you've known—up to this point in your life, you've believed that your identity as a chess piece is your only possible vantage point.

But what if, instead, you took the perspective of the chessboard itself? As the board, you are in direct contact with all the chess pieces. This means you are directly experiencing the thoughts and feelings and memories (both positive and negative) from either side of the board, but as the board, you're not necessarily rooting for one side or another. You're intimately connected with the chess pieces, but you aren't embroiled in any of the battles. After all, as the chessboard you'll see each side win hundreds or thousands of times. No matter the outcome, there is no damage or cost to you. The board always resets and you remain, a constant witness to interactions between the chess pieces, supporting the game as a whole.

In the same way, self-as-context allows you to disconnect from judgments and memories about who you are and what your life ought to be like. Accessing your observational self—your vantage as the chessboard—is especially useful for those who have survived trauma because a part of you transcended the trauma and came through unharmed (even if your body and your emotions were harmed during the trauma).

This next exercise uses a powerful combination of techniques to access your self-as-context through a metaphor visualization followed by a very specific type of mindfulness exercise.

〜

Now let's do an exercise to find the transcendent you—the chessboard you. Sitting in a chair, with your feet on the floor, take a few deep breaths and make yourself comfortable. As you continue to breathe in through your nose and out through your mouth, shift your attention from your environment to your body. Bring your attention to your feet. Notice the sensations of your feet touching the floor. Notice if there is any tension there or if they feel relaxed. If there is tension, wiggle your toes or press your feet into the ground for a few seconds, then let go. How do your feet feel now? Notice if there are any changes in the sensation of your feet.

As you notice these different sensations in your feet, be aware that you're noticing and observing. There's the way your feet feel (tense, relaxed, numb, and so on) and then there's the part of you noticing how your feet feel. The way your feet feel will change all the time. Sometimes they will be relaxed, and sometimes they will be tense. These feelings and sensations will come and go, but the part of you that notices these sensations is always there, and it's always the same.

Now turn your mind to a recent thought that you've had that bothered you. Perhaps it's a memory of an argument you had with a friend or family member. Maybe it's a self-judgment about a mistake you made or something you wish you hadn't done. Notice how these thoughts and memories make you feel. If you can, describe those feelings, perhaps with emotion words (such as happy, sad, angry, frustrated) or with the physical sensations they bring up for you. Say this description out loud or write it down in your journal.

For example, John has been quite irritable lately because work has been crushing and he has gotten some tough feedback from his boss. When he came home, he unleashed his frustration on his wife and yelled at her for something so mundane he couldn't even remember what he was so upset about. When she became upset as well, he doubled down on his reactions and defended raising his voice at her. He refused to apologize and didn't speak to her for the rest of the night. As he reflected on this, he noticed feelings of regret, sadness, and guilt. He experienced physical sensations of a knot developing in his stomach when he recollected how poorly he acted toward her that night. He wrote these observations down in his journal.

Next, turn your attention to the part of you that noticed these thoughts and memories in the first place. These thoughts and memories may be difficult to think about and can be painful to remember in any detail. To do so may cause you struggle, stress, heartache, or regret. But notice that there is a part of you that is contemplating these thoughts and memories. This is a separate but connected part of you that sees these memories in your mind's eye; however, it isn't caught up in the memories themselves or what they mean. You are simply watching, observing, and taking notice of these thoughts and memories and what kind of feelings they bring up in you.

It's important to remember that while these thoughts and memories are a part of you, they are nowhere near the whole of you. There's so much more to you than any of these negative thoughts and memories. There's the part of you that is transcendent and watching this all unfold but is unscathed and unblemished. This is the transcendent you that has been there from the very beginning of your existence. No matter what happens to you in your life, you are not simply the sum of your thoughts, feelings, behaviors, and memories. You are much more than that. Your transcendent self is the part of you that has seen you through all the positive and negative experiences of your life but remains a constant, in its pure form. This is the chessboard you—the you that notices and observes but isn't tethered to any specific experience while still acknowledging that these experiences have happened.

Return to this exercise anytime you need a bit of stabilization and want to bolster your resistance against the tendency toward chaos.

DAILY WORKOUT: IMPROVE YOUR DISTRESS TOLERANCE SKILLS

The primary goal of distress tolerance skills is to prevent self-destructive or harmful behaviors that people might engage in when they are overwhelmed by distress or find themselves caught up in chaos. When Surveillance Specialists are under extreme stress, and especially if that stress is related in some way to their past traumatic experiences, they may find themselves in cycles of chaos, disorganization, and dysregulation. Trauma survivors in particular are more likely to engage in high-risk behaviors because they're used to living in a state of provocation. Feelings of self-blame may lead them to take actions that are self-harming or self-neglecting, like alcohol and drug misuse, binge eating, and not taking care of themselves (not showering, exercising, or eating well). When under stress, Surveillance Specialists may try to block out these feelings by overusing escapist coping such as watching hours of TV, oversleeping, and using anything at their disposal to stop feeling. Needless to say, when Surveillance Specialists are under high levels of stress, their emotional regulation can go out the window, and they have a harder time bouncing back from challenging situations.

When people are under extreme stress, their fight-flight-freeze response gets activated. During these times, it can be very difficult to practice effective coping strategies when they are already agitated and on guard.[25] Distress tolerance skills are meant to be used in these high-stress situations, are quick to produce positive effects, and can help the person lower the intensity of their emotional pain and suffering. They're meant to lessen the internal struggle that people feel when they're in a very difficult situation that isn't going to change anytime soon through no fault of their own (like the terminal illness of a loved one, or living with a family member who is going through their own severe mental health struggles). After they've achieved some semblance of calm and they're out of the acute fight-flight-freeze stage, they can then use other coping strategies that are more likely to produce positive outcomes over the long run.

Dialectical behavior therapy (DBT) distress tolerance skills help you to manage painful emotions without needing to resist or change them. This is especially helpful when there may not be much you can do to change the situation or the actions of other people. It's a way to lessen the pain and struggle while being able to find some semblance of peace in the middle of a crisis. Distress tolerance is one of the four modules of DBT, developed by Dr. Marsha Linehan.[26] They are also called "crisis survival skills" because they can help people navigate a perceived or actual crisis and reduce or avoid destructive behavior that takes the person away from healing and may lead to a worsening of the crisis.

⌐⌐

Work on one of the following distress tolerance techniques every day to build your psychological resilience and learn to cope more effectively with chaos. Each time you find yourself drawn to chaos and repeating past ineffective coping behaviors, come back to this section to use one or more of these techniques. They will help you tolerate the emotional distress you are feeling until you become calmer and able to act in ways that will promote healing and produce positive outcomes. Once you are feeling more settled, you can then use any of the other coping strategies in this book or other therapeutic resources you have found helpful to you.

These distress tolerance skills, aptly summarized with the acronym IMPROVE,[27] are all about gaining improvement in the moment.

Imagery: Imagine yourself dealing successfully with the crisis you are currently experiencing. Envision a fantasy world that is calming, and take yourself there. Shut out anything that can hurt you. Imagine painful emotions draining out of you, like water out of a pipe.

Meaning: Ask yourself, "What is the meaning in this painful situation?" or "What can I learn from this experience?" Is there some purpose or value to the pain I am feeling? Focus on one small positive aspect of the current painful situation. Write down a brief description of the difficult situation along with one positive aspect of it in your journal and read it out loud to yourself.

Prayer: Prayer can come in any form that you are comfortable with. Open your heart to something bigger than yourself. This can be God, the universe, your community, or a transcendent version of yourself. Ask for strength to manage this pain, let go of whatever you can't control, and only focus on the things you can do in the current moment.

Relaxation: Try progressive muscle relaxation by tensing and relaxing, one at a time, each major muscle group throughout your body. Engage in a relaxing ritual like a hot shower, or massage your own neck and hands. Practice stillness by sitting on your couch for a few minutes at a time with no other stimulation (no music, TV, or looking at your phone) to soothe your nervous system.

One thing in the moment: Focus your attention on what you are doing right now, rather than engaging in worries about the future or regrets about the past. Observe one thing in your physical environment and describe it in as much detail as you can. Set a timer for five minutes and free-write your thoughts in your journal.

Vacation: Take a brief vacation by visualizing a trip you're looking forward to or one you enjoyed in the past. Do something indulgent like using scented lotion or eating a small portion of comfort food. Dress up in one of your favorite outfits and take photos. Prepare a plate of food the way it would be presented at an upscale restaurant. Take a break from work and responsibilities and do something that brings you pure joy, like playing video games, watching a funny TV show, or doing a hobby you've neglected recently.

Encouragement: Use self-affirmations to cheer yourself on. Some of my favorites: "You got this," "This pain won't last forever," "I can manage this crisis," "I am doing the best I can," and "I can improve this moment."

BONUS DAILY WORKOUT: RADICAL ACCEPTANCE

Radical acceptance is a special and effective technique that can help reduce interpersonal chaos. It involves accepting what is happening, even when it's not ideal, when it's stressful, and even if it is painful. It's about accepting what is not under your control and accepting reality in a nonjudgmental way. It's about being less attached to the eventual outcomes, as well as accepting any negative thoughts or feelings you might be experiencing. When you practice radical acceptance, it lessens your suffering during difficult times, builds resilience, and helps you to let go of control.

Sometimes we suffer because we don't accept what is happening and because we try to control things that we really can't control. When you're contending with a tough situation or difficult thoughts and feelings, it is natural to try to push it away, fight against it, be in denial, or try to find some way to change it. Of course, some things can be changed, but often we can't do anything about it. A good example is when you're stuck in traffic. You might have somewhere important to be, but it's impossible to will yourself out of a traffic jam. You may think dodging in and out of different lanes might speed things up, but usually it only results in more aggravation, because while you don't save yourself much time, you've certainly stressed yourself out more by all that weaving and dodging and trying to avoid getting into a car accident.

↜

Next time you find yourself in a situation where you notice the urge to try to control or change something that is very stressful or unpleasant, take a deep breath and follow these steps:

1. Turn your mind toward the present moment. Take a few deep breaths and acknowledge where you are physically, what you are thinking, and how you are feeling. Without trying to change these aspects, just simply notice them and try to do this without applying any kind of evaluation or judgment to your observations.

2. Ask yourself what you can control—and what you can't—in this situation. Write these down on a piece of paper or in your journal. Writing can often help to organize your thoughts and help you to regulate your emotional response so you don't feel overwhelmed or frantic.

3. Say a favorite mantra or two to yourself that encourages radical acceptance. Some of my favorites are:
   - I can accept how this is going right now.
   - I can deal with these challenges.
   - This situation is temporary.
   - I have no control over other people—only how I act or react.
   - These feelings will pass.
   - I can control only some of what's happening now—and that's okay.

4. Do something about what you can control—and let the rest go. Look at that list you wrote down of what you can and cannot control. Take action on what you can change, and for the rest, let it all go by breathing out the tension and frustrations they cause you.

SELF-CONCEPT SNAPSHOT

Remember the self-concept snapshot you took in chapter 3? That was your baseline before tackling these exercises. Now that you've worked through these activities, I'd like you to take another snapshot of your self-concept and note any differences. Read the statements below and choose the option that best describes you.

1 = not true, 2 = sometimes or partially true, 3 = mostly or definitely true

- If I had the opportunity, I wouldn't change many things about myself.
- I have confidence in my decision-making.
- I don't worry excessively about what others think of me.
- I like myself even when I am in conflict with someone else.
- I value myself even when I make mistakes.
- I believe my efforts contribute to my success.
- I have control over my reactions to difficult situations.
- I like myself.
- I can start and finish projects without others' help and approval.
- I have a clear sense of who I am.
- I have positive and admirable traits.
- I can overcome challenges when I try hard.

Did your score improve after the exercises? It's helpful to do this checkup once every few weeks to see how your self-concept improves as you continue to gain insight and work through the exercises in this chapter along with any other chapters that you feel may apply to you (for example, if you feel that disorganized attachment is your predominant style but you also have a secondary attachment style).

THE JOURNEY AHEAD

Congratulations on finishing the exercises in this chapter! Remember that you did not become a Surveillance Specialist overnight, and you may benefit from reviewing and reworking these discovery and coping strategies—perhaps even with the support of a health care professional to guide you through the exercises—as you learn and grow.

At this point in your journey, you should find yourself struggling less with your fear of intimacy and vulnerability and recognizing that closeness and connection do not have to mean danger or a loss of self. You'll also notice shifts in the ambivalence you feel toward others, and learn not to paint the world in broad, largely negatively tinted strokes. Healthier boundaries will become easier for you to set and to respect, and you will improve your ability to create a social world that is less unpredictable, as well as to continue to learn to rely on others without feeling the need to push them away when they want to connect with you.

As you learn to resolve the conflicting emotional responses that arise when you seek comfort and assistance from others, you'll also notice that you're starting to effectively regulate your emotions and manage stress better. As you continue the work, you'll find a reliable safe haven in others who deserve your trust, as well as in yourself. After all, this all comes back to self-trust, which is going to grow stronger each time you visit these exercises or review your journal, where you'll see the progress toward a stronger and more resilient self-concept.

Check your self-concept frequently to assess where your progress is at any given time, especially when you are going through challenges in a major area of life. Repeat the exercises that work best for you, and incorporate them into your weekly routines. Once your self-concept is around a score of 24 or higher, this is a great time to tap into the tips in the conclusion, "Your Resilient Self." For more self-concept boosters, see appendix C on page 329.

It is also helpful to read through the chapters on other attachment styles to gain insight into how you relate to other attachment styles. These chapters will help improve your relationships and the quality of your connection with people whose styles differ from your own.

Additionally, please refer to appendix A for exercises that will help you to identify triggers for insecure attachment behaviors and what to do in the moment to manage the situation more effectively.

CONCLUSION

Your Resilient Self

You started this journey perhaps not realizing the extent to which your attachment style was impacting your present life. Now, having gotten to know yourself better—having understood how and why you have become Fiercely Independent, a Worried Warrior, or a Surveillance Specialist, along with the working models that have historically driven your self-concept—you've started to heal. A big part of that healing journey has been meeting, and listening to, your inner child to discover what they need to feel safe, secure, and hopeful for the future. That is what this journey has been about. Not only attending to the day-to-day interference that your attachment style can insert into your life, but to clear the path to reach toward the future and fulfill your dreams—and to do so from a place of the secure attachment you've found with yourself.

You now know how to attain and hold on to secure attachment. Secure attachment and all the benefits that come with it can be yours, but it takes continued effort and awareness. Because insecure attachment is formed at such an early age, your mind is likely to fall into the trap of assimilating new information into the existing ideas, frameworks, and schemas that reflect your insecure attachment, rather than accommodating new experiences by modifying or adjusting existing ideas in response to that new information. In other words, you are likely to fall into old behavioral patterns and self-defeating thoughts not only because you have been doing so for so long but also because your mind uses that default program to understand and respond to the world.

It's not easy to come face-to-face with your attachment wounds, and it shows incredible strength that you've made this effort. You've already taken the first steps toward the life you want by picking up this book, deepening your self-understanding, and earnestly working on the exercises that will help you build a strong self-concept and a secure attachment style. The resolve that brought you this far is a huge testament to the kind of person you are. Although you may periodically question your own abilities, you can draw on the part of you that believes positive change is possible if you put your mind to it. That self-belief is one of the most important things I hope you take away from this book, because it is the basis for a more resilient, well-rounded self-concept that can weather any storm ahead.

On your continued attachment healing journey, remember that your old ways of seeing the world and the views you have of yourself took years and even decades to form, so it will take some time to change your thinking and engage in the new behaviors that will follow. Your habitual response to challenging situations has been as Fiercely Independent, a Worried Warrior, or a Surveillance Specialist, but you can make the shift to becoming a Connected Explorer. Such fundamental change is difficult and can feel a bit precarious at first, but with time and practice, you will gradually find that new ways of thinking are not only possible but have become your new normal.

Because true and permanent transformation happens over time, I encourage you to keep working on these exercises—especially when you find some of those old insecure attachment patterns starting to creep into your life again. If you find yourself entertaining negative thoughts from the past, you're absolutely not the first person to do so, but it is important for you to call them out when you notice them and to refocus your attention on how to get back to a place where you feel stronger and more centered. The antidote to overcoming that negative interference is revisiting this book and your journal entries to find the information that can reshape your perspective and engaging with the exercises that work for you and keeping at it.

Review the chapters that pertain to your (old) attachment style, check in with the self-statements that characterize the style, and focus on the exercises that you feel you need most to bolster your new secure self. Revisiting your timeline exercise in particular is helpful to see the shifts in the events you find significant in your life. Hopefully, you'll find that as time goes on and thanks to your efforts, there is much more balance to your purposeful recollections of the most impactful moments. Doing the Wheel of Life exercise every few weeks helps you to know what areas of life are going well and also which might require more of your attention. I highly recommend that you refresh your life visioning every six months or year, so you can track how your work is beginning to shift your dreams for yourself as well as your belief that you can achieve those dreams.

And don't forget to check out appendix A, "Style Triggers and Timely Tips" (page 315), as this guide helps you to identify situations, thoughts, and feelings that bring about unhelpful responses tied to your old attachment style and then teaches you quick exercises to do in the moment. When you can recognize and respond to a trigger, you can prevent getting stuck in a spiral of behaviors that will take you further from your goals.

Whenever you feel your old insecure attachment style getting in the way of your goals—big and small—visualize your older, wiser self giving your inner child a sign of unconditional support and encouragement. Whether that's a pat on the back, a hug, or a verbal affirmation, tell your inner child that you believe in them, you forgive them, you love them, and they have your support no matter what.

I hope that this book has inspired and empowered you to make lasting, positive changes in your life. As we reach our last pages together, I want you to answer one final question: *How do you feel about yourself?* It's a broad question but, ultimately, it's the only one that matters. I hope that your answer is positive and that you have learned to believe in and like yourself. You deserve to know that you can handle anything that comes your way. You deserve to know that you can balance self-reliance and emotional connection, and effect positive outcomes in your life. No matter what has happened to you in the past, you can change what happens from this point forward. I hope you are excited about your future. I'm confident that you have the tools to achieve what you most desire: to form more satisfying and fulfilling partnerships, family relationships, and friendships; to accomplish what you hope for in your career; to attain better physical and mental health; and to achieve your goals and dreams in all aspects of your life.

The gift of secure attachment is yours for the taking. I can't wait to see what you'll do with this newfound knowledge. Whatever it is, know that I am in your corner rooting for you and your inner child.

Style Triggers and Timely Tips

No matter how much work you do on your attachment style, there will always be circumstances that are likely to trigger the working models and self-beliefs of your insecure attachment style. The better you know your triggers, the better prepared you will be to notice when your attachment style is kicking up unhelpful or painful thoughts and emotions, or directing you toward actions that don't serve you well.

Because the work of attachment healing is a slow process, during these times you may find it helpful to practice one or more of the timely tips (see below) so that you can self-regulate and get back on track to feeling safe, secure, and empowered.

COMMON TRIGGERS

No matter whether you are Fiercely Independent, a Worried Warrior, or a Surveillance Specialist, there will be situations or things that you will experience that will threaten to push you to respond to them in unhelpful, insecure attachment ways. Being aware of potential triggers can set you up to meet and deal with them effectively.

Self-Concept

- When a past traumatic or stressful memory comes up
- When a person's treatment of you reminds you of your relationship with your primary attachment figures from childhood
- Being around another insecurely attached person whose behaviors mirror yours
- Feeling empty inside or lacking purpose

Family

- When another family member behaves erratically or unsympathetically
- Having to depend on a family member for safety, protection, or basic needs
- When interactions with certain family members bring up challenging interpersonal dynamics from childhood

Friendships

- When another person expresses a strong negative emotion (anger, deep sadness)
- When another person appears shut down or ices you out
- When a person dismisses your needs as unimportant

Romantic Relationships

- When a partner behaves erratically or acts distant from you
- When a partner attempts to be emotionally closer to you
- Feeling out of control of your feelings, especially as you start to feel more intensely or become more reliant on your partner
- When a partner confronts you with emotional intensity (like significant anger or frustration)

- When a partner makes a big romantic gesture or expresses interest in a future or long-term commitment
- When a partner needs emotional intimacy at a time when you're already stressed or overwhelmed

Work

- Unpredictable situations that don't allow for planning (for example, being told to present at a meeting off the cuff or having a last-minute change to your carefully orchestrated plans)
- Feeling ignored or pushed away by powerful people at work or people who you believe are your friends
- Seeing cliques form among colleagues and feeling left out
- Getting a negative evaluation
- When you are behind on deadlines
- When you are pressured to multitask or work too quickly
- Feeling like others have high expectations of you

TIMELY TIPS FOR WHEN YOU ARE TRIGGERED

It can take some practice, but when something happens that has you feeling like you will respond based on your insecure attachment style, you can counter that feeling and engage in a way that is reflective of your new secure attachment style. The tools below are meant to be quick exercises to use when you find yourself being triggered to act in a way that might be unproductive to your goals and mental wellness. Most of these take less than five minutes to do, and I suggest that you practice each of them a few times, trying them on for size during times when you are not feeling particularly distressed or triggered. For example, you can build a trial of each exercise into your daily self-care practice. Take note of the ones that work the best for you, and then when you find yourself in a difficult situation, it will be much easier to access these exercises from your brain and muscle memory and use them at a time that will be most beneficial to you.

TIPP THE SCALES

This timely tip is called TIPP and comes from dialectical behavior therapy. TIPP stands for:

Temperature. When upset, our bodies tend to run hot. Changing the temperature will help you to experience calm and get out of the fight-or-flight impulse. Cooler temperatures tend to decrease your heart rate. Try holding an ice cube, splashing your face with cold water, going outside for a walk if the weather is cool, or cooling your face with a handheld fan.

Intense Exercise. When you experience an intense or over-whelming emotion, it can be very helpful to expend nervous energy by doing a brief cardio session. Do jumping jacks, run in place, dance to your favorite song, or hop up and down for a couple of minutes.

Paced Breathing. Overwhelming feelings can quicken our breath, which can lead to hyperventilation or other stressful bodily responses. To counter this, pay attention to your breath and slow it down. Try slowing your inhales and exhales with the 4-7-8 method of deep breathing. Inhale through your nose and count to 4. Hold your breath for a count of 7, then breathe out slowly through your mouth for a count of 8. Repeat several more times until you notice that you feel more relaxed and less overwhelmed.

Progressive Muscle Relaxation. Relax the tense muscles in your body by doing this quick exercise. First, do a quick body scan and notice any areas that feel particularly tense. When you notice tension in a muscle (for example, the one in your calf), tighten it, hold for five seconds, then relax it completely and allow it to rest. By squeezing and then relaxing the tense muscle, you will find that the initial tension is released. Repeat this for the different areas of your body where you experience tension.

GROUNDING EXERCISE: 5-4-3-2-1

This exercise can be extremely helpful during intense anxiety or even panic by grounding you in the present when your mind is full of negative, catastrophic thoughts like *I don't deserve good things, I'll never be in a relationship, I'll never have a job where I can be a success.*

Start by taking a few deep breaths to center yourself, and bring your attention to your surroundings with the 5, 4, 3, 2, 1 grounding exercise:

FIVE: Notice and name **5** things you see around you in your immediate environment.

FOUR: Notice and name **4** things you can touch around you and reach out and touch those items.

THREE: Notice and name **3** things you hear. This could be any external sound outside of your body or even one that originates from inside your body (like your tummy rumbling).

TWO: Notice and name **2** things you can smell.

ONE: Notice and name 1 thing you can taste. What does the inside of your mouth taste like? You can also place a small piece of food, a mint, or gum in your mouth and savor the flavor.

GETTING GROUNDED

Try the following grounding exercises the next time you are in a dysregulated emotional state. Each of these takes only a minute or two and can have profound effects on your ability to tolerate and manage stressful feelings.

- While sitting in a chair, dig your heels into the floor, push your back into the seat of your chair, and feel your connection to the floor and the chair in your body.
- Place your feet firmly on the floor and stand up tall. Imagine roots, like the roots of a tree, extending from the bottom of your feet into the ground below you. Like roots are to a tree, these roots below your feet give you strength and stability and connect you with the earth below you.
- Perform some light stretches by pulling your left arm across your chest. Repeat with your right arm. Stretch your arms upward over your head as far as you can. While seated, stretch out your legs and feet in front of you as far as you can and stretch your toes and your calves. Stand up and fold over from your waist and allow your arms to hang down, getting your fingertips as close to your toes as possible.
- Engage your senses one at a time. Light a candle or put some aromatherapy oil on your wrists and inhale deeply. Chew a piece of gum, being mindful of the way it tastes and how it feels in your mouth. Touch something that offers a tactile

experience like a fidget toy, Play-Doh, stress balls, or a stuffed animal. Cuddle up with a weighted blanket. You can also do the 5-4-3-2-1 exercise (above).

- Describe something in your physical environment in detail using all five senses. For example, the lamp on my desk is tall, white, and has a wood base. It feels smooth to the touch. It has no smell or taste. It emits a humming sound when it is on.

- Play a categories game with yourself. Pick a category (like animals, celebrities, names of songs) and list as many as you can starting with the first letter of the alphabet to the last.

- Write in your journal or read something to yourself. Feel the weight and texture of the journal, the writing utensil, or the book (or Kindle or phone) that you're reading from.

- Get outside and listen to the sounds of nature, or turn on a nature sounds app on your phone.

- Think of a familiar activity and go through it step-by-step. This could be something like making a cup of tea, loading paper in the copier, or feeding pets.

- Take a walk outside and notice what you see: *There is a blue mailbox. I just walked by a silver car. The trees have orange and red leaves.*

- Take a bath with bubbles or use a scented bath bomb. Let the warm water relax your muscles and the scent of the water soothe you. You can even light candles to create a spa-like feeling.

- Watch an episode of a favorite comedy performance or show. Laughter is good medicine, and the distraction of the show can help to ground you.

- If you have a dog, cat, or other animal that you can hold and pet, spend some time sitting with them. Feeling the warmth of their fur and, in the case of the cat, the rumbling of their purr can be calming.

- Deeply examine an object—a rock, a shell, a crystal—and try to see as many colors as you can in it, get a sense of its shape (smooth, rough) and weight (heavy, light), so that you can describe it in detail without looking at it.[1]

ACT OPPOSITE OF

All emotions make you want to do something to either express them or act against them, what we call an emotion's urge. Instead of going with your emotion's urge, act opposite of that urge. For example, if being angry makes you want to yell at your partner, act in the opposite of that urge (hugging them instead or saying something kind are two options).

ACT AS IF

Act as if. Even when you're not feeling your best, act as if you were feeling better. For example, if you're feeling sad, smile and say something optimistic to yourself out loud. Or if you're feeling tired, take a quick walk around the block with a little bounce in your step.

THANK YOUR MIND

In Dr. Russ Harris's book *The Happiness Trap*, he describes a technique that pays gratitude to your mind and gets you unstuck from unhelpful thoughts. I've adapted it to use with many of my patients, who really enjoy the simplicity and effectiveness of it. The next time you notice your mind starting to say mean and hurtful things to you, talk back to it with a sense of lightheartedness and playfulness. Give your mind a name (my mind's name is Betty) so when a negative thought comes up, I say, "Thanks, Betty. Thanks for sharing." I don't engage or argue over what the negative thought is. Next I say, "Thank you, Betty, but I'm going to do something else now." Then I turn my attention and energy toward doing whatever matters most to me in the moment, whether it is to keep working at that project without the influence of my inner critic or going ahead and doing what I was thinking of doing and hoping for the best.

Try this exercise the next time your mind tries to spin a tale of doom and gloom about you or threatens to make you feel less secure in who you are. Instead of believing that everything your mind says is true or feeling like you must do battle with your mind, see your mind as your protector and not your adversary. Align with your mind; let it know you appreciate the input but that you're not going to be distracted by the negative talk and will move on to something that really needs your attention.

DO WHAT YOU CAN, AND LET THE REST GO

Try this timely tip the next time you struggle with feeling empowered. Open your journal to a new page and write a few words or sentences about the problem you're currently facing. Then ask yourself, "What are the things I can change?" and jot down those ideas.

Don't edit yourself at this stage; simply brainstorm all the things you can influence, for example, changing your perspective, using coping skills that you learned in this book or elsewhere, or behaviors and actions you can take that can improve the situation (even if the improvement is temporary).

Then ask yourself, "What are the things I can't change?" and jot those down. Again, don't edit yourself; write down everything that you can think of that is out of your control, like someone else's actions, how someone else might think or feel, or the outcome of the situation if there isn't anything you can do to alter what happens.

Now review the side of the page that has all the things you can't change. Take a deep breath, and let those things go. We often get stuck trying to think our way out of things over which we have no control. We spend time worrying about them, even obsessing over them, but they are not things we can do anything about.

Next, write these things that are out of your control on a loose piece of paper under the title "Things I Can't Change," and rip the paper into pieces and throw them away as a symbolic goodbye to these ideas. Then, focus on your notes under the things you can change, and put your attention on doing each of them, one at a time, to improve your situation.

YES, BUT

The way you talk to yourself can have a big impact on how you feel. Reframe negative self-talk into realistic but encouraging statements using the "Yes... but..." formula. Acknowledge something that isn't going so well right now, and then acknowledge something that is going well or something that you are in the process of doing to improve your circumstances. For example, "**Yes**, I made a mistake yesterday at work and it caused my boss to be upset, **but** I am going to address what happened and rework the project, and ask my boss about any other ways I can improve on my work." "**Yes**, my friend is being incredibly rude and unempathetic right now, **but** I can step away from this and focus on my work—then decide how I want to talk to this friend later tonight."

Self-Compassion Strategies

Self-compassion is vital to any healing process since it helps you to acknowledge and validate your pain and suffering without judging yourself for having difficult emotions or engaging in actions you later regret. It helps reduce self-criticism by encouraging self-kindness and self-acceptance. It helps you to separate your self-worth from your past experiences and builds your confidence as you march toward relationship, career, and other personal goals.

The best part is, self-compassion is a skill that can be reinforced through a variety of strategies and tools. You'll find some of my favorites here. Whether you want to build self-compassion as an ongoing practice or you're looking for a quick way to intervene with your inner critic, these strategies can help:

- Practice compassionate self-talk: Use kind, supportive, and nonjudgmental language when talking to yourself.
- Acknowledge difficult moments: Say to yourself, "Wow, this is really a struggle. This is hard."
- Three things: Say out loud or write down in your journal three things you're thankful for each day.

- "No" is a complete sentence: Practice saying no to things that you don't want to do or that aren't within your top values.
- Remember our common humanity: No matter how alone you feel, remember that suffering and struggle are universal human experiences, and somewhere in the world, there are other people who feel similar to you.
- Seek support from others: It can be hard to ask for help, but try to ask for what you need from at least one person you trust.
- Write a compassionate letter to yourself. Think of a situation that caused you painful feelings. Write a letter to yourself about the situation without placing blame on anyone.
- What would a friend say? Think of what you would say to someone you care about and love if they were facing a similar difficult situation. Now try to say these encouraging and loving messages to yourself.
- Soothe your inner child. Visualize your inner child and ask your inner child, "What do you need most right now?" Find some way to meet your inner child's request or needs in this moment.
- Celebrate your positive qualities. Write down the things you like about yourself, including your strengths, skills, talents, or personal traits. Read this list often and add to it as you see fit.
- Acknowledge your accomplishments. Take time to reflect on your achievements big and small, and celebrate your successes (even if it's just a verbal affirmation to yourself for a job well done), no matter how small they may seem. You should celebrate the intermediary steps that you achieve on the way to a bigger goal, for example. Or celebrate when you get the first thing done from your to-do list in the morning by literally giving yourself a pat on the back.
- Treat yourself. Give yourself a small reward. Treat yourself

to something you enjoy like a nice meal or thirty minutes of online window shopping.

- Share your successes with others. Tell someone you trust about something you are proud to have done today, whether it's keeping your cool with someone who tends to become argumentative with you or starting a new exercise regimen.
- Practice lovingkindness meditation. There are many scripts for this that allow you to visualize sending love, kindness, and well-wishes to others and yourself that you can access online. Here is my version:

LOVINGKINDNESS MEDITATION

Begin by getting comfortable in a chair with your feet on the floor, or sit on the floor. Take a few deep breaths and close your eyes. Become more aware of your breath and how with each inhale it connects to and nourishes your body, and with each exhale, you breathe out stress, tension, and negative feelings.

Notice your thoughts, and bring a gentle curiosity to them. Instead of judging yourself for thinking certain thoughts or allowing certain thoughts to fill your mind, simply observe them, note that they are there, and move on.

Now imagine a person whom you care about and who supports you. Imagine this person is here in front of you. Begin to send loving kindness to this person by saying to them either out loud or silently, *May you be safe, may you be happy, may you be healthy, may you live in peace, and may you receive what you desire in life.* Notice the feelings and sensations that arise as you send these kind thoughts to this person whom you care for.

Now recall a person with whom you may be in conflict, or you could think about someone with whom you've had conflict in the past and with whom you haven't yet had a resolution to your argument or disagreement. Imagine this person is here in front of you. Begin to send loving kindness to this person by saying to them either out loud or silently—*May you be safe, may you be happy, may you be healthy, may you live in peace, and may you receive what you desire in life.* Notice the feelings and sensations that arise as you send these kind thoughts to this person with whom you are in conflict.

Now bring your attention back to yourself. Focus on your breathing and the sensations in your body. Begin to send loving kindness to yourself by saying either out loud or silently—*May I be safe, may I be happy, may I be healthy, may I live in peace, and may I receive what I desire in life.* Notice the feelings and sensations that arise as you send these kind thoughts to yourself.

Now think about the larger community that you are a part of. Imagine your family, your co-workers, your friends, and anyone else you include in your community, including yourself. Offer all of them and yourself loving kindness with these words—*May we be safe, may we be happy, may we be healthy, may we live in peace, and may we receive what we desire in life.*

Take a few additional deep breaths and allow your attention to come back into the room.

APPENDIX C

Self-Concept Boosters

From your journey throughout this book, you know that attachment greatly shapes your self-concept. Even if you have a secure attachment style, your self-concept is important to work on continuously, and I suggest that you build some of these exercises into your weekly self-care routine. It's a great way to nurture a strong, resilient self-concept that will help to bolster your new, secure attachment style.

These exercises can also come in handy when you're feeling stuck or down about yourself and need a quick self-confidence boost. You can try one on right before a difficult conversation with a loved one, preceding an important meeting or a big presentation at work, before you head out to a social function where you may not know many people, or when you're questioning whether you can meet the goals you've set for yourself today.

FIVE FINGERS EXERCISE

Take several deep breaths and close your eyes. Touch your thumb to your index finger and bring to mind a memory when you felt cherished and appreciated by another person. Allow yourself to take in this memory and experience how you felt when you recognized this gratitude from another person.

Touch your thumb to your index finger again and recall a time when you felt proud of something that you did. Reflect on the details of this experience and pay attention to the thoughts you had about yourself.

Touch your thumb to your middle finger and consider a time when you felt really cared for by another person. Immerse yourself in that memory and mindfully experience all the emotions this brings up for you.

Touch your thumb to your ring finger and think about one of your most favorite attributes about yourself. Ask yourself how this attribute has helped someone else in their time of need.

Finally, touch your thumb to your pinkie finger and think about a time when you persevered during a challenge. Remember how it felt to overcome this challenge and remind yourself that you can do this again, no matter what comes your way.

POWER POSE

The "power pose" is an idea that was popularized by a study conducted by social psychologist Amy Cuddy and her colleagues.[1] In the study, Cuddy and her team found that assuming certain body postures for just two minutes increased feelings of power and confidence. In her original research, Dr. Cuddy found that holding high-power poses affected hormone levels (specifically, testosterone and cortisol) in the body, leading to increased feelings of personal power and confidence.

To do the original high-power pose studied by Dr. Cuddy, stand up straight and tall with your feet shoulder-width apart and your arms raised above your head in an open V shape. Make sure your chest is open, your shoulders are back, and hold this position for two minutes or longer. You can try this position while looking at yourself in the mirror and repeating a positive affirmation to yourself. You can even work this power pose into your daily morning routine for a boost of energy and to strengthen your resolve to reach the goals you've set for yourself that day.

WRITE YOURSELF A RECOMMENDATION LETTER

This letter can be directed to anyone who you think would want to know about you and what makes you special, interesting, and one-of-a-kind. Set aside some time to free-write in your journal, and make sure this letter includes specific examples of each of the below.

1. Your **positive traits**, characteristics, and qualities.
2. Your most **important values**.
3. Your **strengths** regarding how you relate to those you care about in your life.
4. Your **capabilities for tackling work or school-related tasks** and a specific example of how you overcame a recent challenge in this area.
5. Your **ability to manage activities of daily living** (personal hygiene, sleep, eating, exercise, necessary chores and responsibilities, and any other ways you take care of your personal needs).
6. Your **skills in managing interpersonal conflict** and a specific example of how you dealt with a recent argument with someone in your life.

7. **Effective coping strategies** you engage in and an example of
    how you coped with a recent difficulty.

Give yourself plenty of time to reflect, and don't feel you need to
answer every question or write the whole letter in one sitting. If you
have trouble writing positive things about yourself, try to write the
letter as if you were someone else who is giving their enthusiastic
endorsement of you. You can add specificity to this recommendation
letter if you feel like there is an area of your life (work, romantic relationships, personal goals) where you need your self-esteem buttressed.

Once you finish the letter, put it in a visible place where you can
easily locate it and read it. Aside from coming back to your journal to
review it, you can put a copy of the letter up on a mirror in your bath-
room or tucked away in a frequently accessed drawer in your desk.

MY HERO COMIC STRIP

This exercise, creating a comic strip featuring yourself as the hero,
will help you to visualize yourself overcoming a challenge in your
life and show you how to utilize your strengths to solve a problem.
By using storytelling about an issue, you can actively engage in the
problem-solving process, which can then help the problem in real
life feel less threatening.

This comic strip will illustrate a problem that you're currently
experiencing (or one that you encountered in the past) and show
how you become the hero of your own story to solve this problem.
You can make this comic strip as short or as long as you want, but to
make sure you have the room to develop a story from beginning to
end, start by drawing four boxes across two of your journal pages
(two squares per journal page).

In the first box, draw yourself encountering a problem (and yes, it's totally okay to use stick figures, draw abstractly, or do whatever you find is the easiest way to express this content without getting overly stuck on perfection or judging your creation).

In the second box, draw the primary antagonist or obstacle represented by this problem.

In the third box, draw yourself doing something to confront this antagonist or obstacle, using one of your special superpowers. Your superpower can be anything: a skill you know you possess, a characteristic that someone has complimented you on, a coping strategy that you've learned in this book or elsewhere that you know works well for you to manage stress, the way you've managed a previously challenging situation and overcome it, or a top value that you know you try your hardest to adhere to daily, to name a few ideas.

In the final box, draw yourself defeating this antagonist or obstacle and/or what happens to you after this problem is solved.

Now go back and caption each of the drawings or write thought bubbles for the characters representing what they're thinking or saying, and fill out the comic strip as much as you want with other details, like drawing objects in the background, coloring your comic strip, or fine-tuning how you and the other characters look. Review the comic strip and take special note of how you conquered the problem presented and what skills or strengths you used to do so. Finally, ask yourself, how much of this story can I take with me into the real world to solve the actual problem?

AFFIRMATIONS FOR EMPOWERMENT

You don't have to wait for someone else to tell you about your abilities and worth. You can claim your power by making positive statements about yourself to yourself. Positive affirmations can work to reinforce ideas of personal empowerment, and they can also be used as a preventative tool so that when you come across difficulties, you can resist feeling helpless and overwhelmed.

There are several keys to using affirmations effectively:

- Choose affirmations that you can sink your teeth into (see below for some suggestions). Don't choose generalized platitudes that are too broad or don't specifically apply to you.
- Choose affirmations that are realistic and practical, and that you can buy into. Positive affirmations that are too far-reaching or seem too good to be true won't work well because your mind won't adopt them as a truth.
- Choose affirmations that you can rotate from day to day. Select a few of your favorite affirmations that apply to different thoughts, feelings, and situations. Write them in your journal so you have them ready.
- Focus on no more than one affirmation daily. More than that and they'll just become all muddled and blurred together. Choose an affirmation each morning that deals specifically with how you're currently thinking and feeling, or that addresses the situations you're likely to come across that day.

Start each morning by selecting your affirmation of the day and reading it aloud to yourself. Write it down on an index card or on a clean note page of your phone app and read it to yourself a few times throughout the day. At the end of the day, read the affirmation to yourself once more and recall at least one specific example of when you demonstrated the sentiment behind this affirmation. Following are some of my favorite affirmations for self-empowerment, but please feel free to write your own.

- I am confident and strong.
- I can communicate my needs effectively.
- I can still take values-based action even if I am in pain.
- I am in control of this situation.
- I won't let negative thoughts take me away from what I must do.
- I won't let others' criticisms hurt my self-esteem.
- I am worthy even when I make mistakes.
- I can ask for help—it's not a sign of weakness.
- I can reach my goal _____ (fill in the blank) today.
- I can handle the stressful situation _____ (fill in the blank) today.

ACKNOWLEDGMENTS

To Sheila Curry Oakes, thank you for your significant, brilliant contributions to this book. It has been marvelous to work with you again and our collaboration fit just like an old glove after working together on *Stop Self-Sabotage*.

To my husband, Pablo David Gavazza, thank you for being my soulmate and my greatest confidant. Thank you for supporting my dreams and for always cheering me on.

To my parents, Renee and Robert Ho, thank you for honoring my aspirations and goals, and for teaching me the values of hard work, generosity, and resilience.

To my sister Maria Ho, thank you for your love, kindness, and empathic nature. I cherish our bond immensely, and I can't imagine a better sister than you in this world.

To Wendy Sherman, my incredible literary agent, I am grateful for your wise guidance and your continued belief in me and my work. None of this would be possible without you.

To Hannah Robinson, thank you for taking a chance on me once again and for being so enthusiastic about this book. I am grateful for all the time, dedication, and attention that you've spent shaping this project to be at its best and providing your valuable insights.

To Nana Twumasi and the entire Balance team, thank you for providing me with such a phenomenal platform for my book and for making my dream come true.

To my maternal grandmother, Sai Chen Lin, thank you for showing me unconditional love from the minute I was born, and for the secure attachment bond with you that is the foundation of so much in my life.

Finally, thank you, God, for our family's countless blessings. Thank you for taking such great care of my inner child and for showing me all that is possible with your grace and love.

NOTES

CHAPTER 1

1.   J. Bowlby, *Attachment and Loss*, Vol. 1: *Attachment* (New York: Basic Books, 1969), 194.

2.   K. Lorenz, "Der Kumpan in der Umwelt des Vogels. Der Artgenosse als auslösendes Moment sozialer Verhaltensweisen," *Journal für Ornithologie* 83 (1935): 137–215, 289–413.

3.   M. D. S. Ainsworth et al., *Patterns of Attachment: A Psychological Study of the Strange Situation* (Mahwah, NJ: Lawrence Erlbaum, 1978).

4.   L. A. Sroufe and E. Waters, "Heart Rate as a Convergent Measure in Clinical and Developmental Research," *Merrill-Palmer Quarterly of Behavior and Development* 23 (1977): 3–27.

CHAPTER 2

1.   C. R. Rogers, "A Theory of Therapy, Personality, and Interpersonal Relationships as Developed in the Client-Centered Framework." This paper, published in the *Journal of Consulting Psychology*, explores Rogers's humanistic theory and the concept of the self.

2.   R. F. Baumeister, "Self-Concept, Self-Esteem, and Identity," in V. J. Derlega, B. A. Winstead, and W. H. Jones (eds.), *Personality: Contemporary Theory and Research* (Chicago: Nelson-Hall, 1999), 339–375.

3.   C. Rogers, "A Theory of Therapy, Personality and Interpersonal Relationships as Developed in the Client-Centered Framework," in S. Koch (ed.), *Psychology: A Study of a Science, Vol. 3: Formulations of the Person and the Social Context* (New York: Mc-Graw Hill, 1959).

CHAPTER 3

1.   "Industry Pioneer," Paul J. Meyer: Continuing the Legacy, https://pauljmeyer.com/the-legacy/industry-pioneer/.

NOTES

CHAPTER 4

1. Nathan W. Hudson, William J. Chopik, and Daniel A. Briley, "Volitional Change in Adult Attachment: Can People Who Want to Become Less Anxious and Avoidant Move Closer towards Realizing Those Goals?" *European Journal of Personality* 34, no. 1 (2020): 93–114. https://journals.sagepub.com/doi/full/10.1002/per.2226.

2. E. A. Butler and A. K. Randall, "Emotional Coregulation in Close Relationships," *Emotion Review* 5, no. 2 (2013): 202–210. http://doi.org/10.1177/1754073912451630.

3. Duke Center for Child and Family Policy for the Administration for Children and Families (ACF), "Co-Regulation from Birth through Young Adulthood: A Practice Brief," UNC Frank Porter Graham Child Development Institute. https://fpg.unc.edu/sites/fpg.unc.edu/files/resources/reports-and-policy-briefs/Co-RegulationFromBirthThroughYoungAdulthood.pdf.

4. Judith E. Carroll et al., "Childhood Abuse, Parental Warmth, and Adult Multisystem Biological Risk in the Coronary Artery Risk Development in Young Adults Study," *Proceedings of the National Academy of Sciences* 110, no. 42 (2013): 17149–17153. https://www.pnas.org/doi/abs/10.1073/pnas.1315458110; Darcia Narvaez, Lijuan Wong, and Ying Cheng, "The Evolved Developmental Niche in Children: Relation to Adult Psychopathology and Morality," *Applied Developmental Science* (January 2016). http://dx.doi.org/10.1080/10888691.2015.1128835; Darcia Narvaez et al., "The Importance of Early Life Touch for Psychosocial and Moral Development," *Psicologia: Reflexão e Crítica* 32 (2019): 16. https://www.ncbi.nlm.nih.gov/pmc/articles/PMC6967013/.

5. J. Maselko et al., "Mother's Affection at 8 Months Predicts Emotional Distress in Adulthood," *Journal of Epidemiology and Community Health* 65, no. 7 (2011): 621–625. https://www.ncbi.nlm.nih.gov/pmc/articles/PMC3118641/.

6. Kerstin Uvnas-Moberg and Maria Petersson, "Oxytocin, a Mediator of Anti-Stress, Well-Being, Social Interaction, Growth and Healing," *Zeitschrift fur Psychosomatische-Medizin und Psychotherapie* 51, no. 1 (2005): 57–80. https://pubmed.ncbi.nlm.nih.gov/15834840/.

7. N. Eisenberg (ed.), *The Development of Prosocial Behavior* (New York: Academic Press, 1982); N. Eisenberg and R. A. Fabes, "Prosocial Development," in *Handbook of Child Psychology*, 5th Ed., Vol. 3, eds. W. Damon and N. Eisenberg (New York: Wiley, 1998), 701–778.

8. Kendra Cherry, "The Different Types of Attachment Styles," *VeryWell Mind*, May 26, 2022. https://www.verywellmind.com/attachment-styles-2795344.

9. M. D. S. Ainsworth et al., *Patterns of Attachment: A Psychological Study of the Strange Situation* (Mahwah, NJ: Lawrence Erlbaum, 1978); K. Lyons-Ruth, "Attachment Relationships among Children with Aggressive Behavior Problems: The Role of Disorganized Early Attachment Patterns," *Journal of Consulting and Clinical Psychology* 64, no. 1 (1996): 64–73. doi:10.1037//0022-006x.64.1.64.

10. B. L. Simmons et al., "Secure Attachment: Implications for Hope, Trust, Burnout, and Performance," *Journal of Organizational Behavior* 30, no. 2 (February 2009): 233–247. doi:10.1002/job.585.

11.   Y. R. Hong and J. S. Park, "Impact of Attachment, Temperament and Parenting on Human Development," *Korean Journal of Pediatrics* 55, no. 12 (2012): 449–454. doi:10.3345/kjp.2012.55.12.449; I. L. Mark, M. J. Bakermans-Kranenburg, and M. H. Ijzendoorn, "The Role of Parenting, Attachment, and Temperamental Fearfulness in the Prediction of Compliance in Toddler Girls," *British Journal of Developmental Psychology* 20, no. 3 (September 2002): 361–378. doi:10.1348/026151002320620299; L. E. Brumariu, "Parent-Child Attachment and Emotion Regulation," *New Directions for Child and Adolescent Development* 148 (2015): 31–45. doi:10.1002/cad.20098; E. DiTommaso et al., "Attachment Styles, Social Skills and Loneliness in Young Adults," *Personality and Individual Differences* 35, no. 2 (July 2003): 303–312. doi:10.1016/s0191-8869 (02)00190-3; E. Moss and D. St-Laurent, "Attachment at School Age and Academic Performance," *Developmental Psychology* 37, no. 6 (2001): 863–874. doi:10.1037/0012-1649.37.6.863.

12.   C. Wu, "The Relationship between Attachment Style and Self-Concept Clarity: The Mediation Effect of Self-Esteem," *Personality and Individual Differences* 47, no. 1 (2009): 42–46. https://doi.org/10.1016/j.paid.2009.01.043

13.   A. B. Doyle et al., "Child Attachment Security and Self-Concept: Associations with Mother and Father Attachment Style and Marital Quality," *Merrill-Palmer Quarterly* 46, no. 3 (2000): 514–539. http://www.jstor.org/stable/23093743.

14.   Riza Bayrak, Murat Gülat, and Nesrin Hisli Sahin, "The Mediating Role of Self-Concept and Coping Strategies on the Relationship between Attachment Styles and Perceived Stress," *Europe's Journal of Psychology* 14, no. 4 (2018): 897–913. https://www.ncbi.nlm.nih.gov/pmc/articles/PMC6266532/pdf/ejop-14-897.pdf.

15.   V. Simard, E. Moss, and K. Pascuzzo, "Early Maladaptive Schemas and Child and Adult Attachment: A 15-Year Longitudinal Study," *Psychology and Psychotherapy: Theory, Research and Practice* 84, no. 4 (2011): 349–366. doi:10.1111/j.2044-8341.2010.02009.x; M. Mikulincer et al., "The Association between Adult Attachment Style and Mental Health in Extreme Life-Endangering Conditions," *Personality and Individual Differences* 27, no. 5 (1999): 831–842. doi:10.1016/s0191-8869(99)00032-x; W. H. Bylsma, C. Cozzarelli, and N. Sumer, "Relation between Adult Attachment Styles and Global Self-Esteem," *Basic and Applied Social Psychology* 19, no. 1 (1997): 1–16. doi:10.1207/s15324834basp1901_1; M. Mikulincer, "Adult Attachment Style and Individual Differences in Functional versus Dysfunctional Experiences of Anger," *Journal of Personality and Social Psychology* 74, no. 2 (1998): 513–524. doi:10.1037/0022-3514.74.2.513; M. Mikulincer, "Attachment Working Models and the Sense of Trust: An Exploration of Interaction Goals and Affect Regulation," *Journal of Personality and Social Psychology* 74, no. 5 (1998): 1209–1224. doi:10.1037/0022-3514.74.5.1209; R. Banse, "Adult Attachment and Marital Satisfaction: Evidence for Dyadic Configuration Individuals with Secure Attachment Effects," *Journal of Social and Personal Relationships* 21, no. 2 (2004): 273–282. doi:10.1177/0265407504041388.

16.   Fei Shen, Yanhong Liu, and Mansi Brat, "Attachment, Self-Esteem, and Psychological Distress: A Multiple-Mediator Model," *The Professional Counselor* 11, no. 2 (2021): 129–142. https://files.eric.ed.gov/fulltext/EJ1300191.pdf.

17.   G. Gleeson and A. Fitzgerald, "Exploring the Association between Adult Attachment Styles in Romantic Relationships, Perceptions of Parents from Childhood and Relationship Satisfaction," *Health* 6, no. 13 (2014). https://file.scirp.org/Html/6-82 02945_47883.htm.

18.   K. K. Little and L. E. Sockol, "Romantic Relationship Satisfaction and Parent-Infant Bonding during the Transition to Parenthood: An Attachment-Based Perspective," *Frontiers in Psychology* 11 (2020). https://www.frontiersin.org/articles/10.3389 /fpsyg.2020.02068/full.

19.   Marisa G. Franco, "The Trait That 'Super Friends' Have in Common," *The Atlantic*, August 25, 2022. https://www.theatlantic.com/family/archive/2022/08/making -keeping-friends-attachment-theory-styles/671222/.

20.   C. Hazan and P. R. Shaver, "Love and Work: An Attachment-Theoretical Perspective," *Journal of Personality and Social Psychology* 59, no. 2 (1990): 270–280. doi: 10.1037/0022-3514.59.2.270.

21.   Shen, Liu, and Brat.

22.   Tchiki Davis, "Shame: Definition, Causes, and Tips," Berkeley Well-Being Institute. https://www.berkeleywellbeing.com/shame.html.

23.   C. L. Burton and G. A. Bonanno, "Measuring the Ability to Enhance and Suppress Emotional Expression: The Flexible Regulation of Emotional Expression (FREE) Scale," *Psychological Assessment*, 28, no.8 (2016): 929–941; T. B. Kashdan et al., "Experiential Avoidance as a Generalized Psychological Vulnerability: Comparisons with Coping and Emotion Regulation Strategies," *Behaviour Research and Therapy* 44, no. 9 (2006): 1301–1320; T. B. Kashdan and J. Rottenberg, "Psychological Flexibility as a Fundamental Aspect of Health," *Clinical Psychology Review* 30, no. 7 (2010): 865–878; T. B. Kashdan, G. Uswatte, and T. Julian, "Social Anxiety and the Experience of Positive Emotion and Anger in Everyday Life: An Ecological Momentary Assessment Approach," *Anxiety, Stress and Coping* 19, no. 4 (2006): 337–357.

24.   Steven Hayes, "The Six Core Processes of ACT," Association for Contextual Behavioral Science. https://contextualscience.org/the_six_core_processes_of_act.

25.   A. Masuda and R. D. Latzman, "Examining Associations among Factor-Analytically Derived Components of Mental Health Stigma, Distress, and Psychological Flexibility," *Personality and Individual Differences* 51 (2011): 435–438.

26.   S. C. Hayes, K. D. Strosahl, and K. G. Wilson, *Acceptance and Commitment Therapy: The Process and Practice of Mindful Change*, 2nd ed. (New York: Guilford Press, 2012).

27.   A. T. Gloster, A. H. Meyer, and R. Lieb, "Psychological Flexibility as a Malleable Public Health Target: Evidence from a Representative Sample," *Journal of Contextual*

Behavioral Science 6, no. 2 (2017): 166–171. https://doi.org/10.1016/j.jcbs.2017.02.003

28. R. Tindle and A. A. Moustafa, "Psychological Distress, Social Support, and Psychological Flexibility during COVID-19," in A. A. Moustafa, ed., *Mental Health Effects of COVID-19* (London: Academic Press, 2021), 89–101. https://www.sciencedirect.com/science/article/pii/B978012824289600012X.

29. Russ Harris, *ACT Made Simple* (Oakland, CA: New Harbinger Publications, Inc., 2009). https://www.actmindfully.com.au/upimages/ACT_Made_Simple_Introduction_and_first_two_chapters.pdf.

30. Harris, *ACT Made Simple.*

31. Harris, *ACT Made Simple.* https://www.actmindfully.com.au/upimages/Making_Self-As-Context_Relevant,_Clear_and_Practical.pdf.

32. J. B. Rotter, "Generalized Expectancies for Internal versus External Control of Reinforcement," *Psychological Monographs: General and Applied* 80, no. 1 (1966): 1–28. doi: 10.1037/h0092976.

33. Ferdi Botha and Sarah C. Dahmann, "Locus of Control, Self-Control, and Health Outcomes," IZA Institute of Labor Economics Discussion Paper Series, May 2022. https://docs.iza.org/dp15306.pdf.

34. Kendra Cherry, "Locus of Control and Your Life," *VeryWell Mind*, December 8, 2022. https://www.verywellmind.com/what-is-locus-of-control-2795434; D. Kesavayuth et al., "Locus of Control, Health, and Health Care Utilization," *Economic Modelling* 86 (2020): 227–238. https://www.sciencedirect.com/science/article/abs/pii/S0264999319302548; M. I. Wallhagen et al., "Impact of Internal Health Locus of Control on Health Outcomes for Older Men and Women: A Longitudinal Perspective," *The Gerontologist* 34, no. 3 (1994): 299–306. https://deepblue.lib.umich.edu/bitstream/handle/2027.42/51483/Wallhagen%20MI,%20Impact%20of%20Internal%20Health,%201994.pdf.

CHAPTER 5

1. J. Stevenson-Hinde and K. Verschueren, "Attachment in Childhood," in P. K. Smith and C. H. Hart (eds.), *Blackwell Handbook of Childhood Social Development* (Hoboken, NJ: Blackwell Publishing, 2002), 182–204.

2. WebMD Staff, "What Is Avoidant Attachment?" Grow by WebMD, https://www.webmd.com/parenting/what-is-avoidant-attachment.

3. M. D. Ainsworth and S. M. Bell, "Attachment, Exploration, and Separation: Illustrated by the Behavior of One-Year-Olds in a Strange Situation," *Child Development* 41 (1970): 49–67; A. Sroufe and E. Waters, "Attachment as an Organizational Construct," *Child Development* 48 (1987): 1184–1199.

4. M. Main, "Analysis of a Peculiar Form of Reunion Behaviour Seen in Some Daycare Children," in R. Webb (ed.), *Social Development in Childhood* (Baltimore: Johns Hopkins, 1977), 33–78.

5. K. Bartholomew and L. M. Horowitz, "Attachment Styles among Young Adults: A Test of a Four-Category Model," *Journal of Personality and Social Psychology* 61 (1991): 226–244. doi: 10.1037/0022-3514.61.2.226).

6. M. Mikulincer and P. R. Shaver, *Attachment in Adulthood: Structure, Dynamics, and Change* (New York: Guilford Press, 2007).

7. T. Sheinbaum et al., "Attachment Style Predicts Affect, Cognitive Appraisals, and Social Functioning in Daily Life," *Frontiers in Psychology* 6 (2015): 296. https://www.frontiersin.org/articles/10.3389/fpsyg.2015.00296/full.

8. Sheinbaum et al., 2015.

9. Sheinbaum et al., 2015.

10. A. Catanzaro and M. Wei, "Adult Attachment, Dependence, Self-Criticism, and Depressive Symptoms: A Test of a Mediational Model," *Journal of Personality* 78 (2010): 1135–1162.

11. G. Bosmans, C. Braet, and L. Van Vlierberghe, "Attachment and Symptoms of Psychopathology: Early Maladaptive Schemas as a Cognitive Link?" *Clinical Psychology and Psychotherapy* 17 (2010): 374–385.

12. V. Illing et al., "Attachment Insecurity Predicts Eating Disorder Symptoms and Treatment Outcomes in a Clinical Sample of Women, *Journal of Nervous and Mental Disease* 198 (2010): 653–659.

13. T. Ein-Dor et al., "Together in Pain: Attachment-Related Dyadic Processes and Posttraumatic Stress Disorder," *Journal of Counseling Psychology* 57 (2010): 317–327.

14. B. Meyer and P. A. Pilkonis, "An Attachment Model of Personality Disorders," in M. F. Lenzenweger and J. F. Clarkin (eds.), *Major Theories of Personality Disorder* (New York: Guilford Press, 2005), 231–281; W. J. Livesley, "Classifying Personality Disorders: Ideal Types, Prototypes, or Dimensions? *Journal of Personality Disorders* 5 (1991): 52–59.

15. Mikulincer and Shaver, 2007.

16. E. Berant, M. Mikulincer, and P. R. Shaver, "Mothers' Attachment Style, Their Mental Health, and Their Children's Emotional Vulnerabilities: A Seven-Year Study of Children with Congenital Heart Disease, *Journal of Personality* 76 (2008): 31–66.

17. P. Wink, "Two Faces of Narcissism," *Journal of Personality and Social Psychology* 61 (1991): 590–597.

18. C. Wu, "The Relationship Between Attachment Style and Self-Concept Clarity: The Mediation Effect of Self-Esteem," *Personality and Individual Differences* 47, no. 1 (2009): 42–46. https://www.sciencedirect.com/science/article/abs/piiS0191886909000579.

19. Sheinbaum et al., 2015.

20. Sheinbaum et al., 2015.

21. M. Solomon and S. Tatkin, *Love and War in Intimate Relationships: Connection, Disconnection, and Mutual Regulation in Couple Therapy* (New York: W. W. Norton, 2011).

CHAPTER 6

1. Albert Ellis, "Unconditional Self-Acceptance" (video), https://www.youtube.com/watch?v=DQgpsvpfMXg.
2. "Flow," APA Dictionary of Psychology, https://dictionary.apa.org/flow.
3. Arne Dietrich, "Functional Neuroanatomy of Altered States of Consciousness: The Transient Hypofrontality Hypothesis," *Consciousness and Cognition* 12 (2002): 231–256.
4. C. G. Jung, *Aion: Researches into the Phenomenology of the Self* (Abington, UK: Routledge, 1951).
5. C. G. Jung, "Good and Evil in Analytical Psychology," *Journal of Analytical Psychology* 5, no. 2 (1960): 91–100.
6. L. Hay, *Mirror Work: 21 Days to Heal Your Life* (Carlsbad, CA: Hay House, 2016).

CHAPTER 7

1. J. R. Abela, S. A. Skitch, R. P. Auerbach, and P. Adams, "The Impact of Parental Borderline Personality Disorder on Vulnerability to Depression in Children of Affectively Ill Parents," *Journal of Personality Disorders* 19, no. 1 (2005): 68–83; P. R. Shaver, D. A. Schachner, and M. Mikulincer, "Attachment Style, Excessive Reassurance Seeking, Relationship Processes, and Depression," *Personality and Social Psychology Bulletin* 31, no. 3 (2005): 343–359; P. Muris et al., "Self-Reported Attachment Style, Attachment Quality, and Symptoms of Anxiety and Depression in Young Adolescents," *Personality and Individual Differences* 30, no. 5 (2001): 809–818; S. M. Safford et al., "The Relationship of Cognitive Style and Attachment Style to Depression and Anxiety in Young Adults," *Journal of Cognitive Psychotherapy* 18, no. 1 (2004): 25–41.
2. M. D. S. Ainsworth, *Patterns of Attachment: A Psychological Study of the Strange Situation* (Psychology Press, 1978).
3. J. J. Exline et al., "People-Pleasing through Eating: Sociotropy Predicts Greater Eating in Response to Perceived Social Pressure," *Journal of Social and Clinical Psychology* 31, no. 2 (2012): 169–193. doi:10.1521/jscp.2012.31.2.169.
4. L. Campbell and T. Marshall, "Anxious Attachment and Relationship Process: An Interactionist Perspective," *Journal of Personality* 79, no. 6 (2011): 917–947.
5. Chia-Huei Wu, "The Relationship between Attachment Style and Self-Concept Clarity: The Mediation Effect of Self-Esteem," *Personality and Individual Differences* 47, no. 1 (2009): 42–46.
6. A. Lee and B. L. Hankin, "Insecure Attachment, Dysfunctional Attitudes, and Low Self-Esteem Predicting Prospective Symptoms of Depression and Anxiety during Adolescence," *Journal of Clinical Child and Adolescent Psychology* 38, no. 2 (2009): 219–231.
7. P. R. Shaver, D. A. Schachner, and M. Mikulincer, "Attachment Style, Excessive Reassurance Seeking, Relationship Processes, and Depression," *Personality and Social Psychology Bulletin* 31, no. 3 (2005): 343–359.

8.   S. D. Jayamaha, Y. U. Girme, and N. C. Overall, "When Attachment Anxiety Impedes Support Provision: The Role of Feeling Unvalued and Unappreciated," *Journal of Family Psychology* 31, no. 2 (2017): 181–191.

9.   Hazan and Shaver, 1990.

10.   E. G. Hepper and K. B. Carnelley, "Adult Attachment and Feedback-Seeking Patterns in Relationships and Work," *European Journal of Social Psychology* 40, no. 3 (2010): 448–464.

11.   H. Braunstein-Bercovitz, "Self-Criticism, Anxious Attachment, and Avoidant Attachment as Predictors of Career Decision Making," *Journal of Career Assessment* 22, no. 1 (2014): 176–187.

CHAPTER 8

1.   L. Campbell and L. Marshall, "Anxious Attachment and Relationship Processes: An Interactionist Perspective," *Journal of Personality* 79, no. 6 (2011): 1219–1249.

2.   M. Wei et al., "Adult Attachment, Depressive Symptoms, and Validation from Self versus Others," *Journal of Counseling Psychology* 52, no. 3 (2005): 368–377.

3.   A. Bender and R. Ingram, "Connecting Attachment Style to Resilience: Contributions of Self-Care and Self-Efficacy," *Personality and Individual Differences* 130 (2018): 18–20.

4.   M. Mikulincer and P. R. Shaver, "Attachment Theory and Emotions in Close Relationships: Exploring the Attachment-Related Dynamics of Emotional Reactions to Relational Events," *Personal Relationships* 12, no. 2 (2005): 149–168.

5.   M. P. Leiter, A. Day, and L. Price, "Attachment Styles at Work: Measurement, Collegial Relationships, and Burnout," *Burnout Research* 2, no. 1 (2015): 25–35.

6.   M. Mikulincer and P. R. Shaver, "The Attachment Behavioral System in Adulthood: Activation, Psychodynamics, and Interpersonal Processes," in M. Zanna (ed.), *Advances in Experimental Social Psychology*, Vol. 35 (New York: Academic Press, 2003), 53–152.

7.   A. Dreisoerner et al., "Self-soothing Touch and Being Hugged Reduce Cortisol Responses to Stress: A Randomized Controlled Trial on Stress, Physical Touch, and Social Identity," *Comprehensive Psychoneuroendocrinology* 8 (2021): 100091. https://www.ncbi.nlm.nih.gov/pmc/articles/PMC9216399/.

8.   D. Church et al., "Clinical EFT as an Evidence-Based Practice for the Treatment of Psychological and Physiological Conditions: A Systematic Review," *Frontiers in Psychology* 13 (2022): 951451. https://pubmed.ncbi.nlm.nih.gov/36438382/.

9.   "The Voo Sound," PositivePsychology.com. https://positive.b-cdn.net/wp-content/uploads/2020/11/The-Voo-Sound.pdf.

10.   R. C. Fraley et al., "Adult Attachment and the Perception of Emotional Expressions: Probing the Hyperactivating Strategies Underlying Anxious Attachment," *Journal of Personality* 74, no. 4 (2006): 1163–1190.

11.   A. Richardson, "Mental Imagery: A Review of the Evidence," *The Psychologist* 30 (2017): 34–38; J. E. Driskell, C. Copper, and A. Moran, "Does Mental Practice

Enhance Performance?" *Journal of Applied Psychology* 79, no. 4 (2017): 481–492; S. E. Williams and J. Cumming, "Sport Imagery and Performance: A Meta-Analysis." *Journal of Applied Sport Psychology* 24, no. 9 (2012): 288–297.

CHAPTER 9

1. S. Doi, T Fujiwara, and A. Isumi, "Association between Maternal Adverse Childhood Experiences and Mental Health Problems in Offspring: An Intergenerational Study," *Developmental Psychopathology* 33, no. 3 (2021): 1041–1058.

2. M. Main and E. Hesse, "Parents' Unresolved Traumatic Experiences Are Related to Infant Disorganized Attachment Status," in M. T. Greenberg, D. Cicchetti, and E. M. Cummings (eds.), *Attachment in the Preschool Years* (Chicago: University of Chicago Press, 1990), 161–181.

3. K. Lyons-Ruth, E. Bronfman, and E. Parsons, "Maternal Frightened, Frightening, or Atypical Behavior and Disorganized Infant Attachment Patterns, *Monographs of the Society for Research in Child Development* 64 (1999): 67–96.

4. E. Tronick et al., "Infant Emotions in Normal and Pertubated Interactions." Paper presented at the biennial meeting of the Society for Research in Child Development, Denver, CO, April 1975; E. Z. Tronick, "Things Still to Be Done on the Still-Face Effect," *Infancy* 4, no. 4 (2003): 475–482; E. Tronick et al., "The Infant's Response to Entrapment between Contradictory Messages in Face-to-Face Interaction," *Journal of the American Academy of Child & Adolescent Psychiatry* 17, no. 1 (1978): 13.

5. K. A. Brennan, P. R. Shaver, and A. E. Tobey, "Attachment Styles, Gender and Parental Problem Drinking," *Journal of Social and Personal Relationships* 8, no. 4 (1991): 451–466. doi:10.1177/026540759184001.

6. D. Out, M. J. Bakermans-Kranenburg, and M. H. Van Ijzendoorn, "The Role of Disconnected and Extremely Insensitive Parenting in the Development of Disorganized Attachment: Validation of a New Measure," *Attachment & Human Development*, 11, no. 5 (2009): 419–443.

7. C. George and J. Solomon, "Attachment and Caregiving: The Carving Behavioral System," in J. Cassidy and P. R. Shaver (eds.), *Handbook of Attachment: Theory, Research and Clinical Applications* (New York: Guilford Press, 1999), 649–670.

8. R. L. Paetzold, W. S. Rholes, and J. L. Kohn, "Disorganized Attachment in Adulthood: Theory, Measurement, and Implications for Romantic Relationships," *Review of General Psychology* 19, no. 2 (2015): 146–156. doi:10.1037/gpr0000042.

9. M. Main and J. Stadtman, "Infant Response to Rejection of Physical Contact by the Mother," *Journal of the American Academy of Child Psychiatry* 20, no. 2 (1981): 292–307. https://doi.org/10.1016/S0002-7138(09)60990-0.

10. Main and Stadtman, 1981, 293.

11. R. Duschinsky, "The Emergence of the Disorganized/Disoriented (D) Attachment Classification, 1979–1982," *History of Psychology* 18, no. 1 (2015): 32–46. https://www.ncbi.nlm.nih.gov/pmc/articles/PMC4321742/.

12. J. Solomon and C. George, "The Disorganised Attachment-Caregiving System,"

in Judith Solomon and Carol George (eds.), *Disorganized Attachment and Caregiving* (New York: Guilford Press, 2011), 25–51.

13. "Boundary," *APA Dictionary of Psychology*. https://dictionary.apa.org/boundary.

14. P. M. Crittenden and M. D. S. Ainsworth, "Child Maltreatment and Attachment Theory," in *Child Maltreatment* (Cambridge: Cambridge University Press, 1989), 432–463. doi:10.1017/cbo9780511665707.015.

15. J. A. Simpson et al., "Working Models of Attachment, Support Giving, and Support Seeking in a Stressful Situation," *Personality and Social Psychology Bulletin* 28, no. 5 (2002): 598–608. doi:10.1177/0146167202288004.

16. J. A. Simpson, W. S. Rholes, and J. S. Nelligan, "Support Seeking and Support Giving Within Couples in an Anxiety-Provoking Situation: The Role of Attachment Styles," *Journal of Personality and Social Psychology* 62, no. 3 (1992): 434–446. doi:10.1037/0022-3514.62.3.434.

17. W. S. Rholes, J. A. Simpson, and M. Friedman, "Avoidant Attachment and the Experience of Parenting," *Personality and Social Psychology Bulletin* 32, no. 3 (2006): 275–285. doi:10.1177/0146167205280910.

18. W. S. Rholes, J. A. Simpson, and B. S. Blakely, "Adult Attachment Styles and Mothers' Relationships with Their Young Children," *Personal Relationships* 2, no. 1 (1995): 35–54. doi:10.1111/j.1475-6811.1995.tb00076.x.

CHAPTER 10

1. Scott Barry Kaufman, "Sailboat Metaphor," https://scottbarrykaufman.com /sailboat-metaphor/.

2. Kaufman.

3. Steve Hein, "Human Emotional Needs," https://eqi.org/needs_long.htm.

4. E. J. Cassell, "Compassion," in C. R. Snyder and S. J. Lopez (eds.), *Handbook of Positive Psychology* (Oxford: Oxford University Press, 2002), 434–445.

5. Making Caring Common Project, "Loneliness in America," Harvard University, https://mcc.gse.harvard.edu/reports/loneliness-in-america; R. O'Sullivan et al., "Impact of the COVID-19 Pandemic on Loneliness and Social Isolation: A Multi-Country Study," *International Journal of Environmental Research and Public Health* 18, no. 19 (2021): 9982. https://www.mdpi.com/1660-4601/18/19/9982.

6. National Academies of Sciences, Engineering, and Medicine, *Social Isolation and Loneliness in Older Adults: Opportunities for the Health Care System* (Washington, DC: The National Academies Press, 2020). https://doi.org/10.17226/25663.

7. O. D. Steen et al., "Loneliness Associates Strongly with Anxiety and Depression during the COVID Pandemic, Especially in Men and Younger Adults," *Scientific Reports* 12 (2022): 9517. https://www.nature.com/articles/s41598-022-13049-9.

8. A. W. M. Spithoven, P. Bijttebier, and L. Goossens, "It Is All in Their Mind: A Review on Information Processing Bias in Lonely Individuals," *Clinical Psychology*

Review 58 (2017): 97–114. https://www.sciencedirect.com/science/article/abs/pii/S027 2735816303336?via%3Dihub.

9. J. Lieberz et al., "Loneliness and the Social Brain: How Perceived Social Isolation Impairs Human Interactions," *Advanced Science* 8, no. 21 (2021): 202102076. https://onlinelibrary.wiley.com/doi/10.1002/advs.202102076.

10. Jancee Dunn, "Day 2: The Secret Power of the 8-Minute Phone Call," *New York Times*, January 2, 2023. https://www.nytimes.com/2023/01/02/well/phone-call-happi ness-challenge.html (accessed August 23, 2023).

11. R. Feldman, Z. Rosenthal, and A. I. Eidelman, "Maternal-Preterm Skin-to-Skin Contact Enhances Child Physiologic Organization and Cognitive Control across the First 10 Years of Life," *Biological Psychiatry* 75, no. 1 (2014): 56–64.

12. J. G. Miller et al., "Children's Dynamic RSA Change during Anger and Its Relations with Parenting, Temperament, and Control of Aggression," *Developmental Psychobiology* 55, no. 8 (2013): 798–806. DOI: 10.1002/dev.21080.

13. J. E. Young, "Schema-Focused Therapy for Borderline Personality Disorder," in *Cognitive Behavior Therapy: A Guide for the Practicing Clinician*, ed. G. Simos (New York: Taylor & Francis Group, 2002), 201–227.

14. A. Arntz, D. P. Bernstein, and J. Jacob, *Schema Therapy in Practice* (Chichester: Wiley-Blackwell, 2012); H. Dadomo et al., "Schema Therapy for Emotional Dysregulation: Theoretical Implications and Clinical Applications," *Hypothesis and Theory*, 2016, retrieved from https://www.frontiersin.org/articles/10.3389/fpsyg.2016.01987/full.

15. S. W. Porge, J. A. Doussard-Roosevelt, and A. K. Maiti, "Vagal Tone and the Physiological Regulation of Emotion," *Monographs of the Society for Research in Child Development* 59 (2–3), 167–186; J. F. Thayer and R. D. Lane, "A Model of Neurovisceral Integration in Emotion Regulation and Dysregulation," *Journal of Affective Disorder* 61, no. 3 (2000): 201–216.

16. T. F. Denson, W. C. Pedersen, and N. Miller, "The Displaced Aggression Questionnaire," *Journal of Personality and Social Psychology* 100, no. 2 (2011): 397–414; C. Vöge and E. L. Gibson, "Emotional Eating: The Role of Adiposity and Mood," *Appetite* 54, no. 3 (2010): 474–476; J. B. Nezlek and P. Kuppens, "Regulating Positive and Negative Emotions in Daily Life," *Journal of Personality* 76, no. 3 (2008): 561–579.

17. "Social Connections Drive the 'Upward Spiral' of Positive Emotions and Health," Association for Psychological Science, May 9, 2013. https://www.psychologi calscience.org/news/releases/social-connections-drive-the-upward-spiral-of-positive -emotions-and-health.html.

18. R. J. S. Gerritsen and G. P. H. Band, "Breath of Life: The Respiratory Vagal Stimulation Model of Contemplative Activity," *Frontiers in Human Neuroscience* 12 (2018): 397. https://www.ncbi.nlm.nih.gov/pmc/articles/PMC6189422/.

19. M. Armstrong et al., "Physiology, Baroreceptors," National Center for Biotechnology Information, https://www.ncbi.nlm.nih.gov/books/NBK538172/.

20. H. Mason et al., "Cardiovascular and Respiratory Effect of Yogic Slow Breathing

in the Yoga Beginner: What Is the Best Approach?" *Evidence-Based Complementary and Alternative Medicine* (2013): 743504. https://pubmed.ncbi.nlm.nih.gov/23710236/.

21.   M. Meier et al., "Standardized Massage Interventions as Protocols for the Induction of Psychophysiological Relaxation in the Laboratory: A Block Randomized, Controlled Trial," *Scientific Reports* 10, no. 1 (2020): 14774.

22.   "Massage for Vagus Nerve Stimulation," OSEA. https://oseamalibu.com/blogs/wellness-blog/massage-for-vagus-nerve-stimulation.

23.   "Making Self-as-Context Relevant, Clear & Practical," ACT for Adolescents. https://www.actmindfully.com.au/upimages/Making_Self-As-Context_Relevant,_Clear_and_Practical.pdf.

24.   R. Harris, *ACT Questions and Answers: A Practitioner's Guide to 150 Common Sticking Points in Acceptance and Commitment Therapy* (Oakland, CA: New Harbinger Publications, 2018), chapter 14.

25.   M. McKay, J. C. Wood, and J. Brantley, *The Dialectical Behavior Therapy Skills Workbook: Practical DBT Exercises for Learning Mindfulness, Interpersonal Effectiveness, Emotion Regulation, and Distress Tolerance* (Oakland, CA: New Harbinger Publications, 2007).

26.   M. M. Linehan, *DBT Skills Training Manual*, 2nd Ed. (New York: Guilford Press, 2014).

27.   Linehan, 2014.

APPENDIX A

1.   https://www.healthline.com/health/grounding-techniques#mental-techniques; https://www.talkspace.com/mental-health/conditions/articles/grounding-techniques-anxiety/; https://www.choosingtherapy.com/grounding-techniques/; https://drsarahallen.com/7-ways-to-calm/.

APPENDIX C

1.   A. J. C. Cuddy, C. A. Wilmuth, and D. R. Carney, "The Benefit of Power Posing before a High-Stakes Social Evaluation," Harvard Business School Working Paper, no. 13-027, 2012.

ABOUT THE AUTHOR

Dr. Judy Ho, PhD, ABPP, ABPdN, is a triple board-certified and licensed clinical and forensic neuropsychologist, a tenured associate professor at Pepperdine University, and author of *Stop Self-Sabotage* (HarperCollins, August 2019), a book detailing a scientifically driven six-step program, which has been translated into seven additional languages around the world.

Dr. Judy maintains a private practice in Manhattan Beach, California, where she specializes in comprehensive neuropsychological assessments and expert witness work. She regularly appears as an expert psychologist on television, podcasts, and radio, and contributes to other media including print and electronic periodicals. She was a co-host on the syndicated daytime television talk show *The Doctors*, co-host of CBS's *Face the Truth*, and host of the *SuperCharged Life* podcast, which focuses on scientific, tangible tips for physical and mental wellness and strategies for motivation and productivity, produced by Stage 29.

Dr. Judy is an avid researcher and a two-time recipient of the National Institute of Mental Health Services Research Award. She hosts an active research program to improve mental health care for high-need populations and is the chair of the Institutional Review Board at Pepperdine University. Her treatment approaches integrate the scientific principles of cognitive behavioral therapy, acceptance and commitment therapy, and dialectical behavioral therapy. She often speaks at national and local events, including research, clinical, and corporate conferences and work-shops for organizations, companies, and schools.

Dr. Judy received her bachelor's degrees in psychology and business administration from the University of California Berkeley and her master's and doctorate from the San Diego State University Department of Psychology/University of California San Diego School of Medicine Joint Doctoral Program in Clinical Psychology. She completed a National Institute of Mental Health–sponsored fellowship at University of California Los Angeles's Semel Institute.

Learn more at https://www.drjudyho.com.